Green Growth Indicators 2017

OECD

BETTER POLICIES FOR BETTER LIVES

This work is published on the responsibility of the Secretary-General of the OECD. The opinions expressed and arguments employed herein do not necessarily reflect the official views of the OECD or of the governments of its member countries or those of the European Union.

This document and any map included herein are without prejudice to the status of or sovereignty over any territory, to the delimitation of international frontiers and boundaries and to the name of any territory, city or area.

Please cite this publication as:
OECD (2017), *Green Growth Indicators 2017*, OECD Publishing, Paris.
http://dx.doi.org/10.1787/9789264268586-en

ISBN 978-92-64-26577-6 (print)
ISBN 978-92-64-26858-6 (PDF)
ISBN 978-92-64-26577-6 (epub)

ISSN 2222-9515 (print)
ISSN 2222-9523 (PDF)

Revised version, July 2017.
Details of revisions available at: *www.oecd.org/about/publishing/Corrigendum_Green_Growth_Indicators.pdf.*

The statistical data for Israel are supplied by and under the responsibility of the relevant Israeli authorities. The use of such data by the OECD is without prejudice to the status of the Golan Heights, East Jerusalem and Israeli settlements in the West Bank under the terms of international law.

Photo credits: © Cover design by advitam for the OECD.

Corrigenda to OECD publications may be found on line at: *www.oecd.org/about/publishing/corrigenda.htm.*

Preface

Green growth is about fostering growth and development, while ensuring that natural assets continue to provide the resources and environmental services on which our well-being relies. Governments that pursue policies designed to promote green growth, need to catalyse investment and innovation that underpin growth and give rise to new economic opportunities. They also need indicators that can raise awareness, measure progress and identify opportunities and risks.

This report updates and extends the set of green growth indicators presented in the 2014 and 2011 editions. It charts the progress that OECD countries and G20 economies have made since 1990. The 2017 edition places greater emphasis on the role of policy action, with enriched discussion on environmentally related taxes and subsidies, technology and innovation, and international financial flows.

Citizens of OECD and G20 countries aspire at better quality of life, but they also increasingly acknowledge that there are limits to the Earth's capacity to support healthy life for all. More ambitious policies are needed to achieve a balance between economic progress and environmental goals. Delivering growth of a quality up to citizens' aspirations will require concerted action both across countries and across all ministries invested in green growth, including finance, economy, industry, trade and agriculture.

This report is the result of work bringing together insights from a wide range of policy areas. Twenty-eight countries including emerging and developing economies have already relied on the OECD green growth measurement framework to develop their own set of indicators. International organisations, including UNSD and those participating in the Green Growth Knowledge Platform routinely draw on the OECD green growth measurement framework.

Major methodological developments since 2014 include new indicators that show how measures of economic productivity could be adjusted to take into account natural resources used and pollution; improved indicators on technological innovation and environmentally harmful subsidies; better measures of population exposure to air pollution and its economic costs.

On-going work focuses on improving measures of raw materials embodied in international trade, better evaluating the sustainability of natural resource use, and better understanding land cover changes. OECD continues to actively engage in global efforts to implement the System of Environmental-Economic Accounting, and provide support to countries as they advance in their efforts to monitor the 2030 Agenda for sustainable development.

We remain committed to working closely with national and international partners to ensure that green growth indicators are analytically sound, and that they support policies that enhance the lives not only of this but also future generations.

Paris, March 2017

Rintaro Tamaki
OECD Deputy Secretary-General

Acknowledgements

This report is an output of the OECD Horizontal Programme on Green Growth. Its elaboration has drawn upon the OECD's expertise with economic and environment policies, statistics, indicators and measures of progress. It has been prepared by the OECD Environment Directorate (ENV) in co-operation with the Statistics Directorate (STD), the Economics Department (ECO), and in consultation with the Centre for Tax Policy and Administration (CTPA), the Directorate for Financial and Enterprise Affairs (DAF), the Development Cooperation Directorate (DCD), the Public Governance and Territorial Development Directorate (GOV), the International Energy Agency (IEA), the Directorate for Science, Technology and Innovation (STI) and the Trade and Agriculture Directorate (TAD).

Preparation of this report was led by Ivan Haščič, with contributions by Miguel Cárdenas Rodríguez, Myriam Linster, Alexander Mackie, Mauro Migotto and Sarah Sentier, and under the supervision of Nathalie Girouard (Head of the Environmental Performance and Information Division of the OECD Environment Directorate). Many other OECD colleagues provided valuable comments. Thanks to Jackie Maher for secretarial and administrative assistance, Clara Tomasini and Elvira Berrueta-Imaz for communication support, and Marielle Guillaud for resource management. The authors are grateful to Janine Treves, Vincent Finat-Duclos and Marisa Gil Lapetra who provided publication and editorial support.

The report has benefitted from consultation with the OECD Working Party on Environmental Information (WPEI) of the OECD Environment Policy Committee (EPOC). The expert advice of ministries and statistical offices in countries proved instrumental for the preparation of the report.

Table of contents

Figures

Executive summary

Our ability to sustain economic and social progress in the long run will depend on our capacity to reduce dependence on natural capital as a source of growth, abate pollution, enhance the quality of physical and human capital and reinforce our institutions. Delivering the quality of growth to which citizens of OECD and G20 countries aspire will require concerted action across countries and within ministries invested in green growth – finance, economy, industry, trade and agriculture, among others.

This report on *Green Growth Indicators* updates previous editions. It integrates the results of recent developmental work on new indicator methodologies and wider country coverage. This applies notably to the indicators on environmentally adjusted multifactor productivity growth, population exposure to air pollution and the related economic costs, land cover change, and technological innovation. Other indicators have been refined, including demand-based CO_2 productivity and environmentally harmful subsidies.

Moreover, greater emphasis is placed on the role of policy action. To that end, the report includes enriched discussion in the chapters on environmentally related taxes and subsidies, technology and innovation, and international financial flows. This is supported by an enhanced visual presentation of the indicators.

Are we becoming more efficient in using natural resources and environmental services?

- The environmental productivity of OECD countries in terms of **carbon**, **energy** and **materials** has improved, but with wide variation across countries and sectors. Carbon dioxide emissions and fossil fuel use have decoupled from economic growth. Most countries, however, have achieved only a relative decoupling. In other words, CO_2 emissions increased at a lower rate than real GDP. Today, OECD countries generate much more economic value per unit of material resources used than in 2000. Efforts to recycle waste are also starting to pay off. Nutrient use in agriculture is improving as well, with surpluses declining relative to production.
- However, once indirect flows such as carbon emissions and raw materials **embodied in international trade** are considered, improvements are often more moderate.
- Despite productivity gains, environmental pressures remain high: carbon emissions continue to rise; fossil fuels continue to dominate the energy mix, sometimes benefiting from government support, and renewables still play only a relatively minor role; the consumption of material resources to support economic growth remains high; and many valuable materials continue to be disposed of as waste.

Is the natural asset base of our economies being maintained?

- The overall pressure on natural resources remains high. Many **ecosystems** have been degraded, biodiversity-rich areas are declining and wildlife is increasingly threatened. A third of global **wild fish** stocks are overexploited. **Wild bird** populations have declined by 28% since the 1980s and by nearly 41% since the 1960s. Many **forests** are threatened by degradation, fragmentation and conversion to other land types.
- Threats to **biodiversity** are particularly acute in countries with a high population density and infrastructure development. Built-up areas have been increasing across the OECD and cover 30% more land than in 1990. Globally, an area the size of the United Kingdom has been converted to built-up areas since 1990. If significant areas of land are not protected from modification, biodiversity will be imperilled. Terrestrial **protected areas** are increasing, but remain insufficient. Many countries still need to expand or establish marine protected area networks.
- Progress has been made with the management of water as the abstraction of renewable **freshwater resources** remained relatively stable despite increasing demand. But in some countries, water stress is high and local water scarcity may constrain economic activity.

Does greening growth generate benefits for people?

- Improvements in air quality have been modest and people's health and quality of life remain at risk. **Air pollution** is the single greatest environmental health risk worldwide. Human exposure to fine particulates remains dangerously high. There has been little improvement in exposure to ground-level ozone and nitrogen oxides that continue to severely affect human health. In the OECD area, exposure to outdoor PM2.5 and ozone is estimated to cause 0.5 million premature deaths each year, with an annual welfare cost equivalent to 3.6% of gross domestic product (GDP).
- Most people in the OECD benefit from **improved sanitation** and almost 80% benefit from **public wastewater treatment**, often using advanced treatment technologies. However, the need to upgrade ageing water supply and sewage systems, and improve access to efficient sewage treatment in small or isolated settlements, remains a challenge.

How does greening growth generate economic opportunities?

- Efforts to implement green growth policies by encouraging innovation and changes in consumer behaviour are accelerating but comparable information about the extent of this change, and the associated jobs and business opportunities, remain difficult to capture statistically.
- Progress has been mixed on the innovation front. Government research and development **(R&D)** spending is rising. However, the share dedicated to environment and energy objectives has remained stagnant. At the same time, research, development and demonstration **(RD&D)** efforts directed at energy are shifting towards renewables. Globally, inventive activity in environment related **technologies** has been slowing down. Long-term incentives are needed to direct innovation towards environmental objectives more effectively.
- Sectors producing **environmental goods and services** command a growing albeit modest share of the economy. The share of trade in environmentally related products is rising, signalling a certain greening of international trade.

- The use of **environmentally related taxes** is growing, but remains modest compared to labour taxes. Their contribution to countries' total tax revenue has actually decreased since 1995. The share of **support to farmers** that potentially exerts the greatest pressure on the environment has decreased, while the share that includes environmental requirements has grown.
- **International financial flows** that support greener growth are evolving. While carbon markets shrank, new opportunities arose with financial institutions issuing **green bonds**. **Development aid** for environmental purposes has continued to rise and aid for renewable energy has surpassed aid for non-renewables.
- Too often, policies lack **coherence**, undermining the transition to green growth. Countries continue to support fossil fuel production and consumption in many ways, at a cost of more than USD 60 billion per year in the OECD area alone, and more than USD 200 billion in BRIICS. Misalignments in the taxation of energy persist. In many countries there is scope to adapt the taxation of motor vehicles to reflect the external costs of vehicle use. The tax rate on diesel fuel should be increased at least to the level of the tax rate on petrol to better reflect the impact of diesel on climate change and local air pollution.

Reader's guide

The OECD green growth indicators enable the monitoring of progress towards four main objectives: establishing a low-carbon, resource-efficient economy; maintaining the natural asset base; improving people's quality of life; and implementing appropriate policy to realise the economic opportunities of green growth.

The conceptual framework

A good understanding of the determinants of green growth and of related trade-offs or synergies must inform policies that promote green growth. These policies need to be supported with appropriate information about the results obtained to-date and the progress still to be made. This requires indicators that speak clearly to policy makers and the public at large. "Green growth is about fostering economic growth and development while ensuring that the natural assets continue to provide the resources and environmental services on which our well-being relies. To do this it must catalyse investment and innovation which will underpin sustained growth and give rise to new economic opportunities" (OECD, 2011a).

Conceptual measurement framework

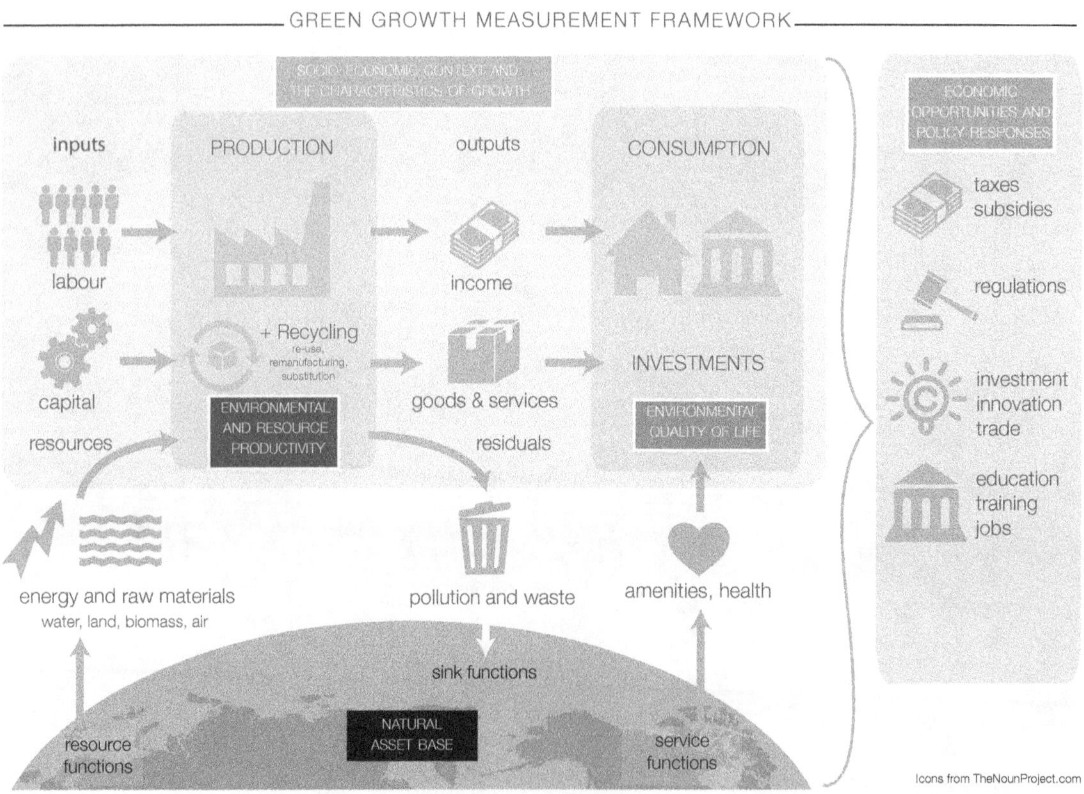

The OECD's approach to monitoring progress towards green growth (first presented in OECD, 2011b) is centred on the economy's production and consumption. It describes the interactions between the economy, the natural asset base and policy actions.

The indicator set

The measurement framework identifies 26 indicators to capture the main features of green growth and monitor progress in four main areas (see *Annex*). These are i) the environmental and resource productivity of the economy; ii) the natural asset base; iii) the environmental dimension of quality of life; and iv) economic opportunities and policy responses. Indicators that describe the socio-economic context and the characteristics of growth complete the picture.

(1) The environmental and resource productivity of the economy

These indicators capture the efficiency with which economic activities – both production and consumption – use energy, other natural resources and environmental services. The indicators in this group reflect key aspects of the transition to a low-carbon, resource-efficient economy:

- carbon and energy productivity – output generated per unit of CO_2 emitted or total primary energy supplied
- resource productivity – output generated per unit of natural resources or materials used
- multifactor productivity adjusted for the use of natural resources and environmental services.

Most resource productivity indicators are **production-based**, accounting for the environmental flows directly "used" or "generated" by domestic production and consumption. They are complemented by **demand-based** indicators that account for environmental flows "used" or "generated" by domestic final demand (the "footprint" approach). Demand-based indicators include environmental flows that are embodied in imports, and deduct the environmental flows embodied in exports. The resulting indicators provide insights into the net (direct and indirect) environmental flows resulting from household and government consumption and investment (final domestic demand).

(2) The natural asset base

These indicators reflect whether the natural asset base is being kept intact and within sustainable thresholds in terms of quantity, quality or value. Ideally they should help identify risks to future growth arising from a declining or degraded natural asset base. Progress can be monitored by tracking stocks of natural resources and other environmental assets along with flows of environmental services:

- the availability and quality of **renewable** natural resource stocks including freshwater, forest and fish resources
- the availability and accessibility of **non-renewable** natural resource stocks, in particular mineral resources, including metals, industrial minerals and fossil energy carriers
- biological diversity and ecosystems, including species and habitat diversity, as well as the productivity of land and soil resources.

(3) The environmental dimension of quality of life

These indicators reflect how environmental conditions and environmental risks interact with the quality of life and well-being of people. They also point out how the amenity services of natural capital support well-being. Further, they can show the extent to which income growth is accompanied (or not) by a rise in overall well-being:

- human exposure to pollution and environmental **risks** (natural disasters, technological and chemical risks), the associated effects on human health and on quality of life, and the related health costs and impacts on human capital and on labour productivity
- public access to environmental services and **amenities**, characterising the level and type of access of different groups of people to environmental services such as clean water, sanitation, green space or public transport.

They can be complemented by information on people's perceptions about the quality of the environment they live in.

(4) Economic opportunities and policy responses

These indicators aim at capturing the economic opportunities associated with green growth (e.g. markets for environmentally related products and associated employment). They monitor policy measures to promote the transition to green growth and to remove barriers to that transition (e.g. environmentally related taxes and subsidies, innovation policy). These indicators can help assess the effectiveness of policy in delivering green growth:

- technology and innovation that are important drivers of growth and productivity in general, and of green growth in particular
- investment and financing that facilitate the uptake and dissemination of technology and knowledge, and contribute to meeting the development and environmental objectives
- production of environmental goods and services that reflect an important, albeit partial, aspect of the economic opportunities that arise in a greener economy
- prices, taxes and transfers that provide signals to producers and consumers and help internalise negative environmental externalities, and which are complemented by indicators on regulation and on management approaches
- education, training and skills development.

The socio-economic context and the characteristics of growth

This group of indicators provides important background information. It helps track the effects of green growth policies and measures on growth and development. It also links the green growth indicators to social goals, such as poverty reduction, social equity and inclusion.

A dynamic process

The indicator set identified is neither exhaustive nor final. It has been kept flexible so that countries can adapt it to different national contexts. The set will be further elaborated as new data become available, as concepts evolve and as policy applications of the indicators provide feedback.

Headline indicators

The 2011 OECD report on Green Growth Indicators foresaw development of a small set of headline indicators to aid communication with policy makers, the media and citizens. The report recognised that presenting a large set of indicators helped describe the multi-dimensional nature of green growth. However, this approach also ran the risk of not presenting a clear message. The idea of developing a single, composite indicator was considered, but rejected. While a composite indicator is easy to communicate, it is difficult to aggregate the data components; how the components are chosen and weighted depends on judgements that may legitimately differ (OECD, 2002). Thus it was decided to develop a small, well-balanced, representative set of "headline" indicators to track a few central elements of green growth.

To be considered, the indicators had to meet the following criteria:

- capture the interface between the environment and the economy
- communicate easily to multiple users and audiences
- align with the OECD measurement framework for green growth
- are measurable and comparable across countries.

On this basis, six headline indicators were identified, plus a placeholder for a future headline indicator on economic opportunities and policy responses. The proposed list of headline indicators is not necessarily final. As the measurement agenda advances, new data may become available and the list may need to evolve accordingly. Some proposed headline indicators are not yet fully measurable, but were retained to drive the measurement agenda.

Headline indicators

Environmental and resource productivity	
Carbon and energy productivity	1. CO_2 productivity
Resource productivity	2. Non-energy material productivity
Multifactor productivity	3. Environmentally adjusted multifactor productivity
Natural asset base	
Renewable and non-renewable stocks	4. Natural resource index
Biodiversity and ecosystems	5. Changes in land cover
Environmental quality of life	
Environmental health and risks	6. Population exposure to air pollution ($PM_{2.5}$)
Economic opportunities and policy responses	
Technology and innovation Environmental goods and services Prices and transfers Regulations and management approaches	*Placeholder: no indicator specified*

About this edition

The indicators presented in this report build on data provided regularly by OECD member countries, as well as from other international sources and peer-reviewed research. The indicators are accompanied by a short text that explains the policy context and the main challenges. It also describes the *main trends and recent developments* that can be observed. This is followed by a description of the definitions underlying the indicators, and the most pressing *measurement and interpretation* challenges. The data sources are provided below graphics as well as at the end of each chapter together with additional references. Each graphic is complemented with a *statlink* providing access to the underlying data. Further details on definitions are provided in a *glossary*.

Country and time coverage

This edition covers OECD member countries, accession candidates and G20 economies – **46 countries** in total. The indicators presented cover **1990-2015** (or latest available year), data availability permitting.

The cut-off date

This publication is based on information and data available to the OECD Secretariat up to **December 2016** and on comments from national delegates received by January 2017.

The online database

- OECD green growth indicators homepage: ***http://oe.cd/ggi***
- OECD online database with selected green growth indicators: ***http://oe.cd/ggi-data***

Recent developments

This edition integrates results of the recent developmental work on green growth indicators. Current efforts are focused on the following:

- **Earth observation and other geospatial data** often provide a unique source of relevant information that is commensurable across countries and at the national and sub-national levels. There are opportunities for monitoring land cover, natural resources and environmental sinks, and for assessing environmental risks. Importantly, Earth observation data can be combined with socio-economic data, thereby improving the policy relevance of the indicators. (For more information, see *http://oe.cd/earth-observation*).
- The OECD database on **Policy Instruments for the Environment**. Such data are pivotal for better understanding the role of policy in the transition to green growth (see *http://oe.cd/pine*). Drawing on this database and other sources, the OECD has also developed an indicator of environmental policy stringency (EPS). Currently, the EPS index covers primarily climate and air pollution policies in energy and transport, but efforts are on-going to integrate also water pollution policies (see *http://oe.cd/eps*).
- Implementation of the **System of Environmental-Economic Accounting (SEEA)**, the international statistical standard for environmental accounting (UN, 2014). This allows combining economic and environmental data in a framework consistent with the System of National Accounts (SNA). The OECD has developed a small set of SEEA core tables that help compiling internationally comparable data for calculating selected green growth and environmental indicators. It works with other international partners to establish global databases with environmental accounts. The current focus is on natural asset accounts and on air and greenhouse gas emission accounts. These accounts will allow calculation of the natural resource index and the environmentally adjusted multifactor productivity growth. They will also populate the input-output tables needed for calculating the demand-based indicators for carbon and material productivity. Further, they will allow breakdown of macro-level environmental data by industry.

Comparability and interpretation

The indicators presented here are of varying relevance for different countries. They should be interpreted in light of the context in which they were produced. National averages can mask variations *within* countries. In addition, care should be taken when making international comparisons in cases when definitions and measurement methods vary among countries. Finally, the indicators rely on data sources and measurement methods that hold a level of uncertainty. Differences between two countries' indicators are thus not always statistically significant. When countries are clustered around a relatively narrow range of outcomes, it may be misleading to establish an order of ranking.

Unless specified otherwise, the following is applied across all chapters:

- All **monetary values** (gross domestic product [GDP], revenues, prices, etc.) shown in this publication are expressed in constant 2010 USD using purchasing power parities (PPPs). They are deflated using the best available deflator – the GDP deflator for most macro-level variables (e.g. tax revenue) or the Consumer Price Index for household-level indicators (e.g. fuel tax-rates). PPPs are the rates of currency conversion that equalise the purchasing power of different countries by eliminating differences in price levels between countries. Conversion by means of PPPs allows comparisons across countries that reflect only differences in the volume of goods and services purchased.
- The **GDP** data for OECD countries come from OECD (2016a) *National Accounts Statistics*. Missing data points are estimated using GDP growth rates from OECD (2016b) *Economic Outlook: Statistics and Projections* and World Bank (2016) *World Development Indicators*.
- Unless otherwise specified, the **population** data used in this report come from OECD (2016c) *Employment and Labour Market Statistics*.

Acronyms and abbreviations

Signs

n.a. : not available n.d. : no date

Country aggregates

OECD Europe	Includes all European member countries of the OECD: Austria, Belgium, the Czech Republic, Denmark, Estonia, Finland, France, Germany, Greece, Hungary, Iceland, Ireland, Italy, Latvia, Luxembourg, the Netherlands, Norway, Poland, Portugal, the Slovak Republic, Slovenia, Spain, Sweden, Switzerland, Turkey and the United Kingdom.
OECD	Includes all member countries of the OECD: countries of OECD Europe plus Australia, Canada, Chile, Israel, Japan, Mexico, New Zealand, the Republic of Korea and the United States.
BRIICS	Brazil, Russian Federation, India, Indonesia, People's Republic of China, South Africa.
ROW	Rest of the world

Note: Country aggregates may include Secretariat estimates.

Country codes

OECD member countries											
AUS	–	Australia	ESP	–	Spain	ISR	–	Israel	NZL	–	New Zealand
AUT	–	Austria	EST	–	Estonia	ITA	–	Italy	POL	–	Poland
BEL	–	Belgium	FIN	–	Finland	JPN	–	Japan	PRT	–	Portugal
CAN	–	Canada	FRA	–	France	KOR	–	Korea, Republic	SVK	–	Slovak Republic
CHE	–	Switzerland	GBR	–	United Kingdom	LUX	–	Luxembourg	SVN	–	Slovenia
CHL	–	Chile	GRC	–	Greece	LVA	–	Latvia	SWE	–	Sweden

CZE	–	Czech Republic	HUN	–	Hungary	MEX	–	Mexico	TUR	–	Turkey
DEU	–	Germany	IRL	–	Ireland	NLD	–	Netherlands	USA	–	United States
DNK	–	Denmark	ISL	–	Iceland	NOR	–	Norway			
OECD accession candidates											
COL	–	Colombia	CRI	–	Costa Rica	LTU	–	Lithuania			
Selected G20 economies											
ARG	–	Argentina	CHN	–	China, People's Rep.	IND	–	India	SAU	–	Saudi Arabia
BRA	–	Brazil	IDN	–	Indonesia	RUS	–	Russian Federation	ZAF	–	South Africa
Other											
WLD	–	World	EU	–	European Union	EU28	–	European Union incl. 28 member states			

Abbreviations and acronyms

cap	Capita	Mtoe	Million tonnes of oil equivalent
CBD	UN Convention on Biological Diversity	N	Nitrogen
CCS	Carbon capture and storage	NACE	Classification of economic activities in the European Union
CDM	Clean Development Mechanism	NMVOC	Non-methane volatile organic compounds
CH_4	Methane	NO_2	Nitrogen dioxide
CO_2	Carbon dioxide	NOx	Nitrogen oxides
DAC	Development Assistance Committee, OECD	ODA	Official development assistance
DALYs	Disability-adjusted life years	O_3	Ozone
DEU	Domestic extraction used	P	Phosphorus
DMC	Domestic material consumption	PEFC	Programme for the Endorsement of Forest Certification
EAMFP	Environmentally adjusted multifactor productivity	PM	Particulate matter
EEZ	Exclusive economic zone	PPPs	Purchasing power parities
EGS	Environmental goods and services	R&D	Research and development
ENVTECH	Environment-related technologies	RD&D	Research, development and demonstration
EUR	Euro (Eurozone's currency)	REDD	(The UNFCCC mechanism for) Reducing Emissions from Deforestation and Degradation
FAO	Food and Agriculture Organization of the UN	RTA	Relative technological advantage
FDI	Foreign Direct Investment	r	Pearson correlation coefficient
FSC	Forest Stewardship Council	R^2	R-squared is a goodness-of-fit measure of a linear regression
GBAORD	Government budget appropriations or outlays for R&D	SDGs	Sustainable Development Goals
GDP	Gross domestic product	SEEA	UN System of Environmental Economic Accounting
GERD	Gross expenditure on R&D	SO_2	Sulphur dioxide
GHG	Greenhouse gas	t	Tonne (metric)
GNI	Gross national income	toe	Tonnes of oil equivalent
ha	Hectare	TPES	Total primary energy supply
ICES	International Council for the Exploration of the Sea	UNCCD	UN Convention to Combat Desertification
IEA	International Energy Agency	UNEP	UN Environment Programme
ISIC	International Standard Industrial Classification	UNFCCC	UN Framework Convention on Climate Change
IUCN	International Union for Conservation of Nature	USD	US dollar
JRC	Joint Research Centre	VAT	Value added tax
kg	Kilogram	VOCs	Volatile organic compounds
km	Kilometre	WHO	World Health Organization
Mt	Million tonnes	$\mu g/m^3$	Micrograms per cubic metre

References

OECD (2017), "Green growth indicators", *OECD Environment Statistics* (database), *http://dx.doi.org/10.1787/data-00665-en* (accessed in March 2017).

OECD (2016a), "Aggregate National Accounts, SNA 2008 (or SNA 1993): Gross domestic product", *OECD National Accounts Statistics* (database), *http://dx.doi.org/10.1787/data-00001-en*.

OECD (2016b), "OECD Economic Outlook No. 100 (Edition 2016/2)", *OECD Economic Outlook: Statistics and Projections* (database), *http://dx.doi.org/10.1787/7fa317bf-en*.

OECD (2016c), "Labour force statistics: population projections", *OECD Employment and Labour Market Statistics* (database), *http://dx.doi.org/10.1787/data-00538-en* (accessed in January 2017).

OECD (2011a), *Towards Green Growth*, OECD Green Growth Studies, OECD Publishing, Paris, *http://dx.doi.org/10.1787/9789264111318-en*.

OECD (2011b), *Towards Green Growth: Monitoring Progress: OECD Indicators*, OECD Green Growth Studies, OECD Publishing, Paris, *http://dx.doi.org/10.1787/9789264111356-en*.

OECD (2002), *Aggregated Environmental Indices: Review of Aggregation Methodologies in Use*, OECD Publishing, Paris, *www.oecd.org/officialdocuments/displaydocument/?cote=env/epoc/se(2001)2/final&doclanguage=en*.

OECD (n.d.), Earth Observation for Decision-Making, webpage: *http://oe.cd/earth-observation*.

OECD (n.d.), Policy Instruments for the Environment (database), webpage: *http://oe.cd/pine*.

OECD (n.d.), Environmental Policy Stringency index, webpage: *http://oe.cd/eps*.

UN (2014), *System of Environmental-Economic Accounting 2012: Central framework*, European Commission, Food and Agriculture Organization, International Monetary Fund, OECD, World Bank, United Nations, New York, *http://unstats.un.org/unsd/envaccounting/seeaRev/SEEA_CF_Final_en.pdf*.

World Bank (2016), "World development indicators", *http://data.worldbank.org/data-catalog/world-development-indicators* (accessed in January 2017).

Green Growth Indicators 2017

Progress towards green growth: An overview

This chapter provides an overview of progress towards green growth in OECD and G20 countries. It builds on a cross-thematic analysis of some central elements of green growth. To that end, it uses a small set of headline indicators describing carbon and material productivity, environmentally adjusted multifactor productivity and population exposure to air pollution. These are complemented by indicators on land consumption by buildings, environmentally related innovation and taxation, and on income levels and inequality. For each aspect of green growth covered, it provides an overview of key developments drawing on results from the substantive chapters of the report.

Cross-thematic summary

OECD countries have come a long way towards green growth. Most countries use the available natural resources and environmental services more productively. They have reduced pollution and hence some of the environmental risks to which their populations are exposed. Many countries have stabilised extraction of renewable natural resources (wood, fish, freshwater), and are advancing towards more sustainable management practices. Numerous examples illustrate that progress achieved towards green growth is compatible with maintaining economic prosperity, and can nurture people's well-being.

Several countries are at the forefront of the transition towards green growth, but no country leads on all fronts. In fact, countries often advance in one dimension of green growth while standing still on other fronts. Too often, progress has been insufficient as evidenced by the failure to halt further dwindling of the natural asset base and its degradation. Important challenges remain, to better safeguard our natural resources and further reduce the environmental footprints of our consumption and production. Beyond relative decoupling, economic growth must be completely untied from environmental pressures (absolute decoupling).

Analysis of the 46 countries covered indicates that Luxembourg, Iceland, Denmark, Norway and the Netherlands have achieved the best overall results (Figure 1). These countries consistently rank high across most of the green growth dimensions assessed. **Denmark**, for instance, is a leader in environmental technologies and innovation and also ranks high in using environmental taxation. However, its residents are exposed to more air pollution than those in **Norway** and **Iceland**. **Luxembourg**'s economy has higher material productivity and the country has higher living standards, but performs less well in the distribution of income. Among the non-OECD economies studied, **Colombia** and **Costa Rica** lead the way.

Countries such as Denmark, Estonia, the United Kingdom, Italy and the Slovak Republic achieved the greatest overall improvements towards green growth compared to 2000 (Figure 2). Among these, the **United Kingdom** and **Italy** improved most on material

Figure 1. **Monitoring green growth, relative to the leaders**

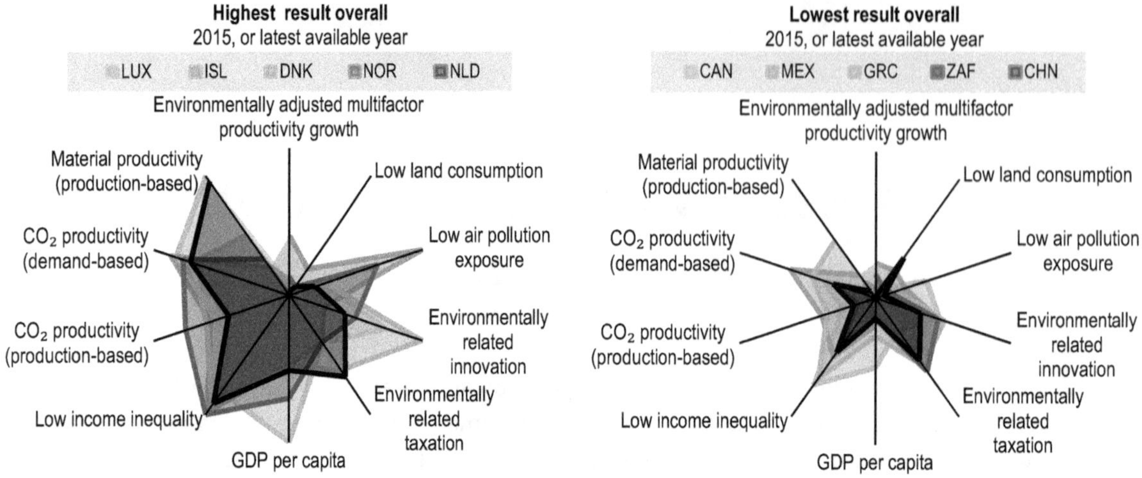

Note: Each axis represents the range of observed results among the 46 countries studied. The best result (leader) is located on the outer frontier of each axis, the worst result is located in the origin. For each indicator, performance of an individual country is then assessed as the "distance to the leader". Overall result is an average across all selected indicators. Countries with missing data are excluded. For more details on the definitions of indicators, see *Notes.*

Source: OECD (2017), "Green growth indicators"; JRC (2016), "Global human settlement layer"; Solt (2016), "The standardized world income inequality database"; World Bank (2016), "World development indicators".

StatLink http://dx.doi.org/10.1787/888933484403

Figure 2. **Progress towards green growth**

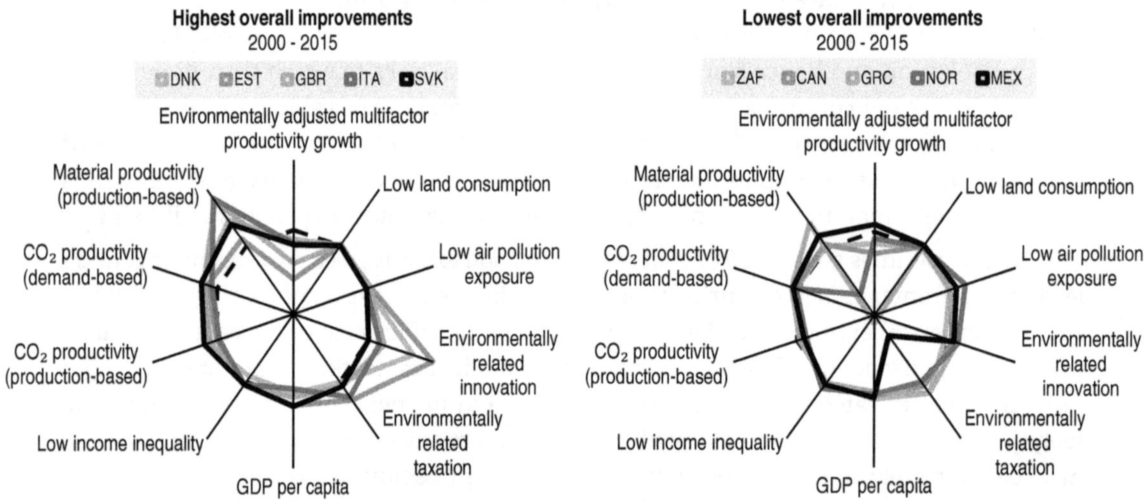

Note: Improvements shown here are determined by comparing results in 2015 to 2000 (as a change in the "distance to the leader"). The black dashed line indicates no change; values below that level indicate deterioration.

Source: OECD (2017), "Green growth indicators"; JRC (2016), "Global human settlement layer"; Solt (2016), "The standardized world income inequality database"; World Bank (2016), "World development indicators".

StatLink http://dx.doi.org/10.1787/888933484410

productivity, the **Slovak Republic** and **Denmark** on carbon productivity, **Italy** and **Estonia** on environmentally related taxation, and **Denmark** and **Estonia** on environmentally related innovation. The top performers vary substantially according to each of the indicators. Most countries achieved improvements in at least some aspects of green growth. This diversity of achievements between countries underlines the need to assess progress towards green growth across a set of multiple indicators.

However, multiple indicators can be complex to interpret and must be placed in a broader growth context (Figure 3). Initial results of a correlation analysis[1] suggest that higher levels of carbon and material productivity are positively associated with lower population exposure to air pollution from fine particulates ($PM_{2.5}$). Moreover, multifactor productivity (EAMFP) growth is correlated with lower land consumption (built-up area per capita) and lower income inequality. This indicates that fostering productivity growth can potentially also generate some desirable environmental and social outcomes.

Figure 3. **Socio-economic context and characteristics of growth**

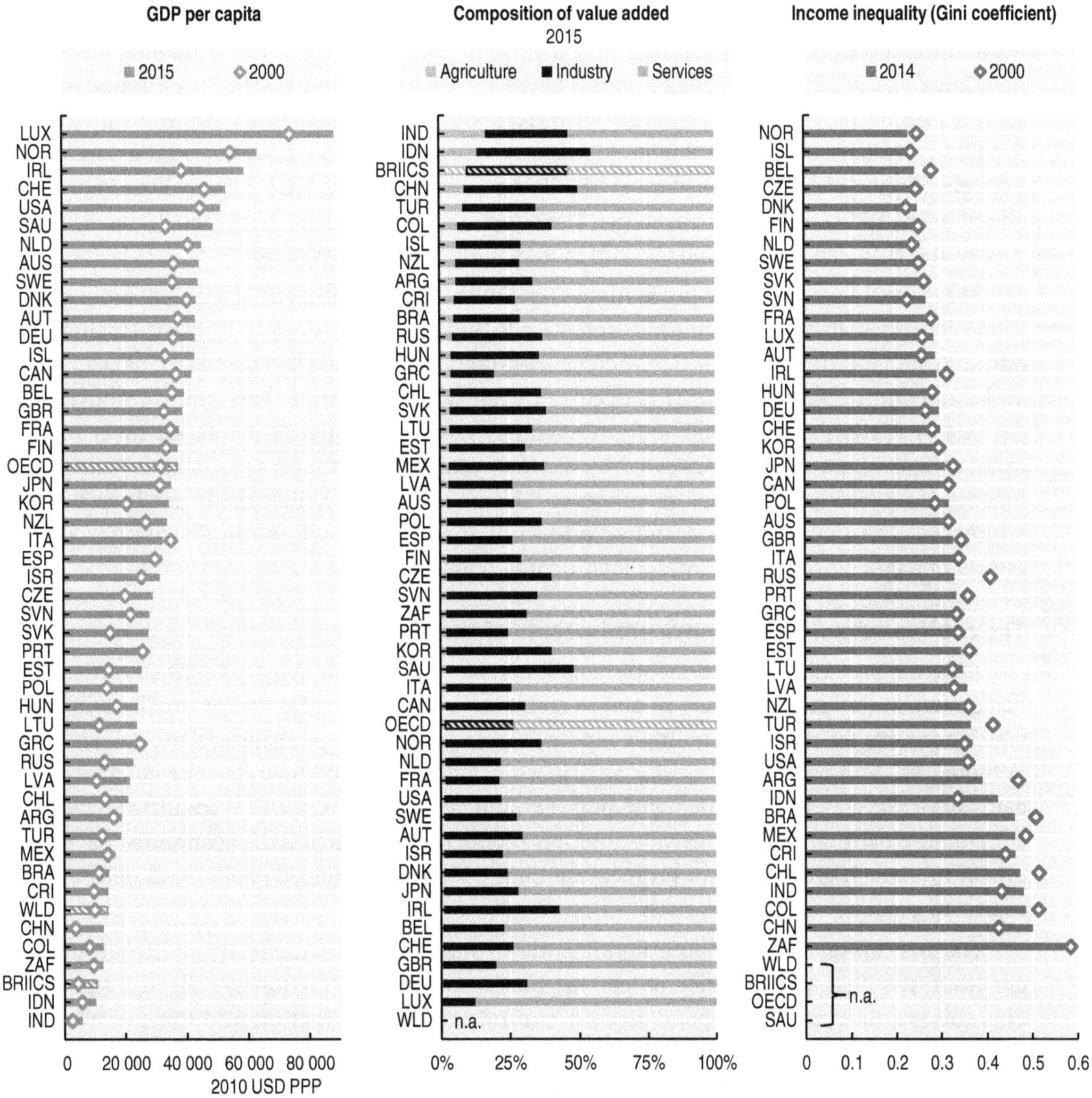

Source: OECD (2017), "Green growth indicators", *OECD Environment Statistics* (database); Solt (2016), "The standardized world income inequality database"; World Bank (2016), "World development indicators".

StatLink http://dx.doi.org/10.1787/888933484425

1. Partial correlation coefficients from pairwise regressions, controlling for country- and time- specific variation.

At the same time, lower land consumption (built-up area per capita) is correlated with higher population exposure to $PM_{2.5}$. This points to some potentially difficult trade-offs. The data also suggest that countries that rely to a greater extent on environmental taxation and foster innovation through environmental technologies tend to achieve higher levels of carbon and material productivity.

Central elements of green growth in focus

The socio-economic characteristics of growth

Large differences across countries have marked economic growth (Figure 3). Between 2000 and 2015, GDP per capita increased by 17% in the OECD area and by 137% in BRIICS economies. It ranged from -7% in Italy and Greece, to over +100% in Latvia, Lithuania, India and China. In the OECD, the service sectors generate most of the value added (73%, compared to 53% in BRIICS). The highest shares of services are in Luxembourg, Greece, the United Kingdom and France. The contribution of industry is highest in Ireland, Korea and the Czech Republic (about 40%), as well as in most BRIICS. Agriculture contributes relatively little value added in the OECD area (2% on average). The agricultural sector contributes much more in Turkey and New Zealand (9% and 6%) and in most BRIICS (10% on average).

Household income inequality is highest in South Africa, China and Colombia; among OECD countries, it is highest in Chile and Mexico. Inequality is lowest in Norway, Iceland and some other European countries. Income inequality has increased in about half of OECD and G20 countries since 2000. This occurred even when countries were going through periods of sustained economic and employment growth. Inequality increased most in Indonesia, China and India, followed by Slovenia, Austria, Germany and Poland. Rising income inequality poses social, environmental and economic challenges. It needs to be addressed when policies are designed and implemented (e.g. when the distributional effects of a green fiscal reform affect low-income households).

The environmental and resource productivity of the economy

Over the past 25 years, the environmental and resource productivity of OECD countries has grown, but with wide variation across countries and sectors. Multifactor productivity, which accounts for the role of multiple inputs (labour, produced capital, natural capital) and outputs (GDP and pollution) provides an important perspective. It shows that productivity gains have played a key role for sustaining economic growth. In fact, OECD countries have generated growth almost exclusively through productivity gains. BRIICS economies have drawn to a much greater extent on increased use of labour, produced capital and natural capital to generate additional growth.

Natural capital can contribute significantly to output growth. About 23% of its output growth in the Russian Federation since 1994 has been due to extraction of subsoil assets. This raises concerns over dependence on natural resource extraction and the need to identify new sources of growth in the long run. Pollution abatement can also affect growth performance. Some countries have achieved economic growth only at the expense of environmental quality.

From the perspective of single inputs and outputs, both the carbon and material productivity of OECD economies has improved. Today, OECD countries generate more economic output per unit of resources consumed. To generate USD 1 000 of GDP in 2015 (or the most recent year available), OECD countries, on average, consume 416 kg of non-energy materials and 111 kg of energy materials (in oil equivalent) (down from 143 kg in 2000). They also emit 256 kg of CO_2 (down from 338 kg in 2000).

Despite a slowdown in the OECD area, global CO_2 emissions continued to grow, up 58% from 1990. Some countries managed to reduce the absolute level of emissions. However, most have achieved only a relative decoupling between emissions and economic growth. In other words, CO_2 emissions increased at a lower rate than real GDP.

Decoupling demand-based CO_2 emissions presents an even greater challenge. Total emissions generated to satisfy domestic final demand in OECD countries have increased faster than emissions from domestic production. As a result, most OECD countries are "net-importers" of CO_2 emissions.

Cleaner production (e.g. through cleaner energy use) can help address both production- and demand-based emissions (consumption of cleaner domestic production). Decoupling demand-based CO_2 emissions is challenging, however, because embodied CO_2 emissions per capita are highly correlated with living standards. Conversely, production-based CO_2 emissions more closely reflect the structure and energy intensity of the economy.

These developments are on par with widespread increases in energy productivity. However productivity levels remain low in many of the major energy consuming countries. OECD countries and BRIICS economies continue to be more than 80% reliant on fossil fuels. Renewables still play only a relatively minor role in the energy mix. Several countries have seen fast increases in coal penetration (both OECD and BRIICS). Further, some countries with potentially important renewable energy resources still show low levels of renewables penetration. Energy productivity could be fostered through continued phasing out of government support for fossil fuel consumption and removing barriers to improvements in energy efficiency.

Materials other than energy carriers represent 78% of the materials mix consumption in the OECD and 87% in BRIICS. Productivity gains have been achieved, but material consumption remains high, often driven by construction materials. Raising the recovery rates of construction minerals could significantly improve efficiency. Once indirect flows (raw materials embodied in international trade) are considered, improvements over longer periods are often more moderate.

Many materials, including valuable materials, end up as waste. However, efforts to move from waste to resources are starting to show results. Increasing material recovery (through recycling and composting) is an important complement to waste reduction efforts. In Europe, about one-third of the 13.4 tonnes of materials consumed every year per person end up in waste. About 17% of this amount is subsequently recovered.

The natural asset base of the economy

Countries' endowment in natural resources varies greatly and intensity of use of many resources is high and rising. Freshwater resources in particular are unevenly distributed and local water scarcity remains of concern. In more than one-third of OECD countries, freshwater resources are under moderate to medium-high stress. Many forests are threatened by degradation, fragmentation and conversion to other types; and many ecosystems have been degraded.

Across the OECD, the conversion of land to artificial surfaces has accelerated. Buildings now cover 30% more land than in 1990. Globally, an area the size of the United Kingdom has been converted to buildings since 1990. Societal changes, population growth and changing urban form (compact vs. fragmented cities) may explain this growth.

Intense urban growth occurs in many already highly urbanised countries. This often brings about a loss of natural resources and agricultural land, soil sealing and negative effects on the water cycle. Land development and the resulting changes in land cover lead to habitat fragmentation and habitat loss. They are thus associated with a decline in the populations of many species and reduced biodiversity. Measures to protect biodiversity and ecosystems such as protected area designations, sustainable resource management, etc. must be complemented with mainstreaming of biodiversity-relevant policy instruments. Environmentally harmful agricultural subsidies must also be phased out.

The environmental dimension of quality of life

Air pollution is the single greatest environmental health risk worldwide. Human exposure to air pollution by fine particulates ($PM_{2.5}$) remains dangerously high in most OECD countries, despite improvements since 1990. Less than one in three OECD countries meet the WHO Air Quality Guideline for annual average $PM_{2.5}$ exposure of 10 micrograms per cubic metre. Exposures to $PM_{2.5}$ continue to rise in China and India and now attain extreme levels. At the same time, there has been little improvement in population exposure to air pollution by ground-level ozone (O_3).

Exposure to these two air pollutants has serious consequences for human health. In the OECD area, exposure to outdoor $PM_{2.5}$ and ozone is estimated to cause around 0.5 million premature deaths each year. This has an annual welfare cost equivalent to 3.6% of GDP. More ambitious policy could thus generate significant benefits.

Economic opportunities from innovation and effective policies

Innovation is a key driver of productivity and economic growth. Efforts to implement green growth policies by encouraging innovation and changes in consumer behaviour are accelerating. Worldwide, the number of inventions in climate change mitigation technologies (especially their applications to buildings, transport and energy generation) have tripled since 2000. At the same time, inventive activity in general (all technologies) has risen only by about 30%.

However, inventive activity has been slowing down across all major environment-related technological domains since 2011. About 90% of green technologies still originate in the OECD, but the contributions of China and India are rising fast. Innovation can help achieve environmental objectives at lower costs and speed up the transition to green growth; it can also lead to new business opportunities and markets.

Providing continuous and long-term incentives for directing innovation towards environmental objectives remains a challenge. Economic instruments are insufficiently used, and policies often lack coherence, thus undermining the transition to green growth.

Research and development budgets are rising in many countries, but the share devoted to environmental and energy objectives remains stagnant. Public budgets for energy-related research, development and demonstration are shifting towards renewables in most OECD countries. Yet, in a handful of countries, support for fossil fuel energy technology keeps rising. In many countries, innovation policies are insufficiently co-ordinated with environmental and resource efficiency policies.

In OECD countries, the share of environmentally related taxes in total tax revenue and compared to GDP is decreasing. Some countries have shifted part of their revenue collection from labour to environmentally related activities. Others have introduced new environmentally related taxes as part of fiscal consolidation. However, most countries have experienced higher increases in their revenue from labour taxes relative to that of the environment. The revenue raise by environmentally related taxes represents only 5.2% of total tax revenue, equivalent to 1.6% of GDP in the OECD area.

At the same time, countries continue to support fossil fuel production and consumption in many ways. This costs more than USD 60 billion per year in the OECD area only, and much more in the rest of the world. Further, there are several impediments to the transition to a low-carbon economy. These include variations in energy tax rates, preferential treatment of diesel fuel and of company cars, exemptions for fuel used in some sectors, and significant gaps in taxation of non-road carbon emissions.

Overall, a better alignment of "green" and "growth" objectives is needed. The main challenges in implementing policy frameworks for green growth include (OECD, 2015):

1. establishing an explicit price on greenhouse gas emissions through taxation or tradable permit systems
2. using pricing instruments to change behaviour with respect to water, waste and transport
3. shifting the tax burden in favour of environmentally related taxation
4. eliminating environmentally harmful discrepancies in tax systems
5. managing subsidies to promote green technologies and phasing out environmentally perverse subsidies
6. supporting the development of green infrastructure
7. orienting innovation systems to advance green growth priorities
8. accelerating improvements in energy efficiency.

Notes

Figure 1 and Figure 2 use the following indicators:

- CO_2 productivity (production-based) calculated as real GDP generated per unit of CO_2 emitted (USD/kg). For more information, see chapter on *Carbon productivity*.
- CO_2 productivity (demand-based) calculated as GDP generated per unit of CO_2 emitted from final demand (USD/kg). For more information, see chapter on *Carbon productivity*.
- Material productivity (production-based) calculated as GDP generated per unit of materials consumed (in terms of Domestic Material Consumption). For more information, see chapter on *Material productivity*.
- Environmentally adjusted multifactor productivity growth (EAMFP) calculated using a growth accounting framework that includes labour, produced capital and natural capital as factor inputs, and pollution as undesirable by-product. For more information, see chapter on *Environmentally adjusted multifactor productivity*.
- (Low) land consumption is calculated as (the inverse of) built-up area per capita. For more information, see chapter on *Land resources*.
- (Low) air pollution exposure is calculated as (the inverse of) mean exposure to outdoor $PM_{2.5}$. For more information, see chapter on *Air pollution, health risks and costs*.
- Environmentally related innovation refers to the share of environmentally related patents on total patents developed by a country's inventors. For more information, see chapter on *Technology and innovation*.

- Environmentally related taxation refers to the share of environmentally related tax revenue on total tax revenue collected in a country. For more information, see chapter on *Taxes and subsidies*.
- Gross domestic product (GDP) per capita, is expressed in USD 2010 using PPPs, per inhabitant. For more information, see *Glossary*.
- (Low) income inequality is calculated as (the inverse of) the Gini coefficient. For more information, see *Glossary*.

References

JRC (2016), "Global human settlement layer", Joint Research Centre, European Commission, *http://publications.jrc.ec.europa.eu/repository/handle/JRC97705*.

OECD (2017), "Green growth indicators", *OECD Environment Statistics* (database), *http://dx.doi.org/10.1787/data-00665-en* (accessed in March 2017).

OECD (2015), *Towards Green Growth?: Tracking Progress*, OECD Publishing, Paris, *http://dx.doi.org/10.1787/9789264234437-en*.

Solt, F. (2016), "The standardized world income inequality database", *Social Science Quarterly*, No. 97/5, SWIID Version 5.1, July 2016, pp. 1267-1281.

World Bank (2016), "World development indicators", *http://data.worldbank.org/data-catalog/world-development-indicators* (accessed in January 2017).

PART 1

The environmental and resource productivity of the economy

Carbon productivity

Energy productivity

Material productivity and waste

Nutrient flows and balances

Environmentally adjusted multifactor productivity

Carbon productivity

Carbon dioxide (CO_2) from the combustion of fossil fuels and biomass accounts for 90% of total greenhouse gas (GHG) emissions. It is thus a key factor in countries' ability to deal with climate change. The stabilisation of GHG concentrations in the atmosphere depends on implementation of coherent national and international policies that aim at structural and technological changes. It depends on countries' ability to further decouple CO_2 and other GHG emissions growth from economic growth, and reduce the overall level of emissions.

Climate change is of global concern for its effects on ecosystems, human settlements and agriculture, and the frequency of extreme weather events. It could have significant consequences for human well-being and socio-economic activities. This, in turn, could affect global economic output.

International production networks and global value chains are increasingly interdependent. This means that domestic mitigation efforts must be placed in a global context. Further, they must build on a good understanding of carbon flows associated with international trade and final domestic demand. With increasing trade flows and the relocation of carbon-intensive production abroad, reductions in domestic emissions can be partially or wholly offset (and sometimes exceed) elsewhere in the world. The links between trade, economic growth and the environment are, however, complex. Policies must account for various factors, including pro-competitive benefits of trade for growth and development.

Achieving the aims of the 2015 Paris Agreement will require structural changes to overcome the carbon dependency of our economies. First, it will require core climate policy instruments, such as an explicit carbon price and phase out of all fossil fuel subsidies. Beyond these steps, governments must align policies across a diverse range of non-climate areas.

Carbon prices are an essential element to decarbonise the economy. They are indispensable to induce cost-effective abatement, to steer investment towards low-carbon infrastructure technologies and to discourage carbon-intensive production and consumption. Globally, countries are far from exploiting the full potential of emissions pricing policies. Most emissions across OECD and BRIICS (Brazil, the Russian Federation, India, Indonesia, the People's Republic of China [hereafter China] and South Africa) are not priced at all, and 90% are priced at less than EUR 30 per tonne of CO_2 (see chapter on *Taxes and subsidies*).

Current policies do not provide stable and sufficient economic incentives for firms to reduce the costs of future mitigation. Nor do they provide incentives for investments that take account of rising climate risks. Introducing a predictable long-term path of carbon prices will allow firms to adapt their investment plans to expected future increases in carbon prices. This is particularly important for investment in long-lived assets.

Figure 1.1. **Global CO_2 emissions from energy use increased**

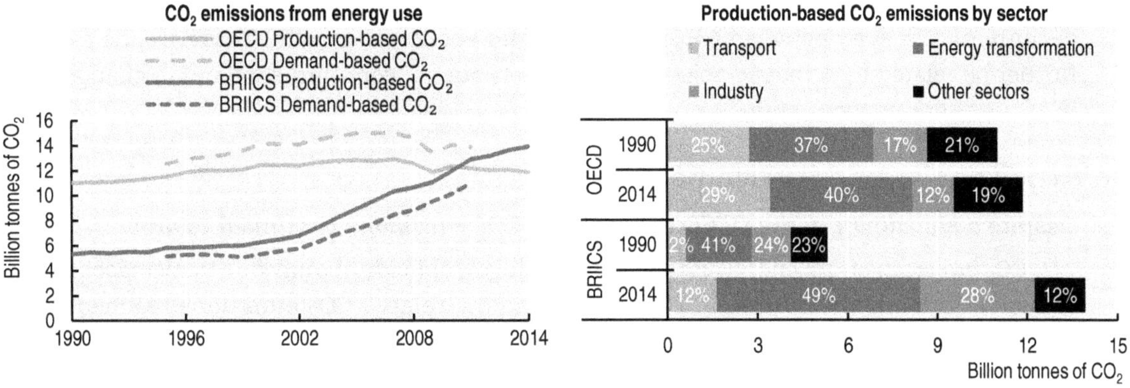

Source: IEA (2016), "CO_2 emissions by product and flow (Edition 2016)", *IEA CO_2 Emissions from Fuel Combustion Statistics* (database); OECD (2015), "Carbon dioxide embodied in international trade", *OECD Structural Analysis Statistics: Input-Output* (database).

StatLink http://dx.doi.org/10.1787/888933484433

Figure 1.2. **CO_2 productivity improved in most countries**

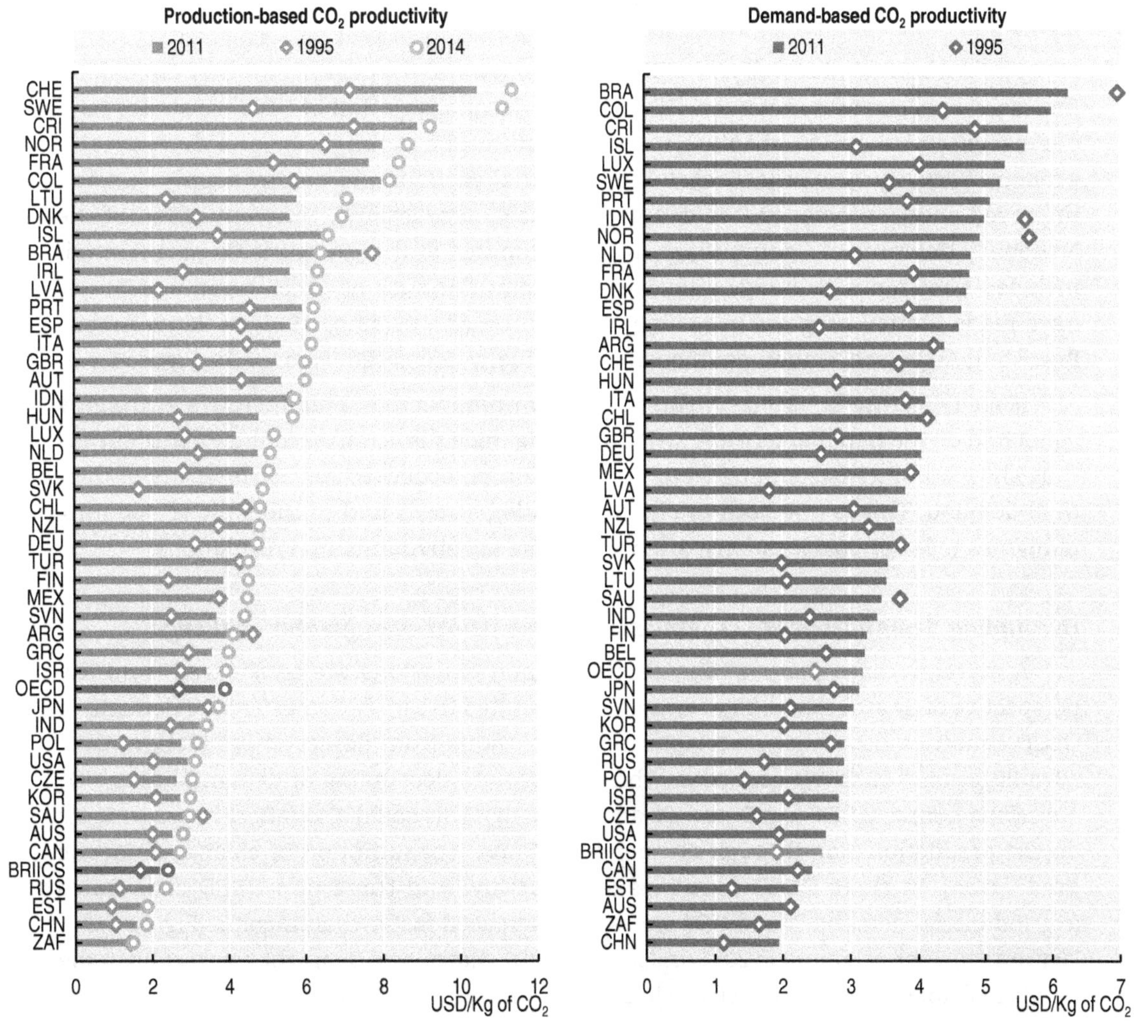

Source: IEA (2016), "CO_2 emissions by product and flow (Edition 2016)", *IEA CO_2 Emissions from Fuel Combustion Statistics* (database); OECD (2015), "Carbon dioxide embodied in international trade", *OECD Structural Analysis Statistics: Input-Output* (database).

StatLink http://dx.doi.org/10.1787/888933484446

Progress towards green growth can be assessed against trends in CO_2 emission productivity from the production and demand (footprint) perspectives, and the level of decoupling achieved between GHG emissions and economic growth. These trends can further be related to domestic objectives and international commitments and to changes in atmospheric concentrations of GHG.

Main trends and recent developments

Despite a slowdown in the OECD area, global CO_2 emissions continued to grow

CO_2 emissions from energy use are still growing worldwide, mainly due to increases in transport and energy sectors. In 2014, global energy-related CO_2 emissions reached a record high of 32.38 billion tonnes, or 58% more than in 1990. Production-based emissions growth has decelerated in OECD countries in the wake of the 2008 financial crises. In part, this reflects an on-going decline in the contribution of industry to overall economic activity. In BRIICS economies, emissions have continued to rise sharply (Figure 1.1).

Most countries have achieved only a relative decoupling between emissions and economic growth, although some managed to reduce emission levels in absolute terms

The carbon productivity of OECD economies has improved, as CO_2 emissions increased at a lower rate than real GDP (relative decoupling). Half of OECD countries have decreased emissions in absolute terms (absolute decoupling). Beyond decreases in economic activity, this reflects shifts in industrial structure, in energy supply mix and improved energy efficiency (see chapter on *Energy productivity*). Nine out of ten of the Nationally Determined Contributions (NDCs) submitted at the 2015 Paris Climate Summit included a reference to energy efficiency. Yet, countries such as Chile, Japan and Turkey have made limited progress in raising carbon productivity since 1995. In Saudi Arabia, Brazil and Argentina, carbon productivity has actually decreased (Figure 1.2a, Figure 1.3a).

Most reporting is based on the production perspective. This includes emissions generated on the national territory without taking trade flows into account. Countries may thus show absolute decoupling from a production perspective, but not in terms of their final demand. This is due both to changing trade patterns and to the shift of polluting industries to lower-cost locations, often with more lax environmental regulations.

Decoupling demand-based CO_2 emissions presents an even greater challenge

A more nuanced picture thus emerges when emissions are considered from the perspective of final demand. Total emissions generated to satisfy domestic final demand in OECD countries have increased faster than emissions from domestic production. Over 1995-2011, only 12 OECD countries achieved absolute decoupling of demand-based CO_2 emissions from real GDP (e.g. Denmark and Germany). This could also reflect improvements on the production side through cleaner energy use (consumption of cleaner domestic production). In three OECD countries (e.g. Norway) and three non-OECD economies (e.g. Indonesia) demand-based CO_2 emissions increased faster than income (Figure 1.2b, Figure 1.3b). High oil prices in 2011 and lower export shares on GDP might partly explain the trends in demand-based productivity in some countries.

Most OECD countries are "net-importers" of CO_2 emissions because these emissions from domestic final demand for goods and services exceed emissions from domestic

Figure 1.3. **Most countries have decoupled CO_2 emissions from economic growth**

OECD and G20

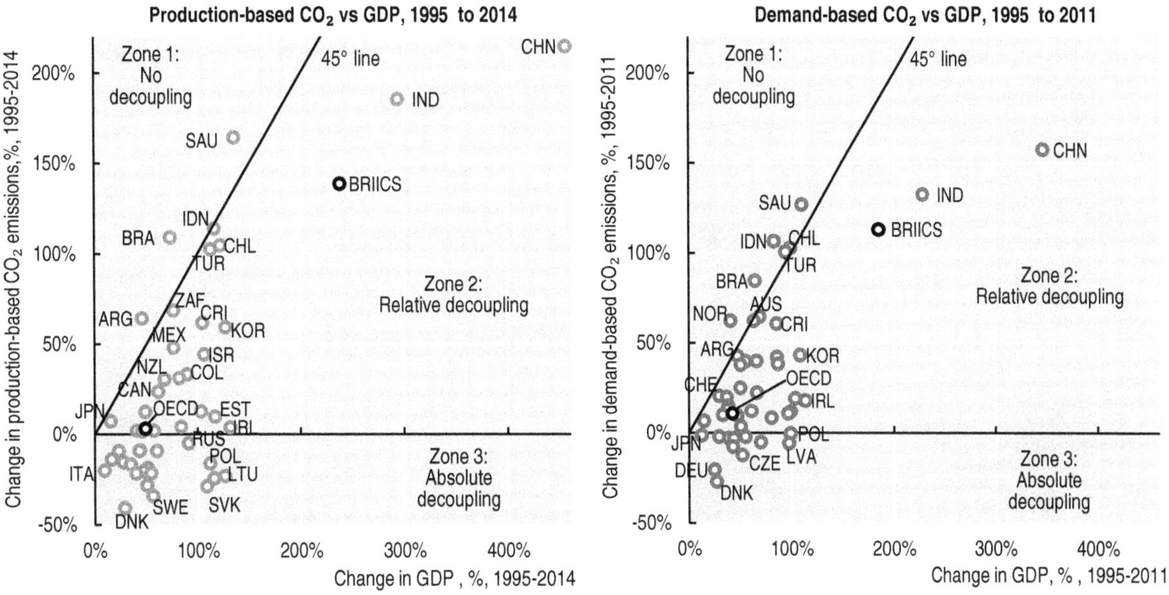

Source: IEA (2016), "CO_2 emissions by product and flow (Edition 2016)", *IEA CO_2 Emissions from Fuel Combustion Statistics* (database); OECD (2015), "Carbon dioxide embodied in international trade", *OECD Structural Analysis Statistics: Input-Output* (database).

StatLink http://dx.doi.org/10.1787/888933484457

Figure 1.4. **Embodied CO_2 per capita is highly correlated with living standards**

OECD and G20

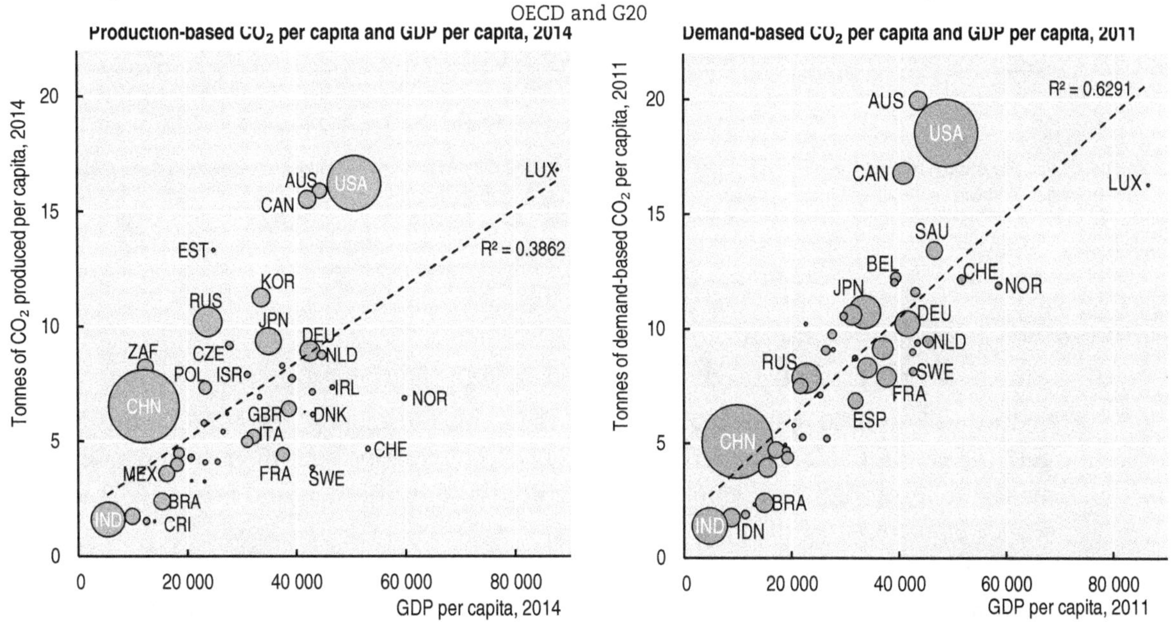

Note: The size of the bubble represents the level of emissions.

Source: IEA (2016), "CO_2 emissions by product and flow (Edition 2016)", *IEA CO_2 Emissions from Fuel Combustion Statistics* (database); OECD (2015), "Carbon dioxide embodied in international trade", *OECD Structural Analysis Statistics: Input-Output* (database).

StatLink http://dx.doi.org/10.1787/888933484465

production (Figure 1.1a, Figure 1.5). This can be partly explained by three factors: i) displacement of energy-intensive production to non-OECD economies; ii) growth of imports (e.g. due to lower prices of imported goods, or higher overall domestic consumption); or iii) imports with a higher carbon footprint. These trends reflect a host of factors, including changes in international production patterns, specialisation in production and changes in the comparative advantages of countries.

Decoupling demand-based CO_2 emissions is challenging because embodied CO_2 emissions per capita are highly correlated with material living standards, more so than production-based CO_2 which more closely reflects the structure and energy intensity of the economy (Figure 1.4).

Figure 1.5. **Most OECD countries are net importers of CO_2**

OECD and G20

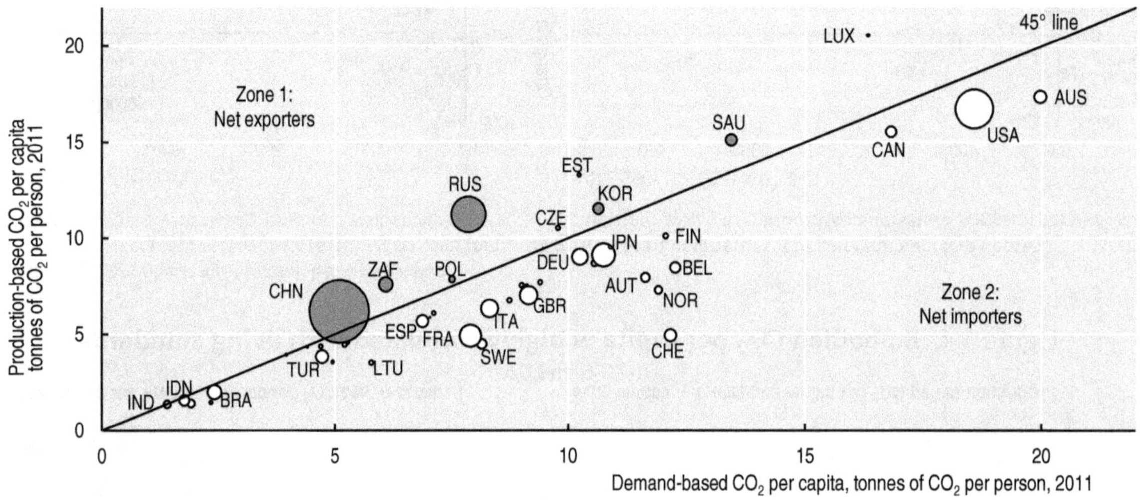

Note: The size of the bubble represents the level of net exports of embodied CO_2. White bubbles indicate negative values of net exports (i.e. net imports). The 45-degree line shows equal emissions of production- and demand-based CO_2.

Source: IEA (2016), "CO_2 emissions by product and flow (Edition 2016)", *IEA CO_2 Emissions from Fuel Combustion Statistics* (database); OECD (2015), "Carbon dioxide embodied in international trade", *OECD Structural Analysis Statistics: Input-Output* (database).

StatLink http://dx.doi.org/10.1787/888933484471

Measurability and interpretation

The indicators presented in this chapter relate to the following:

- **Production-based CO_2 productivity** reflects the economic value generated (in terms of real GDP) per unit of CO_2 emitted. Production-based emissions refer to gross direct CO_2 emissions from fossil fuel combustion, emitted within the national territory. They exclude bunkers, sinks and indirect effects.
- **Demand-based CO_2 productivity** reflects the economic value generated per unit of CO_2 emitted to satisfy domestic final demand. Demand-based CO_2 emissions (or CO_2 embodied in domestic final demand) include the CO_2 from energy use emitted during the various stages of production (in the country or abroad) of goods and services consumed in domestic final demand. Comprehensive data are not available on the monetary values of domestic final demand across all countries shown here. Thus, the indicator is expressed in terms of embodied CO_2 per unit of real GDP. See also *Glossary*.
- **Net exports of CO_2** reflect the difference between the CO_2 from energy use emitted in the production of goods and services in a country, and the CO_2 emitted to satisfy domestic

final demand. "Net exports" are positive if production-based emissions are higher than demand-based emissions. Conversely, if CO_2 emissions embodied in domestic final demand are higher than emissions from production within the national territory, the country is a "net importer" of CO_2.

Carbon productivity indicators inform about the relative decoupling between economic activity and carbon emissions into the atmosphere. They provide insight into how much carbon productivity has improved. They also measure how much of the improvement is due to domestic policies and how much to displacement or substitution effects. The demand perspective helps explain production-based trends.

These indicators should be read in connection with information on total GHG emissions, energy productivity and efficiency, renewable energy sources, energy prices and taxes, and carbon pricing. Their interpretation should take into account the structure of countries' energy supply, trade patterns and climatic factors.

Energy productivity is not the same as carbon productivity, although the two are closely related. As fossil fuel use declines and more "clean energy" technologies are deployed, CO_2 productivity becomes decoupled from energy productivity.

Sources

IEA (2016), "CO_2 emissions by product and flow (Edition 2016)", *IEA CO_2 Emissions from Fuel Combustion Statistics* (database), *http://dx.doi.org/10.1787/data-00430-en* (accessed on 31 January 2017).

OECD (2017), "Green growth indicators", *OECD Environment Statistics* (database), *http://dx.doi.org/10.1787/data-00665-en* (accessed in March 2017).

OECD (2015), "Carbon dioxide embodied in international trade", *OECD Structural Analysis Statistics: Input-Output* (database), *http://stats.oecd.org/Index.aspx?DataSetCode=IO_GHG_2015* (accessed on 31 January 2017).

Wiebe, K.S. and N. Yamano (2016), "Estimating CO_2 Emissions Embodied in Final Demand and Trade Using the OECD ICIO 2015: Methodology and Results", *OECD Science, Technology and Industry Working Papers*, No. 2016/05, OECD Publishing, Paris, *http://dx.doi.org/10.1787/5jlrcm216xkl-en*

Further reading

OECD (n.d.), Carbon dioxide emissions embodied in international trade, webpage: *http://oe.cd/io-co2*.

OECD (n.d.), Measuring trade in value added, webpage: *http://oe.cd/tiva*.

Energy productivity

Energy is an essential input in all economic activities. The structure of a country's energy supply and the efficiency of its energy use are key determinants of environmental performance and economic development. These, in turn, help determine green growth.

Energy supply and use have different environmental effects depending on energy source. They contribute to greenhouse gas (GHG) emissions and to local and regional air pollution. They also impact water quality and land use. There are risks associated with the nuclear fuel cycle and the extraction, transport and use of fossil fuels. The use of renewable energy sources and of low-carbon fuel technologies plays an important role in addressing climate change, as well as energy security.

Energy productivity can be improved by adopting more energy-efficient production technologies and processes, as well as by increasing the energy efficiency of consumer goods and services. However, achievement of environmental and climate policy objectives requires moderation of energy consumption to reduce energy use in absolute terms, not only in proportion to output (see chapters on *Carbon productivity* and *Taxes and subsidies*.)

Progress towards green growth can be assessed in two ways. It can be measured against the energy productivity of the economy and against domestic objectives for energy efficiency. In addition, it can be assessed against the share of renewable sources in energy or electricity supply. Progress can further be assessed against international environmental commitments that have implications for domestic energy policies and strategies.

Main trends and recent developments

Energy use increased the most in the services and transport sectors

Over the past two decades, energy supply of OECD countries has slightly increased and stabilised at 5 billion tonnes of oil equivalent (toe). This increase in supply has occurred despite generally low energy prices in recent years (Figure 2.1). The same level was also recently reached in BRIICS economies (Brazil, Russian Federation [hereafter Russia], India, Indonesia, People's Republic of China [hereafter China], South Africa), following the doubling of energy supply during the same period. These increases are due to a higher aggregate energy demand, principally in the services and transport sectors (OECD) and industry (BRIICS).

Despite widespread increases in energy productivity, productivity levels remain low in many of the major energy consuming countries

Overall, energy productivity has increased in OECD and BRIICS. Remarkably, in eight countries it has more than doubled (China, Ireland, Poland, Estonia, Lithuania, Slovak Republic, Latvia and Luxembourg). In some others, it has actually decreased (Costa Rica, Brazil, Iceland and Saudi Arabia) (Figure 2.2).

Figure 2.1. **Energy use in the OECD increased, particularly in services and transport**

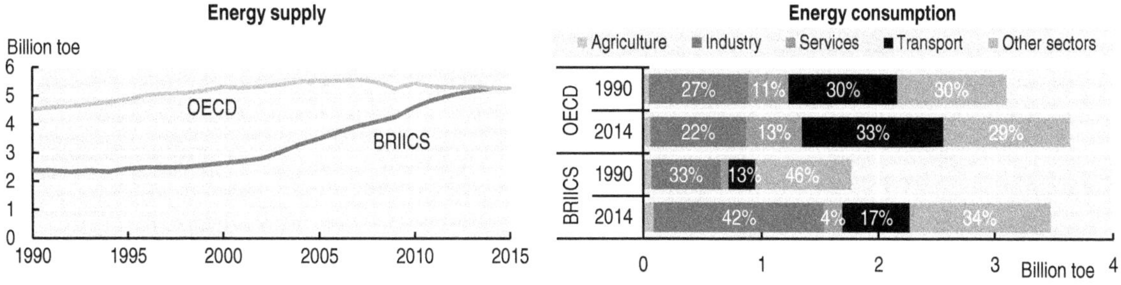

Source: IEA (2016a), "World energy balances", IEA World Energy Statistics and Balances (database).

StatLink http://dx.doi.org/10.1787/888933484487

Figure 2.2. **Energy productivity is growing in most countries, but few use less energy overall**

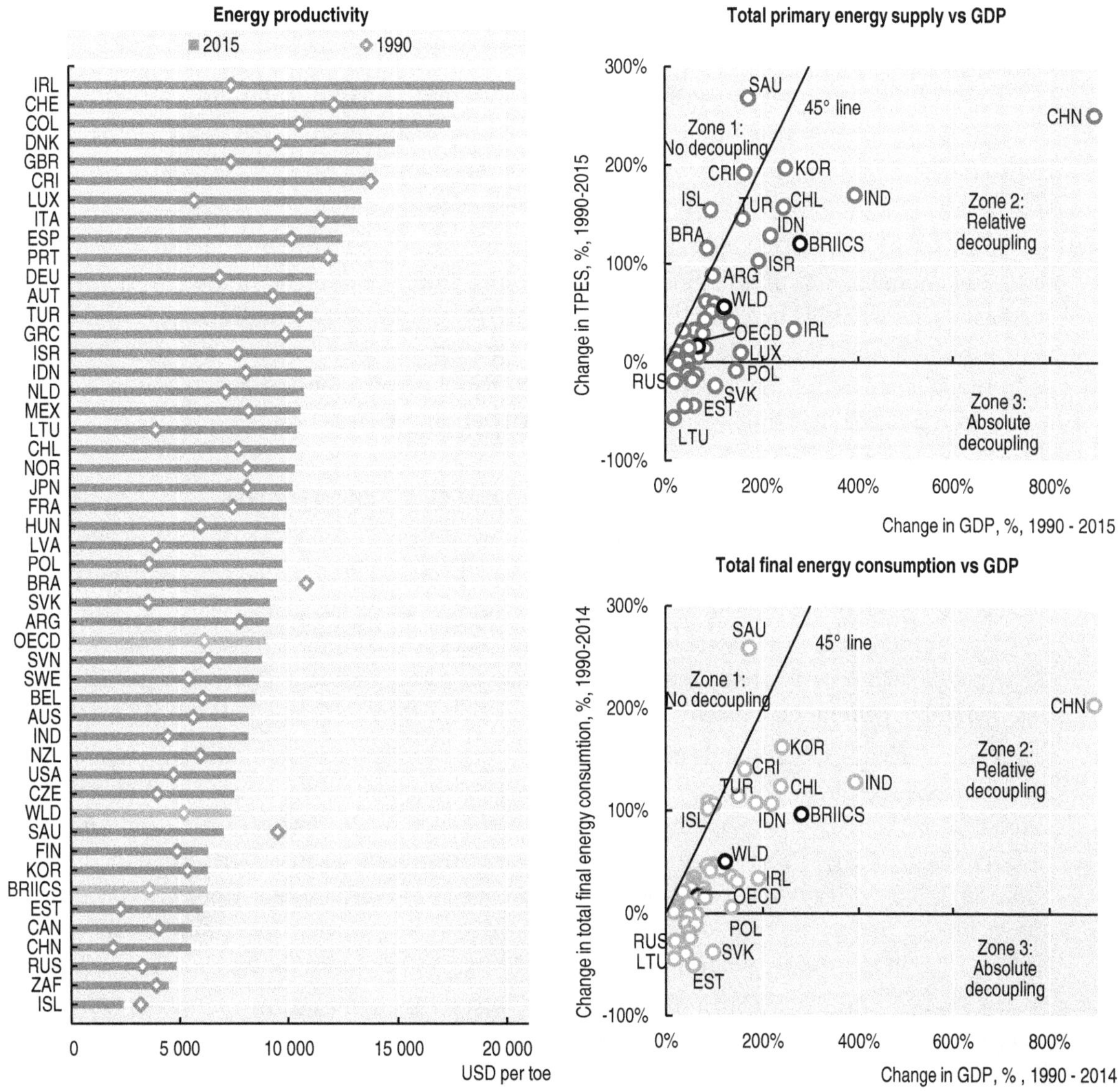

Source: IEA (2016a), "World energy balances", *IEA World Energy Statistics and Balances* (database).

StatLink http://dx.doi.org/10.1787/888933484496

Most countries have achieved a relative decoupling of energy use from GDP growth. This is a consequence of structural changes in the economy and energy conservation measures. In some countries, it also reflects decreases in economic activity and relocation of energy-intensive production abroad. Mandatory energy efficiency regulation now covers about a third of global final energy use, and has helped moderate the effects of low energy prices in recent years (IEA, 2016b). Together with increased use of cleaner and renewable energy sources, this has further contributed to limiting the growth of carbon dioxide (CO_2) emissions from energy use in OECD countries (see chapter on *Carbon productivity*).

Differences among OECD countries in energy productivity remain high. Since 1990, however, the low-productivity countries have been showing signs of catching-up. BRIICS economies such as Russia, South Africa and China, have increased energy productivity; however, their levels of productivity remain low relative to OECD countries. In these countries, government support for fossil fuel consumption is generally high. This creates barriers to improving energy efficiency and productivity (see chapter on *Taxes and subsidies*).

OECD and BRIICS economies continue to rely more than 80% on fossil fuels

The energy supply structure varies considerably by country. Since the 1990s, changes in the fuel mix accompanied growth in primary energy supply in the OECD. Shares from coal and oil fell, while shares from gas and renewables rose.

Even in 2015, the OECD was still 80% reliant on fossil fuels, primarily oil and gas. In BRIICS economies, 83% of energy supply still comes from fossil fuels. Shares from coal increased dramatically, reaching half of their energy supply. Coal penetration grew the fastest in Indonesia, Mexico, Japan (following the nuclear accident in Fukushima), as well as in India, Israel and Estonia (Figure 2.3d). From the climate change perspective this is a worrying trend: coal has the highest carbon density among all fossil fuels.

Renewables still play only a relatively minor role in OECD energy mixes

Several OECD countries have progressed in promoting renewables in their energy mixes. Overall, however, the share of renewables has increased only modestly over the last two decades (9.6% of energy and 23% of electricity supply for the OECD as a whole in 2015). The fastest increases in renewables penetration occurred in some European countries (Figure 2.3a). These increases were mainly due to government policies supporting deployment of generation capacity.

The trend in the OECD stands in stark contrast with developments in BRIICS economies. Renewables shares on total primary energy supply (TPES) have actually plummeted in BRIICS since 1990, particularly in India, China and Saudi Arabia. Although some countries had built renewables capacity, it was insufficient to outpace the growth in fossil fuel capacity. In addition, in countries where renewables largely consist of biomass (e.g. wood, charcoal, straw), its traditional uses by households have been decreasing. Some OECD countries show similar drops in renewables shares, most notably Norway, Mexico and Turkey.

The contribution of renewable sources to electricity generation increased only marginally. Some countries such as Saudi Arabia, South Africa, Korea and Israel have potentially important renewable energy resources. However, they still show remarkably low levels of renewables penetration. (Figure 2.4).

Figure 2.3. **Fossil fuels continue to dominate energy supply**

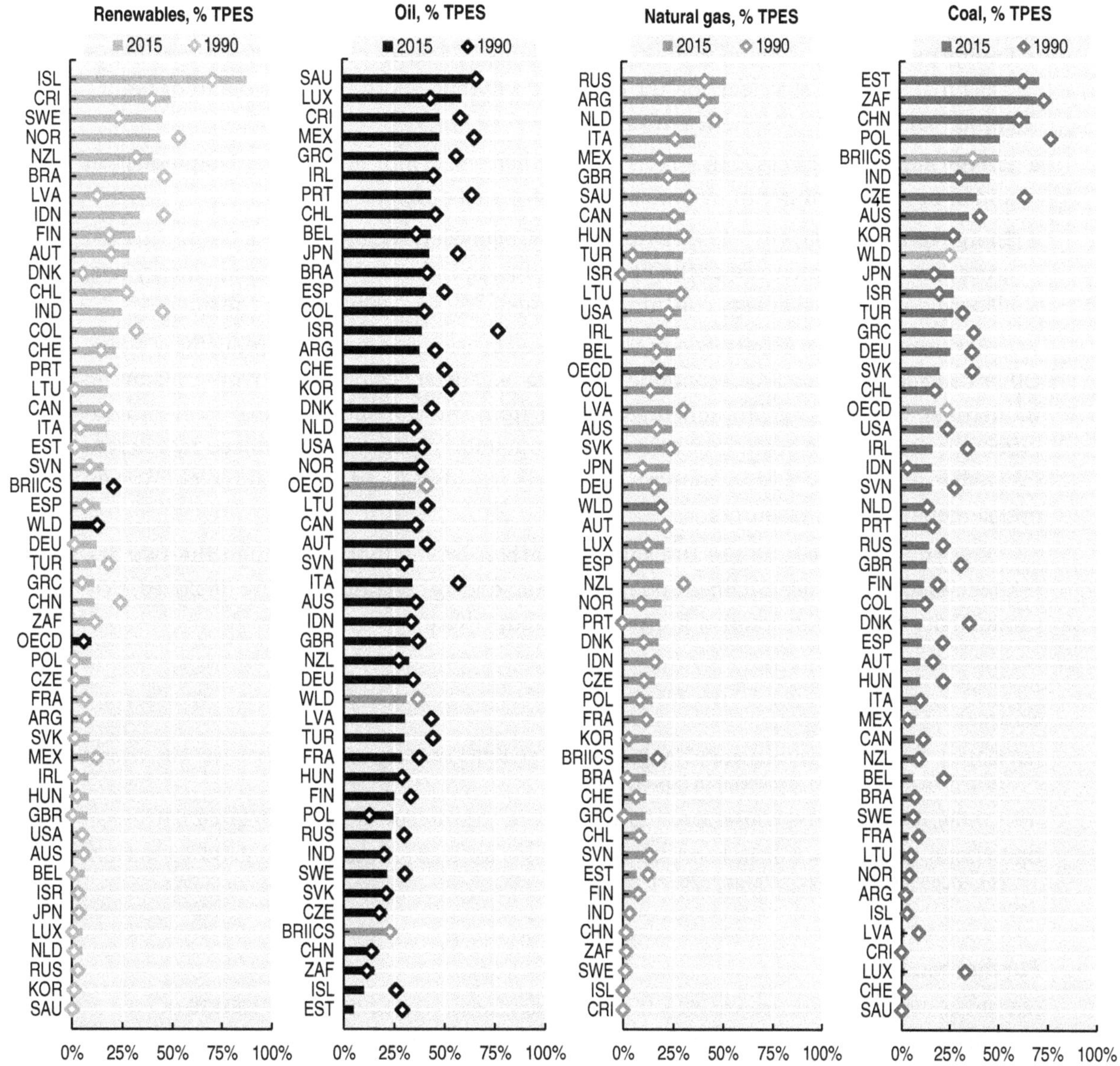

Source: IEA (2016a), *IEA World Energy Statistics and Balances* (database).

StatLink http://dx.doi.org/10.1787/888933484507

Figure 2.4. **Electricity generation from renewables increased only marginally**

Renewable electricity as percentage of total electricity generation

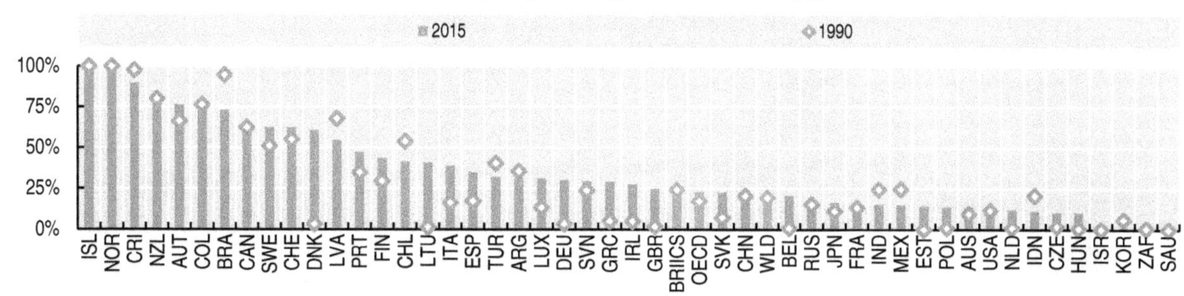

Source: IEA (2016a), *IEA World Energy Statistics and Balances* (database).

StatLink http://dx.doi.org/10.1787/888933484510

Measurability and interpretation

The indicators presented in this chapter relate to the following:

- **Energy productivity**, defined as the output generated (in terms of real GDP) per unit of TPES (USD/toe). It reflects, at least partly, efforts to improve energy efficiency and to reduce carbon and other atmospheric emissions.
- **Energy supply** is expressed in tonnes of oil equivalent. It indicates the sum of production and imports excluding exports and stock changes (see also *Glossary*).
- **Energy consumption** is expressed in tonnes of oil equivalent. Energy used for transformation processes and for own use of the energy producing industries is excluded. Energy use, also called total final energy consumption, largely reflects deliveries to consumers.

A country's energy efficiency must be assessed by more than energy productivity alone. Other considerations include economic structure (e.g. presence of large energy-consuming industries), country size (influencing demand from the transport sector), local climate (affecting demand for heating or cooling) and outsourcing of goods produced by energy-intensive industries. Cross-country comparisons also need to consider countries' endowment in energy resources.

Energy productivity is not the same as carbon productivity, although the two are related. As fossil fuel use declines and more "clean energy" technologies are deployed, CO_2 productivity becomes decoupled from energy productivity.

Sources

IEA (2016a), "World energy balances", *IEA World Energy Statistics and Balances* (database), *http://dx.doi.org/10.1787/data-00512-en* (accessed in January 2017).

IEA (2016b), *Energy Efficiency Market Report 2016*, IEA, Paris, *http://dx.doi.org/10.1787/9789264266100-en*.

OECD (2017), "Green growth indicators", *OECD Environment Statistics* (database), *http://dx.doi.org/10.1787/data-00665-en* (accessed in March 2017).

Further reading

IEA (2016a), *World Energy Investment 2016*, IEA, Paris, *http://dx.doi.org/10.1787/9789264262836-en*.

IEA (2016b), *World Energy Outlook 2016*, IEA, Paris, *http://dx.doi.org/10.1787/weo-2016-en*.

Material productivity and waste

Material resources form the physical foundation of the economy. They differ in their physical and chemical characteristics, their abundance and their value to countries. The use of raw materials from natural resources and the related production and consumption processes have environmental, economic and social consequences beyond national borders. Improving resource productivity and ensuring a sustainable management of material resources is critical from both supply security and environmental perspectives.

The main challenge is to ensure that materials are used efficiently at all stages of their life cycle (extraction, transport, manufacturing, consumption, recovery and disposal) and throughout the supply chain. This will avoid waste of resources, reduce the associated negative environmental impacts (both upstream and downstream) and potentially decrease pressures on primary natural resources. Governments have to provide incentives throughout the entire life cycle (including e.g. at product design) to encourage innovation directed at addressing the environmental externalities of resource use. This implies, for example, internalising the cost of waste management into prices of consumer goods and of waste management services. It also demands integration of materials, product and chemicals policies. Countries have used approaches such as circular economy and 3R policies (reduce, reuse and recycle), sustainable materials management and sustainable manufacturing to improve resource productivity.

Detailed internationally comparable data on material flows remain insufficiently available. As a result, this chapter focuses on aggregate measures of material use.

Main trends and recent developments

Global resource extraction is rising, though more slowly in OECD countries

Worldwide use of most significant materials has been rising for many years and has caused concerns over the environmental effectiveness of their use. In some cases, this has been accompanied by supply uncertainty and price volatility.

Among the OECD and G20 countries, the People's Republic of China (hereafter China) and the United States extract most (non-energy) raw materials. They are followed by India and Brazil (mostly biomass), and South Africa and Canada (mostly metals) (Figure 3.1c). At the world level, used material extraction has been steadily increasing since 1980, by over 200%. Much of this increase is due to non-metallic minerals (including construction minerals and industrial minerals), which grew by more than 300% in 1980-2013. This increase represented almost half of materials extracted in 2013 (see *materialflows.net*).

Productivity gains have been achieved, but material consumption remains high

Materials other than energy carriers represent 78% of the materials mix consumption in OECD member countries and 87% in BRIICS economies (Brazil, Russian Federation, India,

Figure 3.1. **Material productivity is growing in some countries but remains low and stagnant in others**

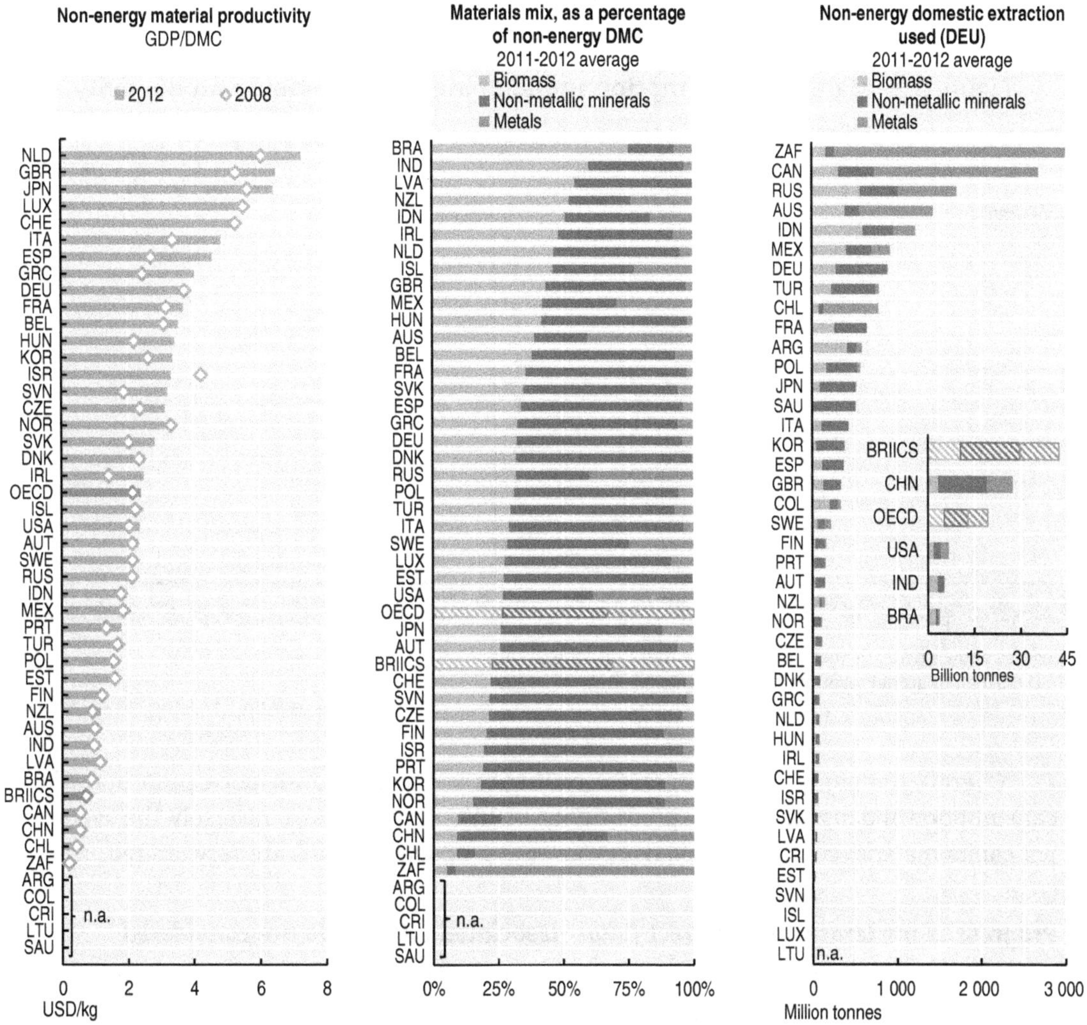

Note: Non-metallic minerals include construction minerals and industrial minerals.

Source: OECD (2016a), "Material resources", *OECD Environment Statistics* (database); Vienna University of Economics and Business (2017) *materialflows.net* online data portal.

StatLink http://dx.doi.org/10.1787/888933484529

Indonesia, China, South Africa). Material productivity has been improving in some OECD countries (especially in some European countries and Korea). However, it remains low and stagnant in BRIICS economies (Figure 3.1a). In 2012, OECD economies generated about USD 2 400 of income (in terms of GDP) per tonne of non-energy materials used. That is more than three times the value generated by BRIICS economies (USD 700 per tonne, using purchasing power parities [PPPs]).

In many European countries, improvements occurred particularly after 2008. This followed the financial crisis that led to less industrial output and less demand for materials in some sectors, particularly construction.

The consumption of non-energy material resources in OECD countries remains high at about 15 kg per year per capita. It is still about 14% higher than in BRIICS economies although the gap is closing (Figure 3.2). Given their weight, construction minerals dominate the non-energy materials mix in many countries and determine general trends. This group of materials features low recovery rates and therefore significant potential for efficiency improvements and greater circularity of flows.

Figure 3.2. **Material consumption remains high despite rising productivity**

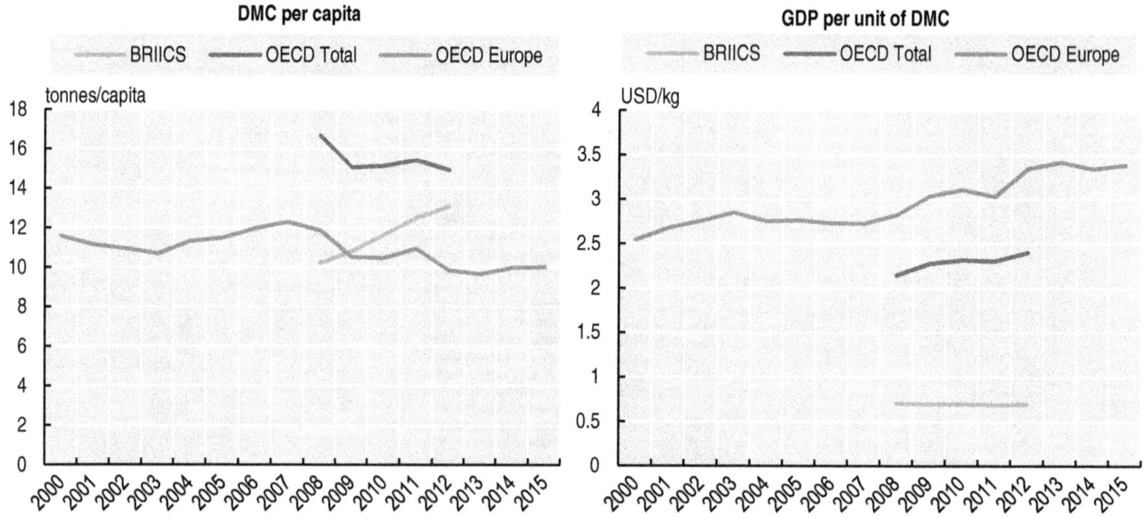

Note: Aggregates shown here are based on estimates to fill missing values.
Source: OECD (2016a), "Material resources", *OECD Environment Statistics* (database).

StatLink http://dx.doi.org/10.1787/888933484531

Overall, the general trend in OECD countries is towards lower per capita material consumption and higher material productivity. In BRIICS economies, conversely, the average per capita material consumption is rising fast and productivity gains are very limited.

Progress is moderate once indirect flows associated with trade are considered

Changing trade patterns and the displacement of resource-intensive production to other countries play a role in productivity gains. According to pilot data, once indirect flows (raw materials embodied in international trade) are considered, improvements in countries that are net importers are often more moderate over longer periods (OECD, 2015; UNEP, 2015). Indirect flows of materials take into account the life-cycle dimension of the supply chain. This includes the upstream natural resource requirements, though the materials are not physically imported. Their environmental consequences occur in the countries where the traded materials originate.

Many materials end up as waste, but efforts to move from waste to resources show results

Over the last two decades, OECD countries have put significant efforts into curbing municipal solid waste generation and encouraging waste prevention in industry. Generation of municipal waste in OECD member countries as a group has increased by 2% since the early 2000s. This shows a modest decoupling from economic growth (gross domestic product [GDP] increased by 12% during the same period) and from population growth (waste per capita fell by 6%). A person living in the OECD generates, on average, 516 kg of municipal waste per year; this is about 40 kg less than in 2000, but still about 10 kg more than in 1990.

In several countries, municipal waste generation intensities decreased by double-digit figures. Most notable were Spain, Iceland and Estonia where per capita amounts fell by over 20% (Figure 3.3a). Seven countries failed to decouple waste generation from economic growth. In Denmark and Norway, per capita waste generation soared in times of moderate economic growth. In some countries such as Portugal waste generation continued to rise despite an economic slowdown.

Figure 3.3. **Municipal waste generation has been slowly decoupling from economic growth**

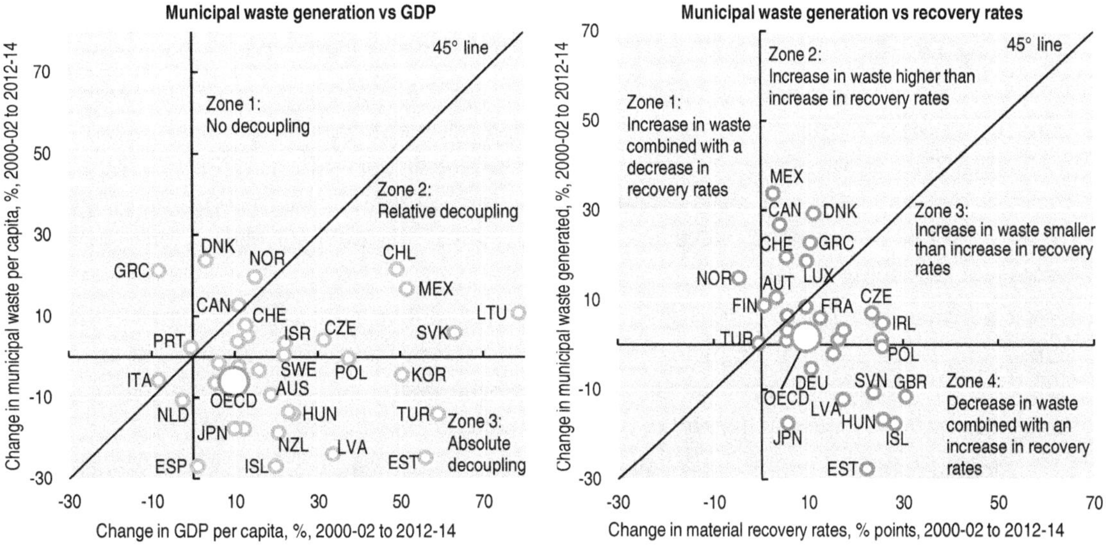

Source: OECD (2016b), "Municipal waste", *OECD Environment Statistics* (database).

StatLink http://dx.doi.org/10.1787/888933484547

Figure 3.4. **Municipal waste landfilling and tax rates, 2013**

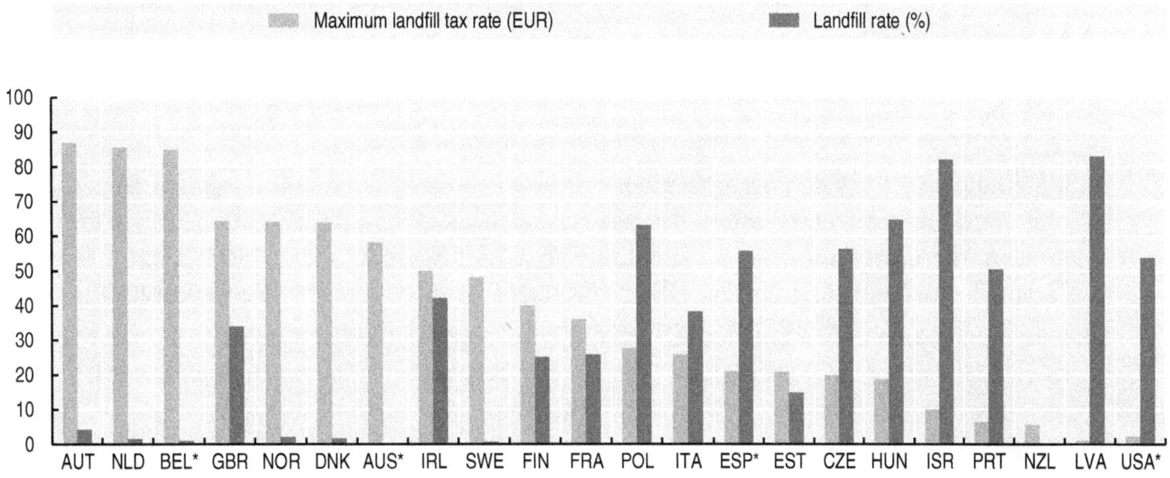

Note: *tax rates refer to Flanders for Belgium, to New South Wales for Australia, to Catalonia for Spain, and to New Jersey, North Carolina, Mississippi and Indiana for the United States.

Source: OECD (2016b), "Municipal waste", *OECD Environment Statistics* (database); OECD (2017a), "Environmental policy instruments", *OECD Environment Statistics* (database).

StatLink http://dx.doi.org/10.1787/888933484552

Increasing material recovery complements efforts to reduce waste amounts. More and more waste is being diverted from landfills and incinerators and fed back into the economy through recycling and composting. Independent of the progress achieved in reducing municipal waste generation, material recovery rates increased in all countries, except Turkey. The average recovery rate of municipal waste treated in the OECD is now 34%, compared to 25% in 2000.

Significant progress can be observed in many central and eastern European countries where recovery rates were extremely low in the early 2000s. Some countries managed to simultaneously reduce municipal waste generation and increase recovery over the past ten years (e.g. Estonia, Hungary and the United Kingdom) (Figure 3.3b).

Landfilling nonetheless remains the major disposal method in many OECD countries. Landfill taxes are often used to encourage waste prevention and material reuse and recycling. The tax rates usually vary by type of waste disposed (i.e. higher tax rates for recoverable waste). The available data suggest that ten countries levy a maximum tax rate of at least EUR 40 per tonne of waste landfilled. They also indicate a correlation between tax rates and landfilling activity.

Countries with low tax rates, such as the Czech Republic, Israel and the United States, landfill more than half of municipal waste. Other factors that play a role include landfill bans for certain categories of waste (e.g. biodegradable waste), the capacity of recovery and recycling facilities, and the density of population and economic activities (Figure 3.4).

More generally, recycling rates have increased for some high-volume materials, such as glass, steel, aluminium, paper and plastics, but remain low for many others. Many valuable materials continue to be disposed of as waste and, if not recovered, are lost to the economy. Unexploited "urban mines" (e.g. electric and electronic equipment) could be an important source of minerals and metals for the industrial sector. They are also a potentially important domestic source of raw materials in the future. In Europe, about one-third of the 13 400 tonnes of materials consumed every year per person end up in waste. About 17% of this amount is recovered.

Measurability and interpretation

The indicators presented in this chapter relate to the following:

- **Material productivity** defined as the monetary value (in terms of real GDP) generated per unit of materials used (in terms of domestic material consumption, DMC). The focus is on non-energy materials (that is, excluding fossil energy carriers). This indicator is complemented by data on the domestic extraction of materials used in the economy (DEU).
- **Municipal waste** defined as household and similar waste collected by or on behalf of municipalities, and originating from households, offices and small businesses. **Material recovery** includes recovery for recycling and composting.
- **Landfill rates of municipal waste** defined as the amounts of municipal waste disposed at landfills as a percentage of amounts treated. They are presented with **landfill tax rates**, (i.e. the tax levied per tonne of municipal waste disposed in landfills). Tax rates vary depending on waste types: **maximum tax rates** apply to waste that could be easily recovered (such as recyclable and compostable waste). Final waste is usually subject to a lower rate.

Measures of material productivity extend productivity measurement and analysis to material resources. They complement measures such as labour and capital productivity.

These measures should be read in conjunction with information on commodity prices, flows of secondary raw materials, waste management practices and costs, and consumption levels and patterns. In general, caution is needed when drawing conclusions based on country-level data. Interpretation should take into account the properties and composition of material groups, as well as countries' endowment in natural resources and the structure of their economy. The indicators presented in this chapter do not reflect environmental impacts.

The data on material flows used to calculate the indicators presented here are estimates, and their coverage and completeness vary by variable and by country. Missing information, including on physical flows of international trade, and a lack of consensus on measurement methods, limit the calculation of some material flow indicators at international level. In particular, more needs to be done to monitor flows of secondary raw materials and to calculate internationally harmonised demand-based indicators that measure the raw material equivalents embodied in international trade of goods and services.

Data on the generation and management of waste also remain weak in many countries. The types of waste covered, the definitions and surveying methods employed may vary considerably among countries and over time. See also *Glossary*.

Sources

OECD (2017a), "Environmental policy instruments", *OECD Environment Statistics* (database), *http://dx.doi.org/10.1787/data-00696-en* (accessed in November 2017).

OECD (2017b), "Green growth indicators", *OECD Environment Statistics* (database), *http://dx.doi.org/10.1787/data-00665-en* (accessed in March 2017).

OECD (2016a), "Material resources", *OECD Environment Statistics* (database), *http://dx.doi.org/10.1787/data-00695-en* (accessed in March 2017).

OECD (2016b), "Municipal waste", *OECD Environment Statistics* (database), *http://dx.doi.org/10.1787/data-00601-en* (accessed in November 2016).

OECD (2015), *Material Resources, Productivity and the Environment*, OECD Publishing, Paris, *http://dx.doi.org/10.1787/9789264190504-en*.

UNEP (2015), "Material flow dataset", *Global Material Flows and Resource Productivity* (database), *http://undatacatalog.org/dataset/material-flow-dataset-0* (accessed in December 2016).

Vienna University of Economics and Business (2017), *materialflows.net* online data portal, *http://materialflows.net/home* (accessed in March 2017).

Further reading

OECD (2017a), "Guidance on compilation of mineral and energy resource accounts", *OECD Working Papers*, forthcoming.

OECD (2017b), Waste prevention: a survey of policies and programmes across the OECD, Report No. ENV/EPOC/WPRPW(2015)13/FINAL.

OECD (2016a), *Policy Guidance on Resource Efficiency*, OECD Publishing, Paris, *http://dx.doi.org/10.1787/9789264257344-en*.

OECD (2016b), *Extended Producer Responsibility: Updated Guidance for Efficient Waste Management*, OECD Publishing, Paris, *http://dx.doi.org/10.1787/9789264256385-en*.

OECD (2008), Recommendation of the Council on Resource Productivity, adopted by the OECD Council on 28 March 2008, document No. C(2008)40, *www.oecd.org/env/40564462.pdf*.

OECD (n.d.), Resource Productivity and Waste, webpage: *www.oecd.org/env/waste*.

UNEP (n.d.), International Resource Panel, webpage: *www.unep.org/resourcepanel*.

Nutrient flows and balances

The sustainability of agro-food systems is at the centre of green growth considerations. There are three main concerns related to sustainability: food security, run-off of nutrients such as nitrogen (N) and phosphorus (P) from commercial fertiliser use and intensive livestock farming, and pesticide residues that may leach into surface water and groundwater and enter the food chain. Farming also contributes to climate change and can lead to deterioration in soil, water and air quality and to loss of natural habitats and biodiversity. These environmental changes can, in turn, have implications for agricultural production and limit the sustainability of agriculture. But farming can also provide sinks for greenhouse gases (GHGs), help conserve biodiversity and landscapes, and help prevent floods and landslides.

The main challenge is to progressively decrease negative impacts and increase environmental benefits associated with agricultural production. In this way, ecosystem functions can be maintained and food security ensured for the world's growing population. This will require two types of interventions. First, the productivity and sustainability of agro-food systems must be improved through, for instance, better land management practices. In addition, pollution discharges from agriculture can be reduced through better management of nutrients (fertilisers and manure). Second, agricultural support measures linked to production that encourage intensive production and exacerbate the rate of biodiversity loss in the world must be addressed. Gains can also be expected from demand-side measures and changing consumption patterns (e.g. dietary preferences for red meat, as well as seasonal and local produce).

Progress towards green growth can be partly assessed against changes in agricultural nutrient balances and intensities. Nutrient balances indicate the level of potential environmental pressures from nutrients in the absence of effective pollution abatement. This is particularly true for soil, water and air.

Main trends and recent developments

Nutrient surpluses declined relative to agricultural output

For many OECD countries, nutrient surpluses declined both in terms of absolute tonnes of nutrients and nutrient surpluses per hectare of agricultural land (Figure 4.1). The rate of reduction in OECD nutrient surpluses has been faster in the early 2000s than before, but has slowed in recent years for nitrogen in some countries. Over the past decade, the value of OECD agricultural production increased by about 55% in real terms. Conversely nitrogen surpluses (tonnes) declined by about 16% and phosphorus surpluses by about 43%. These trends confirm the process of decoupling of agricultural production from environmental pressures related to N and P nutrients. They reflect some improvement in nutrient use efficiency by farmers.

Figure 4.1. **Nutrient surpluses declined**

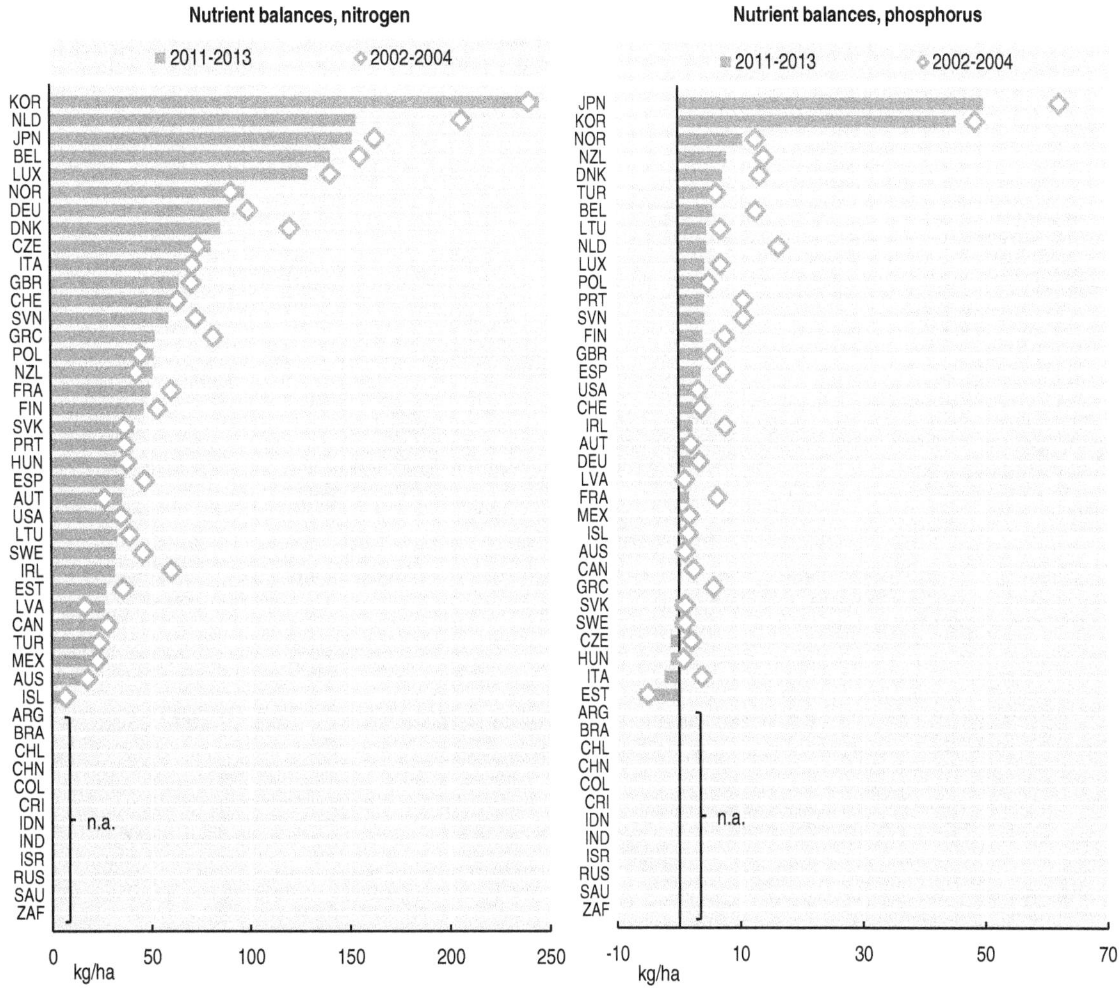

Note: Nutrient balances are expressed in kg/ha of agricultural area.

Source: OECD (2017a), "Agri-environmental indicators: nutrients", *OECD Agriculture Statistics* (database).

StatLink http://dx.doi.org/10.1787/888933484561

The apparent consumption of commercial fertilisers per hectare of agricultural land compared to crop production reveal similar developments. On the one hand, consumption of nitrogen continued to rise (18% more in OECD, signalling relative decoupling). On the other, consumption of phosphate declined (4% less, signalling absolute decoupling) (Figure 4.2).

Yet in some countries fertiliser consumption is high and growing

In BRIICS economies (Brazil, Russian Federation, India, Indonesia, People's Republic of China, South Africa) the apparent consumption of fertilisers per hectare of agricultural land increased sharply over the last decade, both for nitrogen (+36%) and phosphate (+48%) (Figure 4.3). Crop production value increased even faster (+143% in real terms), signalling a relative decoupling. However, the level of commercial fertiliser use per-hectare in BRIICS is, on average, about twice as high as in OECD countries.

There are sizeable variations within and between countries in terms of the intensity of, and trends in, nutrient surpluses and consumption. The variations depend on soil quality, cultivated crops (those that require high nutrient inputs, such as maize and rice)

Figure 4.2. **Most countries have decoupled fertiliser consumption from crop production**

OECD and G20, 2002-04 and 2011-13 averages, percentage changes

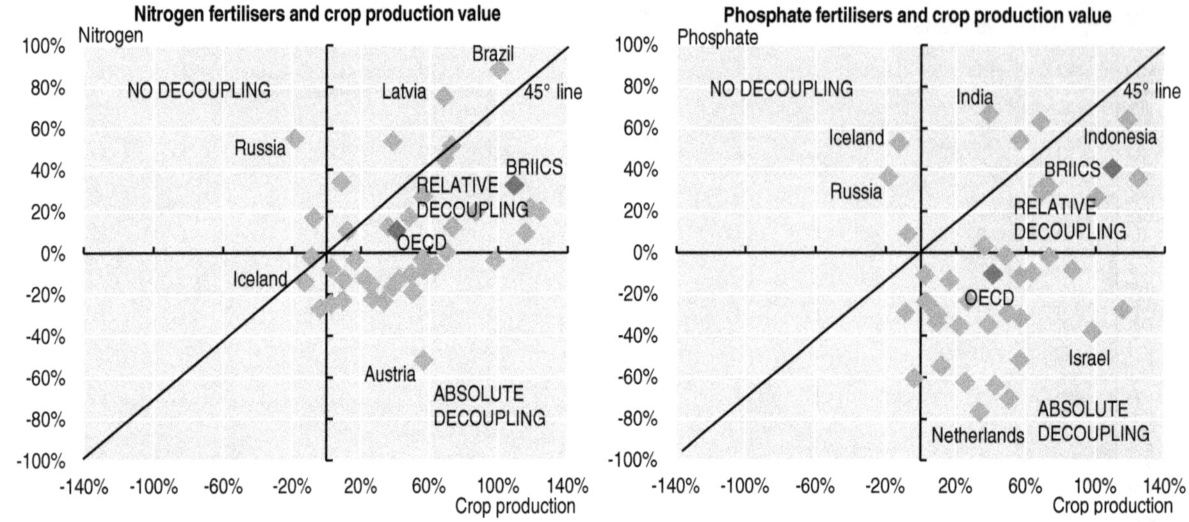

Note: Consumption of commercial fertilisers is expressed in kg/ha of agricultural area. Crop production value is expressed in USD using 2010 prices and PPPs. OECD excludes the Czech Republic.
Source: FAO (2017), FAOSTAT (database).

StatLink http://dx.doi.org/10.1787/888933484574

Figure 4.3. **BRIICS consume almost twice the level of fertilisers per agricultural area as OECD**

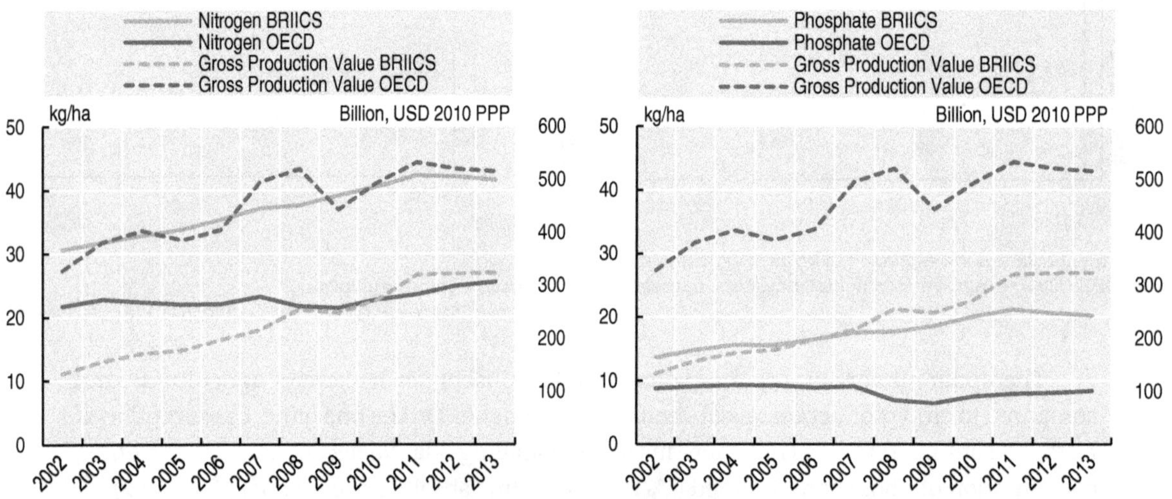

Note: Consumption of nutrients from fertilisers is expressed in kg/ha of agricultural area (left axis). Crop production value is expressed in USD using 2010 prices and PPPs (right axis). OECD excludes the Czech Republic.
Source: FAO (2017), FAOSTAT (database).

StatLink http://dx.doi.org/10.1787/888933484584

and local concentrations of livestock (associated with large volumes of manure) (Figure 4.1, Figure 4.4). Other factors that play a role include countries' weight in international trade (e.g. Brazil is a major exporter of agricultural and food products) and farmers' knowledge about appropriate fertiliser application methods.

Figure 4.4. **Consumption of commercial fertilisers has not decreased sufficiently**

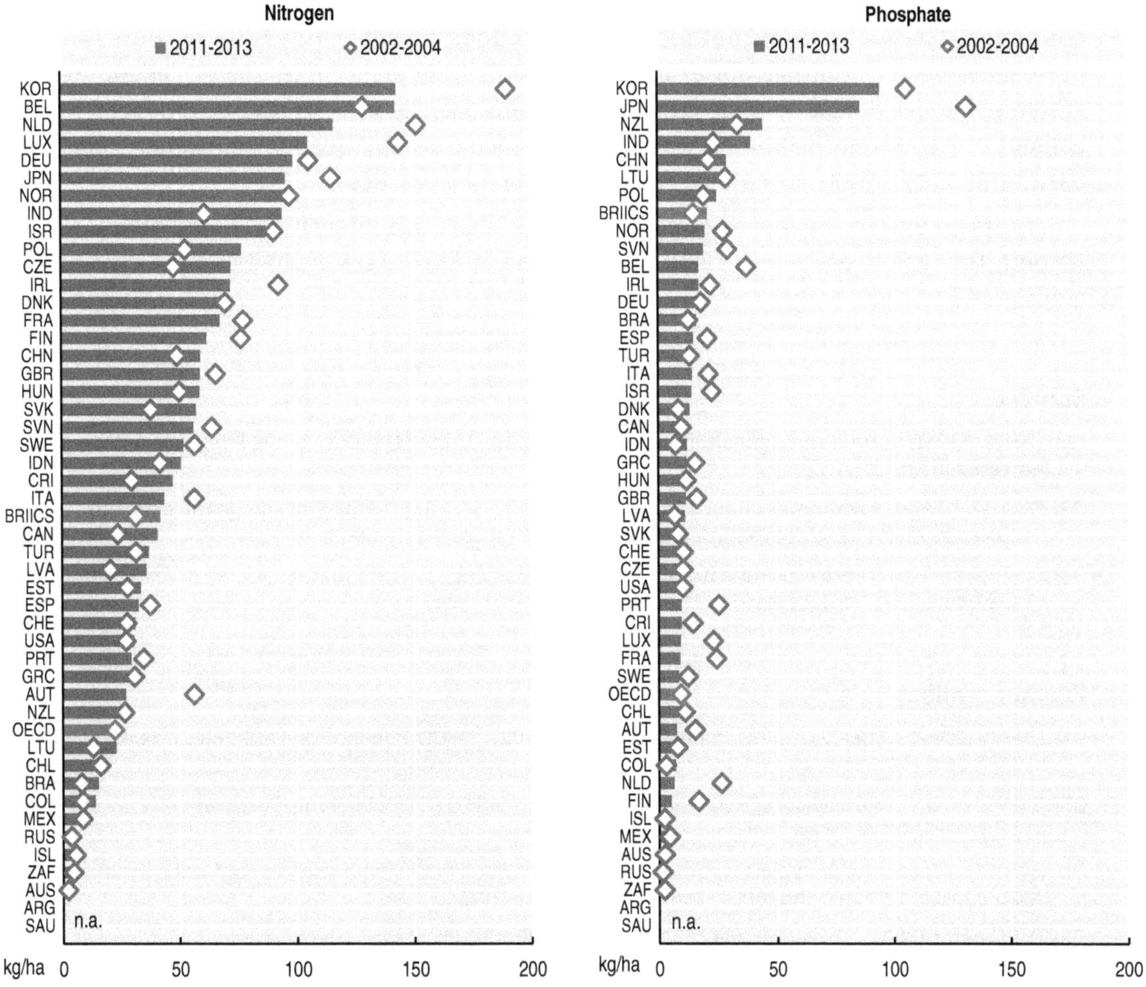

Note: Consumption of nutrients from fertilisers is expressed in kg/ha of agricultural area.
Source: FAO (2017), *FAOSTAT* (database).

StatLink http://dx.doi.org/10.1787/888933484590

Measurability and interpretation

The indicators presented in this chapter relate to agricultural nutrient balances and commercial fertiliser consumption. They include the following:

- **Nitrogen and phosphorus surplus intensities**, expressed as gross nutrient balances in kilograms per hectare of agricultural land; see also *Glossary*.
- **Nitrogen and phosphate fertiliser use**, expressed as apparent consumption of fertilisers per hectare of agricultural land; and compared to the **gross production value** in the agricultural sector.

These indicators describe potential environmental pressures, and may hide important spatial variations. The nutrient indicators are based on nutrient balances from primary agriculture. They do not consider nutrient flows from other food production systems, such as fisheries, or total nitrogen cycles in the economy. Agriculture, however, plays an important role in the nutrient cycle.

Nutrient balances (surpluses or deficits) expressed per hectare of agricultural land help the comparison of the relative intensity of nutrients in agricultural systems between countries. The estimation method used here does however not fully account for differences across countries, for example as regards differences in intensive agriculture systems that use double or triple cropping. Nutrient balance indicators should be read in conjunction with information on water use in agriculture, soil quality, biodiversity, land use, commodity prices, farm management and cropping practices.

Cross-country comparisons of commercial fertiliser use intensities should take into account the type of agricultural land to which the fertilisers are applied and the type of crops grown.

Sources

FAO (2017), FAOSTAT, Food and Agriculture Organization of the United Nations, Rome, *http://faostat.fao.org* (accessed in March 2017).

OECD (2017a), "Agri-environmental indicators: Nutrients", *OECD Agriculture Statistics* (database), *http://stats.oecd.org/Index.aspx?DataSetCode=AEI_NUTRIENTS* (accessed in March 2017).

OECD (2017b), "Green growth indicators", *OECD Environment Statistics* (database), *http://dx.doi.org/10.1787/data-00665-en* (accessed in March 2017).

Further reading

OECD/FAO (2016), *OECD-FAO Agricultural Outlook 2016-2025*, OECD Publishing, Paris, *http://dx.doi.org/10.1787/19991142*.

OECD (2013), *OECD Compendium of Agri-environmental Indicators*, OECD Publishing, Paris, *http://dx.doi.org/10.1787/9789264186217-en*.

OECD (2011), "Measuring progress towards green growth in food and agriculture", in *Food and Agriculture*, OECD Publishing, Paris, *http://dx.doi.org/10.1787/9789264107250-7-en*.

OECD/Eurostat (2007), Gross nitrogen balances handbook, *www.oecd.org/greengrowth/sustainable-agriculture/40820234.pdf*.

Environmentally adjusted multifactor productivity

Rising productivity is a key source of long-run economic growth that can increase material living standards. To capture the role of environmental services, the OECD productivity framework was extended to calculate the environmentally adjusted multifactor productivity (EAMFP) growth. The EAMFP thus measures a country's ability to generate income from a given set of inputs (including also domestic natural resources). At the same time, it accounts for the production of undesirable environmental by-products (pollution).

The EAMFP complements the traditional measure of productivity – multifactor productivity (MFP) – widely used by economic and finance policy makers. It fosters greater consideration of environmental concerns in economic policy decisions. Compared to the MFP, the indicators below allow better identification of the sources of economic growth and better assessment of long-term growth prospects. In fact, if productivity measurement is not adjusted for environmental services, productivity growth can sometimes be overestimated. This is the case in countries where economic growth relies on depletion of natural capital or on heavily polluting technologies. On the other hand, productivity growth can be underestimated in countries that invest in more efficient use of domestic natural resources or abate pollution (e.g. invest in cleaner technologies).

The EAMFP measurement framework remains a work-in-progress. In the current edition, natural capital is limited to subsoil assets (fossil fuels and minerals). Pollution is limited to air emissions (greenhouse gases and air pollutants).

Main trends and recent developments

Productivity gains have played a key role in sustaining economic growth

All OECD and G20 countries have increased their productivity (EAMFP) over the last two decades (Figure 5.1, Figure 5.2a). Countries such as Estonia, Ireland and Lithuania have achieved more than three percentage points of growth thanks to fast-rising productivity. In countries such as Greece and Turkey, slow productivity improvements (less than 0.5 percentage points) have compromised growth.

In relative terms, countries such as Iceland, Finland, Japan or Germany have achieved the bulk of growth (around 80%) essentially via productivity gains (Figure 5.2d). In countries like India and the People's Republic of China (hereafter China), less than 40% of growth performance can be attributed to rising productivity.

Differing reliance on factor inputs is the key reason for different overall growth performance of many OECD and BRIICS economies (Brazil, Russian Federation [hereafter Russia], India, Indonesia, China, South Africa). OECD countries have generated growth

Figure 5.1. **Growth accounting: The sources of growth vary across countries**

Long-term averages (circa 1991-2013)

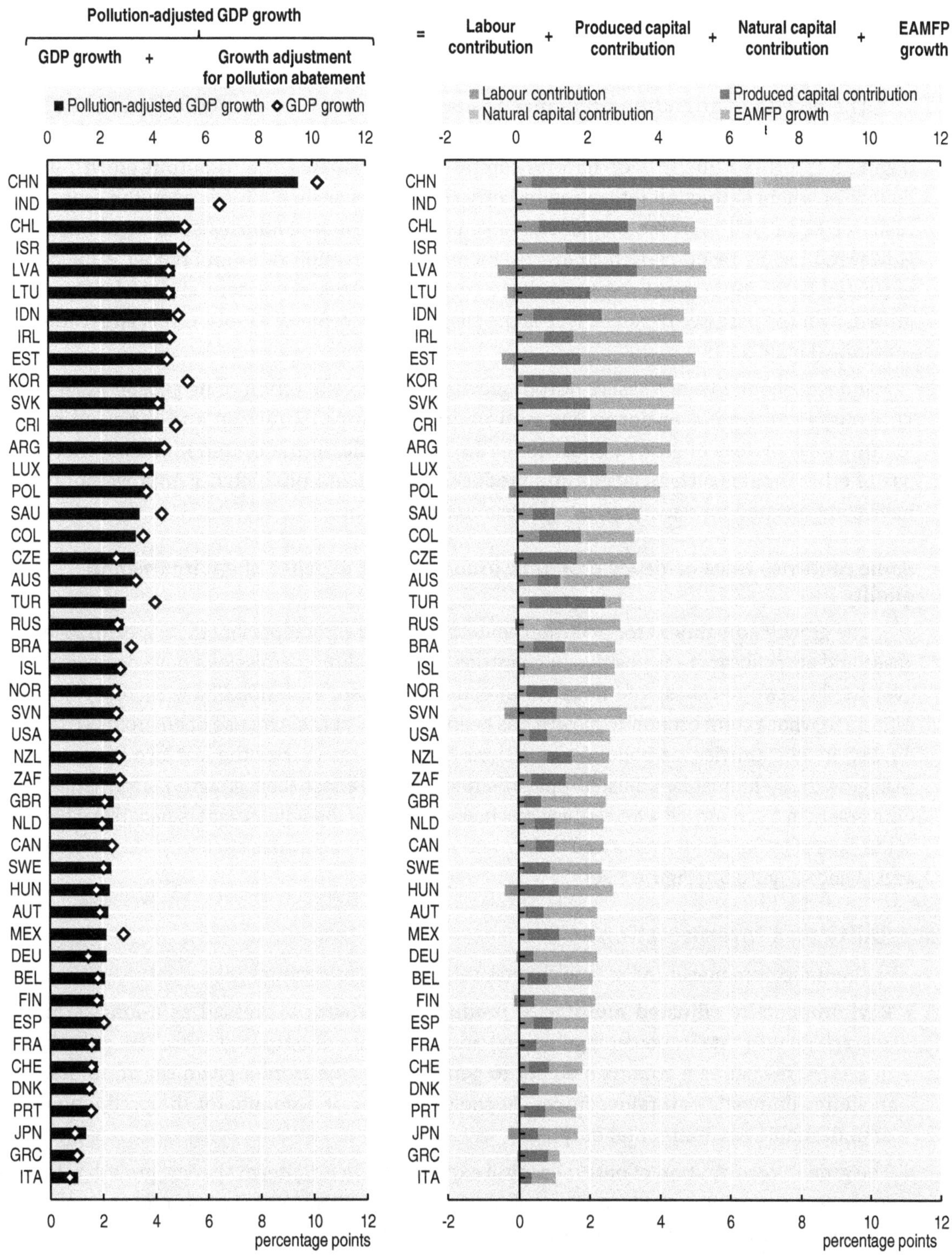

Note: The coverage of environmental services remains partial, currently limited to subsoil assets on the input side and air emissions as undesirable output. In panel B, negative values mean that the contribution of input to output growth has been decreasing.

Source: OECD (2016), "Environmentally adjusted multifactor productivity", *OECD Environment Statistics* (database).

StatLink http://dx.doi.org/10.1787/888933484605

almost exclusively through productivity gains. Conversely, BRIICS economies have drawn more on increased use of labour, produced capital and natural capital to generate additional growth (Cárdenas Rodríguez, Haščič and Souchier, 2016).

Natural capital can contribute significantly to output growth

The growth contribution of (domestic) natural capital – currently represented by subsoil assets – is small in most countries relative to produced capital and labour (Figure 5.1, Figure 5.2b). In fact, natural capital will contribute little to output growth in countries where extraction rates remain fairly constant over time. This is even the case if resource extraction represents a considerable share of GDP in countries such as Canada. However, in some resource-rich countries, increasing extraction rates and higher value of extracted domestic natural resources have contributed to a significant share of output growth over the past two decades. This is the case for Russia, Saudi Arabia, Chile, Israel and Australia (Figure 5.2e).

Indeed, about 23% of Russia's output growth is due to extraction of its subsoil assets. This raises concerns over dependence on natural resource extraction and the need to identify new sources of growth in the long run. Meanwhile, in the United Kingdom, more use of other inputs (such as labour and produced capital) and productivity improvements have compensated for declining natural resource extraction.

Some countries have achieved economic growth at the expense of environmental quality

The growth adjustment for pollution abatement – currently represented by greenhouse gases and air pollutants – is positive in countries where pollution emissions have decreased over the last two decades, and negative in countries where emissions have increased. It reflects to what extent economic growth has been achieved at the expense of environmental quality. In 29 countries, as pollution emissions have decreased over the last two decades, GDP growth rates must be adjusted upwards to correctly reflect their growth performance. Conversely, in 17 countries where emissions have increased, the adjustment is negative. This is the case of India, Saudi Arabia and China, and some OECD countries such as Turkey, Korea and Mexico (Figure 5.1, Figure 5.2c).

Measurability and interpretation

The indicators presented in this chapter relate to the following:

- **Environmentally adjusted multifactor productivity growth** expressed as a long-term average growth rate in percentage points, and as a share of output growth. The growth in EAMFP measures a country's ability to generate income from a given set of inputs, including domestic natural resources. At the same time, it accounts for the production of undesirable environmental outputs.
- The **growth contribution of natural capital** expressed as a long-term average growth rate in percentage points, and as a share of output growth. It measures how much current income growth depends on domestic natural resource use.
- The **growth adjustment for pollution abatement** expressed as a long-term average growth rate in percentage points, and as a share of output growth. It measures to what extent economic growth has been achieved at the expense of environmental quality. See also *Glossary*.

Figure 5.2. **Productivity and the role of environmental services for growth**

Long-term average (circa 1991-2013)

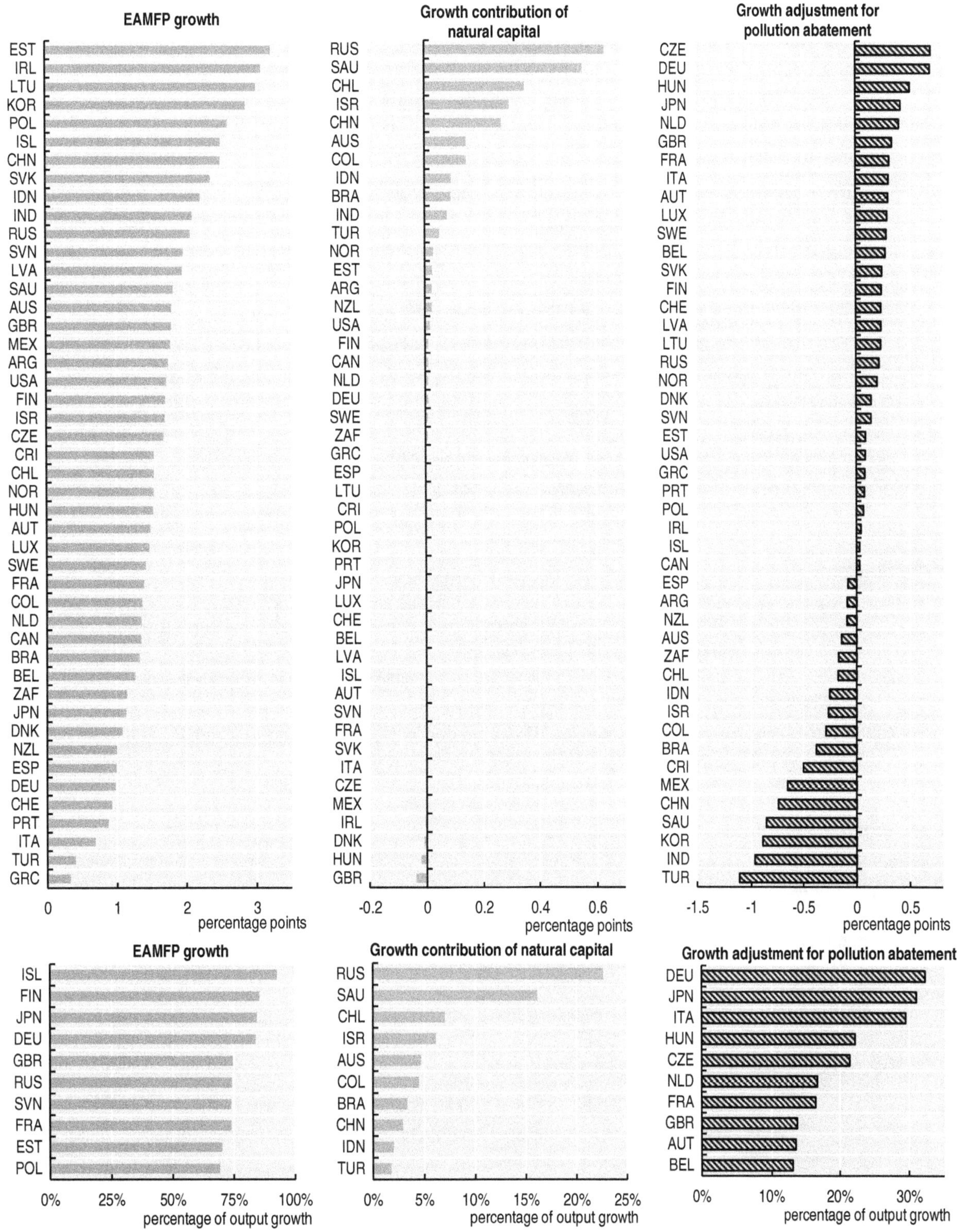

Note: The coverage of environmental services remains partial, currently limited to air emissions and subsoil assets.

Source: OECD (2016), "Environmentally adjusted multifactor productivity", *OECD Environment Statistics* (database).

StatLink http://dx.doi.org/10.1787/888933484611

These indicators should be interpreted with caution. In the current edition, the coverage of environmental services remains partial. It is limited to eight types of air emissions (CO_2, CH_4, N_2O, NMVOC, SO_X, NO_X, CO, PM_{10}) and 14 types of subsoil assets (hard coal, soft coal, gas, oil, bauxite, copper, gold, iron ore, lead, nickel, phosphate, silver, tin and zinc). Many other natural resources (e.g. soil, biodiversity) and many environmental services (e.g. pollination, water purification, avalanche and landslide prevention, landscape amenities, etc.) are not taken into account. Pending better data availability, future work will seek to include more natural resources and environmental services.

In addition, these indicators provide an aggregated picture of the economy. As any other country-level measure, they might hide important sectoral or firm-level differences (see e.g. Albrizio, Koźluk and Zipperer, 2017). These indicators are sensitive to the business cycle. For example, they are volatile in times of economic recession. Analysing long-term trends, as presented here, helps to mitigate these concerns.

The underlying growth accounting framework only allows measurement of changes in productivity ("growth"). It does not permit measurement of productivity levels, or contribution to the level of GDP. This should be kept in mind when comparing across countries. Finally, in growth accounting, inputs and outputs are evaluated from the producers' perspective. The EAMFP framework does not account for environmental damages or the social costs of pollution. Therefore, it is not a measure of social welfare.

Sources

Cárdenas Rodríguez, M., I. Haščič and M. Souchier (2016), "Environmentally Adjusted Multifactor Productivity Growth: Methodology and Empirical Results for OECD and G20 Countries", *Green Growth Papers* No. 2016/04, OECD Publishing, Paris, *http://dx.doi.org/10.1787/5jlr2z7ntkf8-en*.

OECD (2017), "Green growth indicators", *OECD Environment Statistics* (database), *http://dx.doi.org/10.1787/data-00665-en* (accessed in March 2017).

OECD (2016), "Environmentally adjusted multifactor productivity", *OECD Environment Statistics* (database), *http://dx.doi.org/10.1787/55a11744-en* (accessed in December 2016).

Further reading

Albrizio, S., T. Koźluk and V. Zipperer (2017), "Environmental policies and productivity growth: Evidence across industries and firms", *Journal of Environmental Economics and Management*, Vol. 81, January, pp. 209-226, *http://dx.doi.org/10.1016/j.jeem.2016.06.002*.

Brandt, N., P. Schreyer and V. Zipperer (2014), "Productivity Measurement with Natural Capital and Bad Outputs", *OECD Economics Department Working Papers*, No. 1154, OECD Publishing, Paris, *http://dx.doi.org/10.1787/5jz0wh5t0ztd-en*.

OECD (2016), *OECD Compendium of Productivity Indicators 2016*, OECD Publishing, Paris, *http://dx.doi.org/10.1787/pdtvy-2016-en*.

OECD (2015), *The Future of Productivity*, OECD Publishing, Paris, *http://dx.doi.org/10.1787/9789264248533-en*.

OECD (n.d.), "Greening productivity measurement", webpage: *http://oe.cd/eamfp*.

OECD (n.d.), "Measuring environmentally adjusted total factor productivity for agriculture", webpage: *http://oe.cd/eatfp*.

Green Growth Indicators 2017

PART 2

The natural asset base

Land resources

Forest resources

Freshwater resources

Biodiversity, ecosystems and wildlife resources

Land resources

Land and soil resources are essential components of the natural asset base of the economy and of ecosystems. They are both a private property and a (global and local) common; they are critical for the production of food and other biomass, support recreational activities and, more generally, provide a physical foundation for all economic activity. The way land is used and managed influences everything in the environment. This ranges from biodiversity and ecosystem services (including erosion risk, flood protection, etc.) to soil, water and air quality, and greenhouse gas (GHG) emissions.

The market value of land varies by location. Where demand is low, land is relatively abundant. Elsewhere, many competing demands on land lead to its relative scarcity and drive up its price. Unregulated development driven by the desire to maximise market value leads to conversion of land to the highest-value use. This process, however, fails to account for the ecological value of land. For instance, urban settlements historically developed along navigable streams, sacrificing riparian and wetland ecosystems. Nowadays, in many developed countries, urban expansion mainly occurs at the expense of farmland. Exploitation of natural resources (unsustainable logging, mineral extraction), construction of transport infrastructure, and agricultural expansion continue to be the main drivers of deforestation worldwide.

These underlying drivers and the resulting land cover change are leading contributors to the loss of biodiversity and ecosystem services globally (CBD, 2010). Land development and the resulting changes in land cover lead to habitat fragmentation and loss. They are thus associated with a decline in the populations of many species and reduced biodiversity (Karousakis, 2012). Conversions of agricultural land to artificial land (which include at least partial soil sealing) irreversibly degrade soil and lead to the cumulative loss of productive agricultural land.

The main challenge is to keep a balance between economic, social and environmental objectives. This includes managing land in a manner that directs development away from greenfield and biodiversity-sensitive locations. Land management should also preserve the essential ecosystem functions of the land and the soil, and integrate land-preservation considerations into sectoral policies. This can be achieved using regulation (e.g. spatial planning, land-use zoning, urban growth boundaries and protected area networks) or economic instruments (e.g. conservation easements or payments for ecosystem services, land taxes, biodiversity offsets, and the phasing out of environmentally harmful agricultural subsidies). However, the environmental effectiveness and cost-efficiency of these approaches may differ markedly.

This chapter focuses on land cover and land-cover change, drawing on information from global land monitoring that has become available only recently. Future editions will aim to address some of the other important issues such as status of soil resources and land

Figure 6.1. **Land cover and land cover conversion**

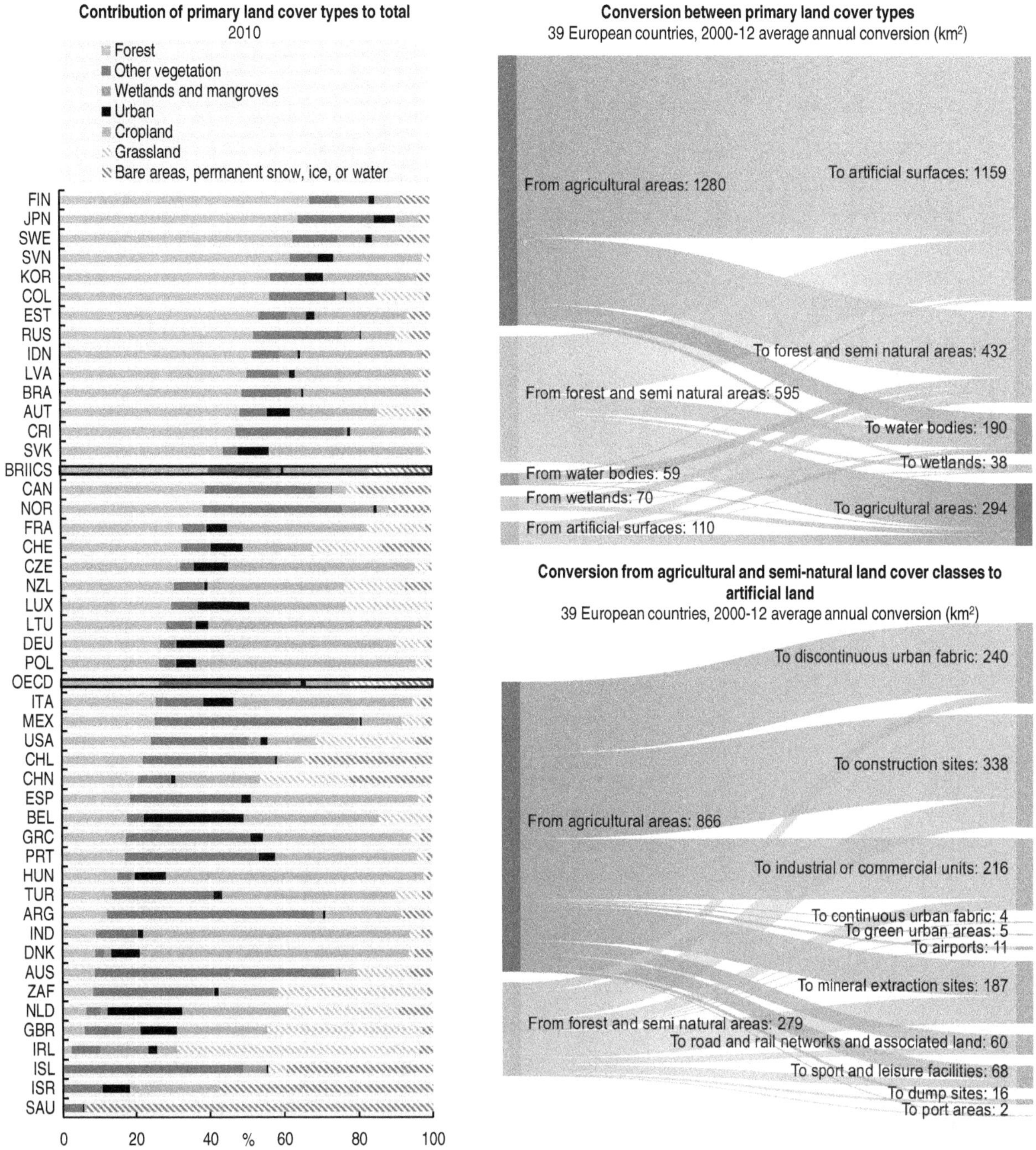

Note (Panel A): Classes have been combined for presentation purposes. Grasslands include agricultural land use types like pasture. Reference period is 2008-12, however the underlying datasets are informed by sensor data from 2003-12. For detailed definitions, see ESA (2016).

Note (Panel B): Minimum change mapped in underlying datasets is 0.05 km^2, smaller changes are not recorded and not included here. 0.05 km^2 is approximately the size of a new housing development of 250 dwellings at medium housing density. It is therefore likely that these rates of change are considerably underestimated. For detailed definitions see EEA (2016).

Source: OECD calculations based on the CCI-LC datasets (ESA, 2016) and the CORINE-LCC datasets (EEA, 2016).

StatLink http://dx.doi.org/10.1787/888933484623

degradation, changes in land use, habitat loss and fragmentation, and the impacts of land dynamics on human well-being, pending better availability of internationally harmonised indicators.

Main trends and recent developments

Across all the OECD, built-up areas now cover 30% more land than in 1990

In most OECD countries, natural and semi-natural vegetated land (forests, grasslands, wetlands, shrubland and other vegetated land) covers 30% to 80% of the area (Figure 6.1a, Figure 6.2). At the global scale, these land cover types are essential for provision of ecosystem services and conservation of biodiversity. In some countries such as Denmark and India, cropland is dominant (> 70%). Across all OECD countries, built-up areas now cover 1.11% of the total land area, a 30% increase since 1990.

Globally, an area the size of the United Kingdom has been converted to built-up areas since 1990 (244 000 km^2) (Figure 6.4e). Note that "built-up" here refers only to buildings, excluding all other types of urban land such as paved surfaces (roads, parking lots), commercial and industrial sites (ports, landfills) and urban green spaces (parks, gardens); consequently, the share of "urban area" is much larger.

Urbanisation of agricultural and semi-natural land is the major driver of land-cover change in Europe

In Europe, urbanisation is the main driver of land-cover change (Figure 6.1b). Urban and other artificial development typically occurs on agricultural land (at least 796 km^2 lost annually from 2006 to 2012, corresponding to approximately 100 000 football fields) and on forested and semi-natural land (280 km^2). The second most common type of land cover change is conversion from forests and semi-natural land to agricultural land, and vice versa (e.g. afforestation). Forests and semi-natural land are now converted into agricultural land at a slower rate (from 289 to 144 km^2/year between 2000-2006 and 2006-2012). During the same periods, the rate at which agricultural land was converted into artificial surfaces also declined (from 935 to 796 km^2/year). However, conversions to artificial surfaces remain a serious concern given the existing level of urbanisation in these countries and its cumulative character. Moreover, these land-cover changes have increased the fragmentation of natural and semi-natural land in most European countries (EEA, 2015).

Intense urban growth occurs in many already highly urbanised countries

There are large variations in built-up area share, ranging from 0.04% of total land area in Iceland to almost 17% in the Netherlands (Figure 6.4a). In most countries built-up area growth slowed from 2000 onwards. The Slovak Republic and the United Kingdom were among the few exceptions (Figure 6.4b). There are also large differences in the amount of built-up area per capita both within and between countries. In most countries, the amount of built-up area per capita is increasing (Figure 6.3, Figure 6.4c and Figure 6.5a). Some countries, including Portugal, Belgium and the Netherlands, have high built-up area growth rates, high rates of conversion as a share of total land, a high (and increasing) ratio of built-up area per capita and a relatively large share of land area already built-up. This indicates that urbanisation pressures in these countries are particularly intense.

The disconnect between built-up area growth and population growth may be explained by societal changes (e.g. growth in single-person households due to higher divorce rates,

Figure 6.2. **Share of natural and semi-natural vegetated land, circa 2010**

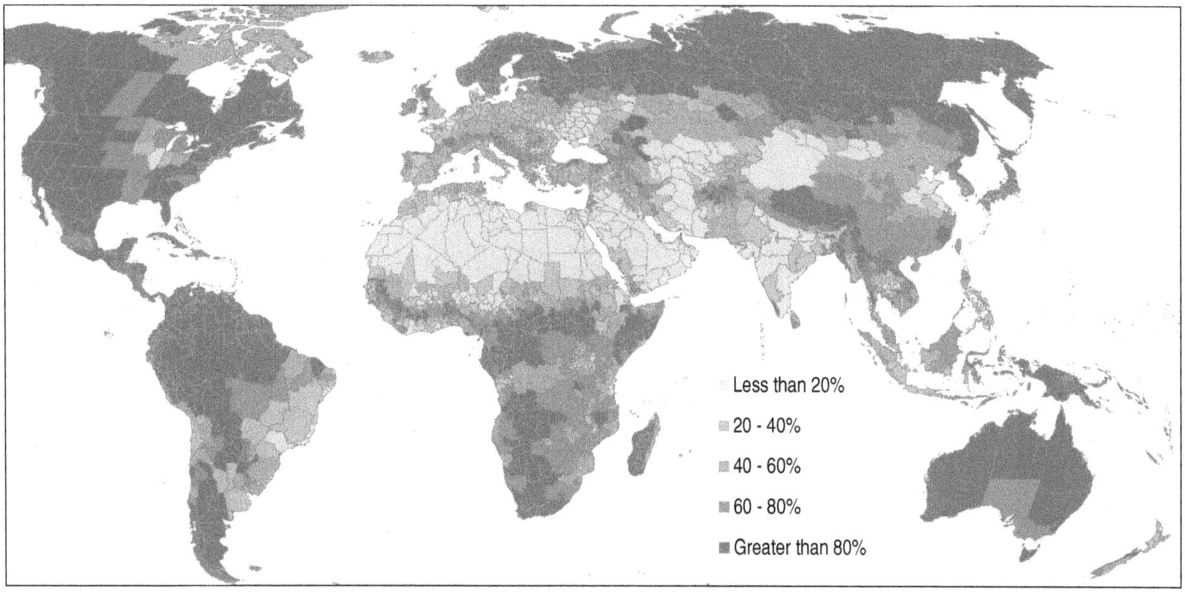

Note: Natural and semi-natural vegetated land includes land cover types such as pasture, orchards and commercial forestry. Cropland, permanent snow and ice and bare land are excluded. Reference period is 2008-12. However, the underlying datasets are informed by sensor data from 2003-12.

Source: OECD calculations based on the CCI-LC datasets (ESA, 2016). Administrative boundaries: FAO (2015).

StatLink http://dx.doi.org/10.1787/888933484637

Figure 6.3. **Built-up area per capita, circa 2014**

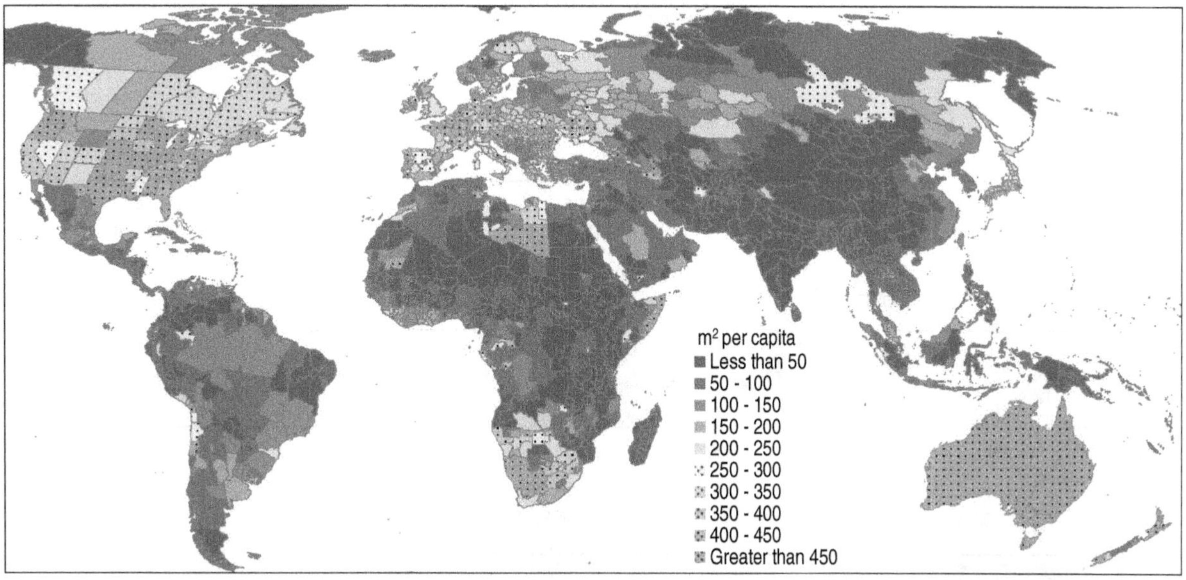

Note: "Built-up" refers only to buildings, excluding all other types of urban land such as paved surfaces (roads, parking lots), commercial and industrial sites (ports, landfills) and urban green spaces (parks, gardens). In some countries, there is large uncertainty in sub-national population estimates due to unavailability of reliable census data.

Source: OECD calculations using JRC (2016) "Global Human Settlement Layer" (38m resolution multi-temporal built-up-area dataset) and CIESIN (2016) "Gridded Population of the World, version 4". Administrative boundaries: FAO (2015).

StatLink http://dx.doi.org/10.1787/888933484647

Figure 6.4. **Urban growth occurs in many already highly urbanised countries**

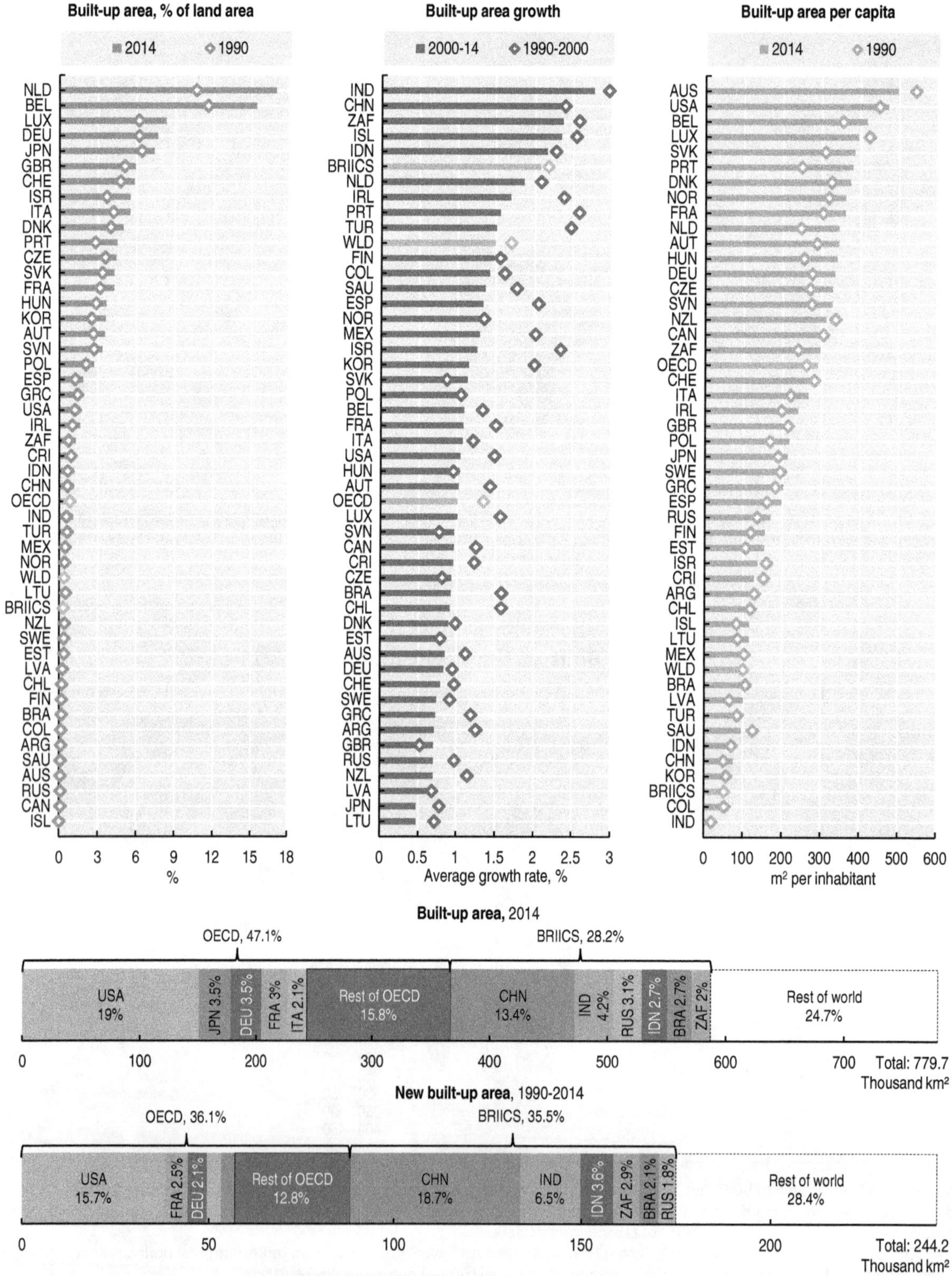

Note: "Built-up" refers only to buildings, excluding all other types of urban land such as paved surfaces (roads, parking lots), commercial and industrial sites (ports, landfills) and urban green spaces (parks, gardens).

Source: OECD calculations using JRC (2016), "Global Human Settlement Layer".

StatLink http://dx.doi.org/10.1787/888933484652

Figure 6.5. **Built-up area growth surpassed population growth in most countries**

OECD and G20

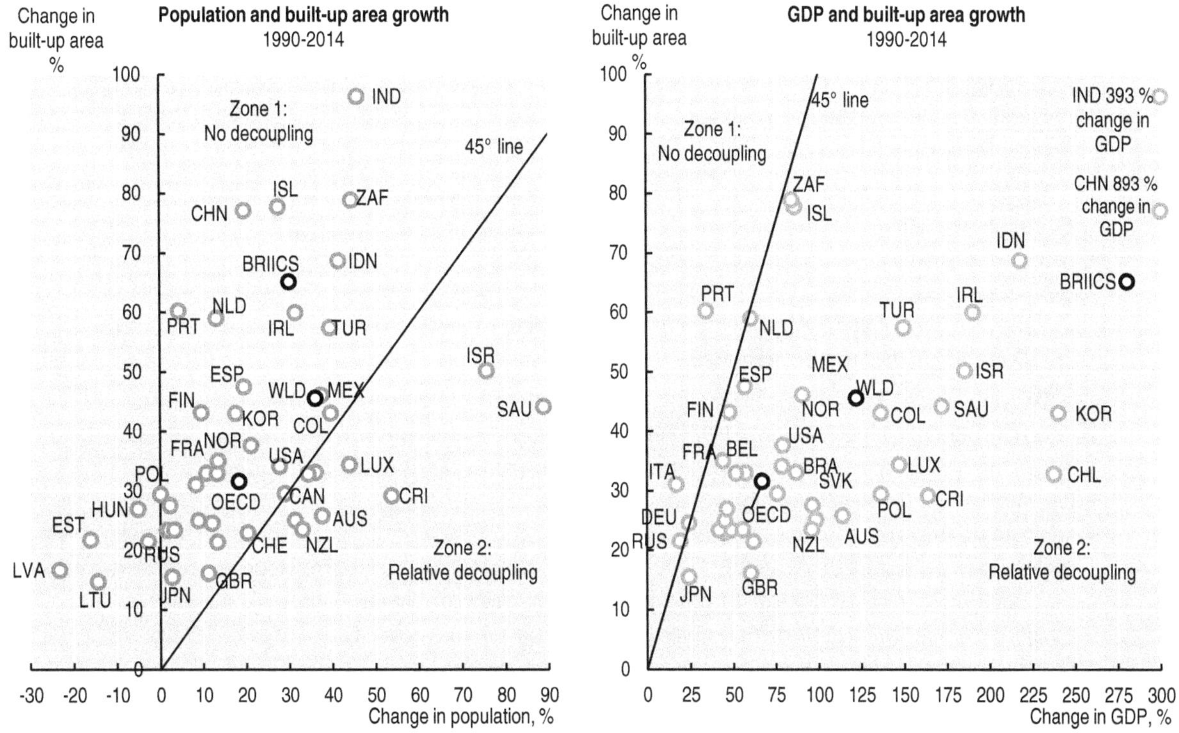

Note: "Built-up" refers only to buildings, excluding all other types of urban land such as paved surfaces (roads, parking lots), commercial and industrial sites (ports, landfills) and urban green spaces (parks, gardens).

How to read this graph (panel A): Countries where the built-up area has grown proportionally more slowly than the population are located in *Zone 2: Relative Decoupling.* It is more likely that these countries have responded to population increases though densification (i.e. more compact and densely populated urban development relative to their 1990 levels) or the re-zoning of industrial and commercial built-up land. Countries where the built-up area has grown proportionally more quickly than the population are located in *Zone 1: No decoupling.* It is more likely these countries have been less successful at dealing with urban sprawl or have seen extensive industrial and commercial development. Countries that saw little, or even negative population growth, *all* nevertheless saw modest levels of ultimately unsustainable built-up area growth. That is especially true of many Central and Eastern European countries. It is also perhaps surprising that some countries with relatively intense urbanisation rates and pressure such as Portugal and the Netherlands have not densified whereas others countries with less intense pressures have densified.

As noted above, describing the changing urban form is important to better understanding these changes in built-up areas (i.e. compact versus fragmented urban development).

Source: OECD calculations using JRC (2016), "Global Human Settlement Layer".

StatLink http://dx.doi.org/10.1787/888933484664

ageing population), lifestyle changes (e.g. increasing demand for larger, detached homes in the urban periphery), the construction of commercial and industrial buildings, and the changing urban form (e.g. compact high-density development along the urban fringe versus fragmented low-density development scattered throughout the suburbs).

Historically, land development has played an important role in economic growth. Recent data suggest a positive correlation between growth in built-up areas and GDP (r = 0.56). However, similar levels of built-up growth are associated with vastly different GDP growth rates (Figure 6.5b). For instance, while Korea, Chile, Finland, France and Italy have all seen about a 30-40% increase in built up areas, their GDP growth rates have been very different. The challenge is to shift to a more sustainable growth model that relies less on built-up area growth.

Box 6.1. **Tropical forest loss continues at alarmingly high rates**

Globally, tropical forests have experienced the greatest tree cover change and the greatest tree cover loss (Hansen et al., 2013). Among OECD and G20 countries, Argentina, Brazil and Indonesia have seen the highest rates of tropical forest loss (11.8%, 6.4% and 10%, respectively) during 2000-12 (measured as greater than 50% tree cover loss in land with at least 50% tree cover in 2000).

Subtropical forests such as those in South Africa, Chile, the People's Republic of China, Australia and New Zealand tend to see high rates of tree cover change due to short-cycle intensive forestry, but with more equal ratios of tree cover loss to gain. On average, temperate forests such as those in Europe and Canada see similar dynamics to subtropical forests. However, they have slightly greater relative tree cover loss, in part because of natural, stand-replacing disturbance regimes.

The above conclusions from Hansen et al. (2013) refer to a biophysical description of tree cover, defined as vegetation at least 5 metres in height and with canopy cover greater than 50%. This type of methodology using remote sensing data can provide harmonised, entirely biophysical land cover information, separate from any consideration of land use. As one advantage, this approach can potentially record *all* changes, including temporary changes, regardless of how anthropogenic or natural the cause. This can complement standard reporting-based statistics on forest land (see chapter on *Forest resources*). Remaining challenges include the following: robustly estimating *net* tree cover gain or loss, identifying policy-relevant information that accounts for the naturally large differences in forest dynamics across different ecological zones, and distinguishing plantation crops and trees in some regions (which might be included as tree cover per the above definition).

Measurability and interpretation

The indicators presented in this chapter relate to:

- **Land cover proportions**, by primary land cover type using data from ESA (2016).
- **Land cover conversions**, quantifying the conversions between the primary land-cover types with particular focus on conversions of natural ecosystems to anthropogenic ones. The indicator is constructed for Europe (EEA, 2016). Similar datasets exist for a few other OECD countries (for a review, see e.g. Diogo and Koomen, 2016), but assessment across a range of cover types at a more global scale is currently not possible due to the considerable technical challenges in producing these kinds of datasets.

  It is however possible to assess the extent of change in **built-up areas** (JRC, 2016) consistently at the global scale. This is presented here for OECD and G20 countries. It is likely that similar datasets with a specific focus on a single land cover class (e.g. forest land, wetlands or permanent water bodies) will yield the most usable information globally in the medium term.

The example indicators presented here are based on several very different land cover and land cover change mapping projects. Each of these has distinct limitations, caveats and classification systems.

Recent efforts to strengthen the global land monitoring capacities (e.g. using remote sensing) now provide a wealth of data. These can play an important role in quantifying global land cover change and related environmental phenomena. Earth observation data are a useful complement to administrative and statistical data and an underexploited resource for monitoring natural assets. It allows the production of internationally comparable indicators with the largest possible coverage of countries.

These improvements increasingly allow identifying *where* changes such as deforestation or urbanisation are most intense. However, land cover changes are the outcome of complex and connected natural and anthropogenic processes that are challenging to characterise; therefore, data gaps remain about the *drivers* of these changes and their impacts (e.g. quantifying the causes of deforestation or the social, demographic and economic trends that promote urban sprawl).

Sources

CBD (2010), *Global Biodiversity Outlook 3*, Convention on Biological Diversity, *www.cbd.int/gbo3*.

CIESIN (2016), Gridded Population of the World, version 4 (GPWv4), Center for International Earth Science Information Network, *http://dx.doi.org/10.7927/H4X63JVC*.

Diogo, V. and E. Koomen (2016), "Land cover and Land Use Indicators: Review of available data", *OECD Green Growth Papers*, No. 2016/03, OECD Publishing, Paris, *http://dx.doi.org/10.1787/5jlr2z86r5xw-en*.

EEA (2016), CORINE Land Cover Change (2000-06 and 2006-12 datasets), European Environment Agency, *http://land.copernicus.eu/pan-european/corine-land-cover*.

EEA (2015), Fragmentation of natural and semi-natural areas, European Environment Agency, Brussels, *www.eea.europa.eu/data-and-maps/indicators/fragmentation-of-natural-and-semi-1/assessment-1*.

ESA (2016), Climate Change Initiative Land Cover (2010 dataset), European Space Agency, *www.esa-landcover-cci.org/*.

FAO (2015), Global Administrative Unit Layers (GAUL) 2014 version, FAO-GeoNetwork, Food and Agriculture Organization of the United Nations, *www.fao.org/geonetwork/srv/en/metadata.show?id=12691* (accessed in March 2016.)

Hansen, M. et al. (2013), "High-resolution global maps of 21st-century forest cover change", *Science*, Vol. 342/6160, American Association for the Advancement of Science, New York, pp. 850-853, *10.1126/science.1244693*.

JRC (2016), Global Human Settlement Layer (GHS_BUILT_LDSMT_GLOBE_R2015B_3857_38_v1_0 dataset), Joint Research Centre, *http://publications.jrc.ec.europa.eu/repository/handle/JRC97705*.

Karousakis, K. et al. (2012), "Biodiversity", in *OECD Environmental Outlook to 2050: The Consequences of Inaction*, OECD Publishing, Paris, *http://dx.doi.org/10.1787/env_outlook-2012-7-en*.

OECD (2017), "Green growth indicators", *OECD Environment Statistics* (database), *http://dx.doi.org/10.1787/data-00665-en* (accessed in March 2017).

Further reading

EEA (2016), *Urban Sprawl in Europe*, European Environment Agency, *www.eea.europa.eu/publications/urban-sprawl-in-europe*.

OECD (2016), *Biodiversity Offsets: Effective Design and Implementation*, OECD Publishing, Paris, *http://dx.doi.org/10.1787/9789264222519-en*.

OECD (2013), *Scaling-up Finance Mechanisms for Biodiversity*, OECD Publishing, Paris, *http://dx.doi.org/10.1787/9789264193833-en*.

UNCCD (2016), *A Natural Fix: A Joined-up Approach for Delivering the Global Goals for Sustainable Development*, UN Convention to Combat Desertification, *www2.unccd.int/sites/default/files/documents/22042016_A%20Natural%20Fix_ENG.pdf*.

Forest resources

Forests are among the most diverse and widespread ecosystems on Earth. Among their functions, they provide timber and other products, and deliver cultural and recreational benefits. Forests also provide ecosystem services, including regulation of soil, air and water. In addition, they are reservoirs for biodiversity, and act as carbon sinks.

Human activities have an impact on the health and diversity of forests. They also affect natural forest growth and regeneration. These impacts have consequences for the economic, environmental and social services that forests provide. Many forest resources are threatened by overexploitation, fragmentation, degradation of environmental quality and conversion to other types of land use. The main pressures from human activities include conversion to agriculture and transport infrastructure, air pollution and forest fires.

The main challenges are to ensure sustainable management of forest resources, avoiding over-harvesting and degradation. This approach maintains timber value and an adequate supply of wood for production activities. It maintains provision of essential ecosystem services. And it preserves social, cultural and spiritual values emanating from forests. Environmental concerns should also be integrated into forestry policies (e.g. eco-certification and carbon sequestration measures). The Reducing Emissions from Deforestation and Forest Degradation in Developing Countries (REDD) mechanism helps mobilise finance to mitigate deforestation and thus greenhouse gas (GHG) emissions.

Main trends and recent developments

Forest resources have slightly increased in most OECD countries

Forests are unevenly distributed. A handful of the most forest-rich countries account for the bulk of the world's forest resources. OECD countries account for about 27% of the world's forest area; the BRIICS for 42% (FAO, 2016). Forest area within the OECD has remained stable or increased slightly since 1990. Worldwide, however, forest area has been slightly decreasing. Fragmentation, degradation of environmental quality and conversion to other land-use types raise concern in many countries.

In almost all OECD countries for which data are available the volume of the stock of trees has grown since the 1990s (Figure 7.1a). Countries with young, immature forests that grow faster have observed the most important increases. These countries include Korea (+187%), Costa Rica (+161%), Spain (+83%) and Denmark (+79%). Reductions can be observed in countries with vast volumes of wooded biomass, mainly due to reductions in their forest area. These countries include Brazil (-8%), Indonesia (-28%) and Argentina (-13%). Variations in forest resource stocks depend on multiple factors, including deforestation, forest fires, degree of forest maturity, tree species distribution, storms, pests and diseases. Increasing carbon concentrations in the atmosphere and changes in climatic conditions

Figure 7.1. **Forest resources are increasingly used and managed in a sustainable way**

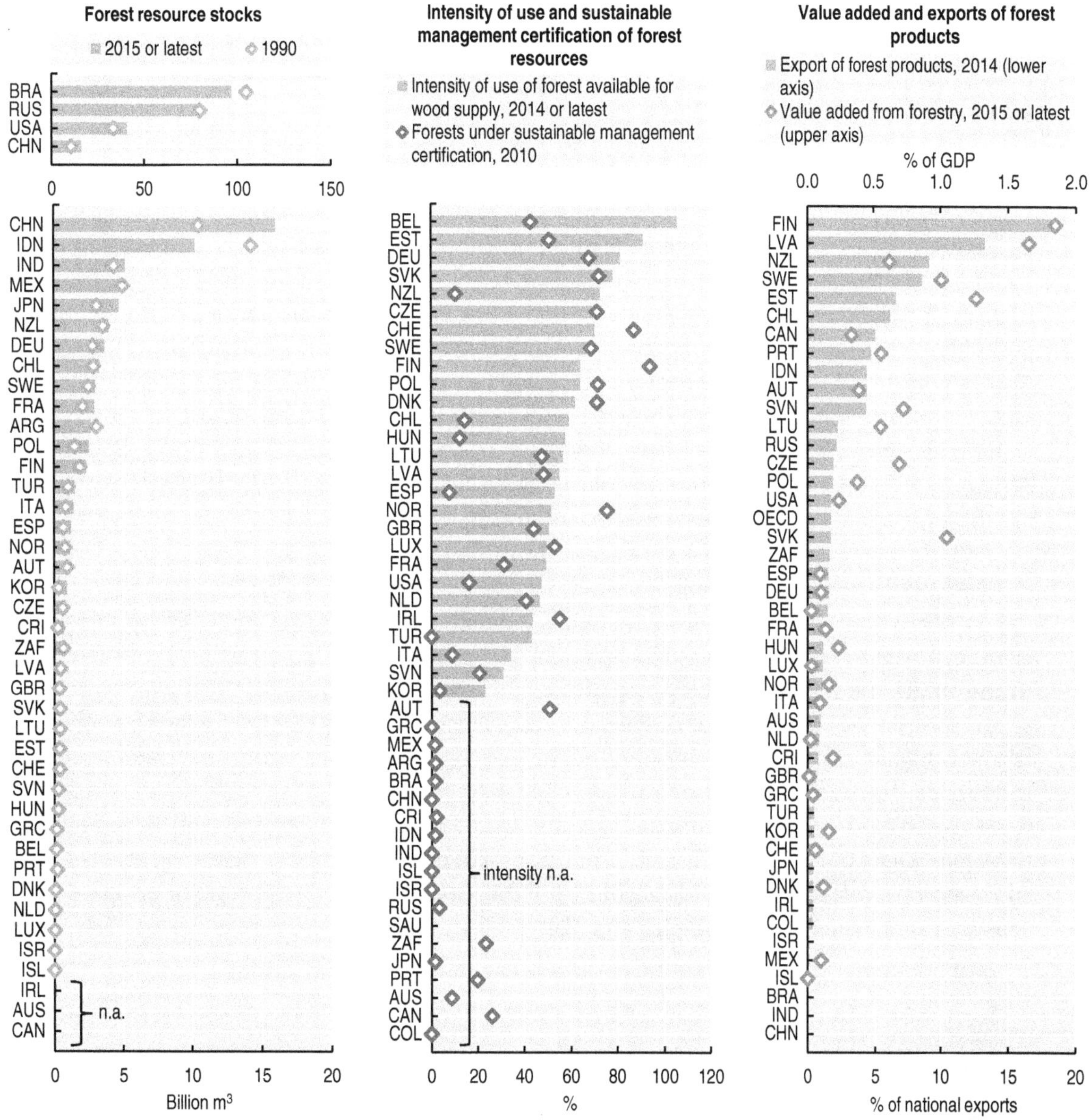

Note: Data prior to 2010 were not considered.

Source: FAO (2015), "Global Forest Resource Assessments 2015"; OECD (2017a), "Forest resources", *OECD Environment Statistics* (database), FAO (2016), "Forestry production and trade", *FAOSTAT* (database).

StatLink http://dx.doi.org/10.1787/888933484670

further affect forests in terms of species composition, productivity and functioning of ecosystems.

The intensity of use of forest resources is relatively stable

The portion of countries' forest resource stock available for wood supply varies considerably. About 83% of forests in Europe are commercially exploitable. This ranges from almost 100% in the United Kingdom to 24% in Cyprus (Eurostat, 2016).

At the national level and in forests available for wood supply, most OECD countries appear to use their forest resources in a sustainable way. Most do not over-harvest their forest resources, maintaining the use intensity below 100%. However, there is significant variation among and within countries (Figure 7.1b). Since the 1990s, intensity of forest use has generally increased in 14 of 25 countries in which longer trends are available. This is partly due to the use of wood as biomass for energy, in line with policy objectives for renewables.

The share of forests under sustainable management certification has been increasing

Increasingly, forest owners adopt sustainable management practices. Certification can be useful for encouraging sustainable forestry practices, but it is not strictly necessary for sustainable management. Countries with a relatively intensive use of the resource have the highest prevalence of certified sustainable management (Figure 7.1b). For example, about 90% of forests in Finland and Switzerland are under sustainable management certification. Certified sustainable forest management is much less prevalent in the most forest-rich OECD countries (including the United States, New Zealand and Mexico) and BRIICS economies (Brazil, Russian Federation, India, Indonesia, People's Republic of China, South Africa). Significant gaps remain worldwide as well. This is partly because certification costs are too expensive for some forest owners and managers.

In most countries, the contribution of forestry to the economy is modest

In seven OECD countries, the commercial exploitation of forest resources contributes significantly to the economy. As such, it generates over 5% of their export value. Elsewhere in the OECD, the forestry and logging sector contributes much less. In most cases, the sector contributes below 0.5% of GDP (Figure 7.1c). The economic weight of forest products is much higher after taking into account the downstream wood-based manufacturing industries. In the EU-28, for example, wood-based industries, though decreasing, represented 7.9% of the manufacturing value added in 2013 (Eurostat, 2016). However, these numbers do not reflect the significant non-market environmental services provided by forest resources. Nor do they account for the vital life-support functions of forest ecosystems on which our economies and well-being depend.

For additional discussion of land cover, see chapter on *Land resources*.

Measurability and interpretation

The indicators presented in this chapter relate to the following:

- **Forest resource stocks** measured as the growing stock of standing trees. It is defined as the volume over bark of all living trees with a minimum diameter of 10 cm at breast height and including the stem from ground level up to a top diameter of 0 cm (excluding branches). The standing volume of growing stock can be converted, by applying biomass expansion factors, into estimates of above and below-ground woody biomass.
- The **intensity of use** of forest resources, measured as fellings in percentage of gross increment. Data refer to forests available for wood supply only. The balance between increment and fellings highlights the sustainability of timber production over time. It also reflects current availability and potential for future availability of timber. To be sustainable the fellings over a given period must not exceed the increment over the same period. See also *Glossary*.

They are complemented by the following:

- The share of forest area under **sustainable management certification** (i.e. Forest Stewardship Council, Programme for the Endorsement of Forest Certification, or other international certification).
- **Exports of forest products** (e.g. round wood, wood panels, pulp and paper) as percentage of total exports and **value added** from forestry and logging (ISIC A02) as percentage of GDP.

The indicators on forest resources give insights into quantitative aspects of forest resources and into the forests' timber supply functions. They present national averages that may conceal important variations among forests. They should be read with information on the "maturity" of the forests and on forest quality (e.g. species diversity, including tree and non-tree species; forest degradation; forest fragmentation).

Data on forest resources and the intensity of their use can be derived from several sources. These include, forest inventories and forest accounts, OECD environmental data and international Forest Resource Assessments (FAO, UNECE) for most OECD countries. Interpretability is limited, however, due to differences in the variables monitored. Historical data often lack comparability or are not available over longer periods.

Sources

Eurostat (2016), "Agriculture, forestry and fishery statistics: 2016 edition", *http://ec.europa.eu/eurostat/documents/3217494/7777899/KS-FK-16-001-EN-N.pdf/cae3c56f-53e2-404a-9e9e-fb5f57ab49e3*.

FAO (2016), "Forestry production and trade", *FAOSTAT* (database), *http://faostat.fao.org* (accessed in December 2016).

FAO (2015), "Global Forest Resource Assessments 2015", *www.fao.org/forestry/fra/en*.

OECD (2017a), "Forest resources", *OECD Environment Statistics* (database), *http://dx.doi.org/10.1787/data-00600-en* (accessed in March 2017).

OECD (2017b), "Green growth indicators", *OECD Environment Statistics* (database), *http://dx.doi.org/10.1787/data-00665-en* (accessed in March 2017).

Further reading

Karousakis, K. (2009), "Promoting Biodiversity Co-Benefits in REDD", *OECD Environment Working Papers*, No. 11, OECD Publishing, Paris, *http://dx.doi.org/10.1787/220188577008*.

OECD (2012), *OECD Environmental Outlook to 2050: The Consequences of Inaction*, OECD Publishing, Paris, *http://dx.doi.org/10.1787/9789264122246-en*.

Freshwater resources

Freshwater resources, whose distribution varies widely among and within countries, are of major environmental and economic importance. Various forces exert pressure on water resources. These include over-abstraction and degradation due to pollution loads from human activities (agriculture, industry, households), changes in climate and weather conditions, and the introduction of invasive species. Over-abstraction of water, in particular, can have significant environmental and socio-economic consequences. These range from low river flows, depleted groundwater and degraded water quality (including salinisation of freshwater bodies in coastal areas), to loss of wetlands, desertification and risks for both food security and economic production.

The main challenges are to ensure sustainable management of water resources, avoiding over-abstraction and degradation. This management model aims to maintain adequate supplies of freshwater of suitable quality for economic activities and human use, and to support aquatic and other ecosystems. To that end, risks related to water quantity and quality must be identified, targeted and mitigated in a coordinated manner.

Water quantity is best managed through a combination of water demand management, water-efficient practices and technologies, and well-designed water allocation. Water quality management requires prevention, reduction and management of water pollution. It must cover all sources (diffuse and point sources) and all water bodies (surface, ground, coastal). Further, it must consider all major existing and emerging pollutants.

Infrastructure and other investments can also affect the natural integrity of rivers, lakes, aquifers and wetlands. In addition, they can influence hydromorphological conditions, the natural water retention capacity of the basins and ecosystem function. Both polluters and users should be kept accountable as much as possible.

This chapter focuses on water quantity issues and on renewable resources.

Main trends and recent developments

Countries' endowment in freshwater resources varies greatly and local water scarcity remains of concern

The availability of renewable fresh water resources and the levels of water stress – intensity of use of available renewable resources – show wide variation among and within countries (Figures 8.1a and 8.1c). Most OECD countries face at least seasonal or local water quantity problems. Several have extensive arid or semi-arid regions where scarce water constrains economic development. In more than one-third of the OECD, freshwater resources are under moderate to medium-high stress. In a few countries, water resources are abundant and population density is low. In some countries such as Saudi Arabia, renewable freshwater resources are limited. In these cases, public water supply has to rely

Figure 8.1. Freshwater endowments and abstraction intensities

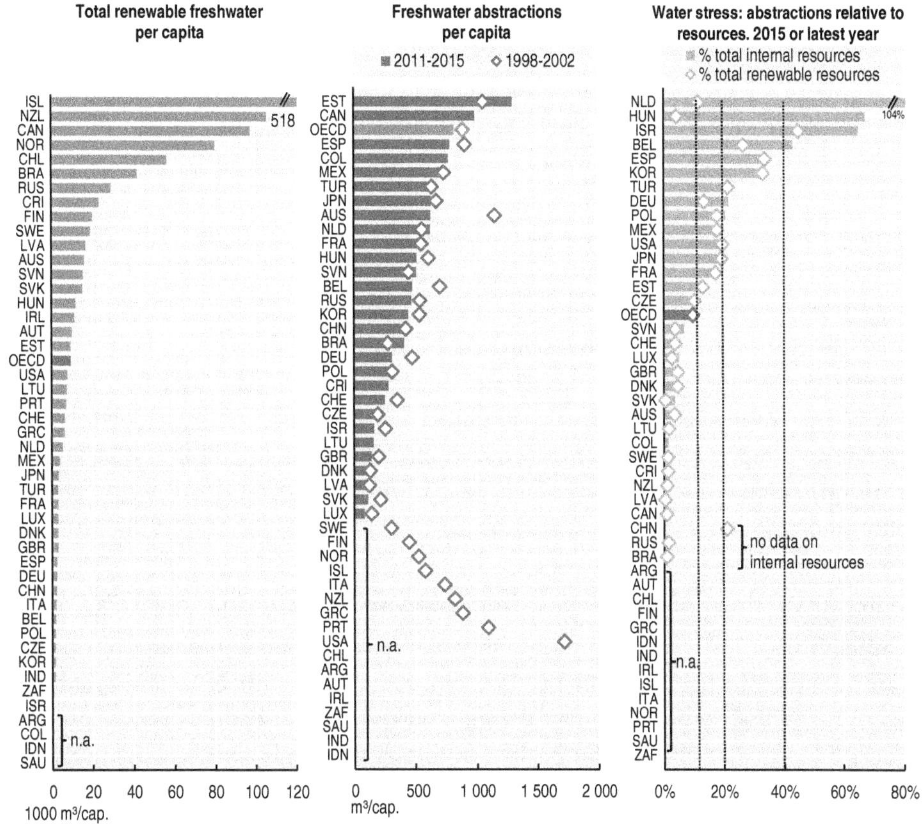

Note: In panel C (water stress): < 10%: low; 10-20%: moderate; 20-40%: medium-high; > 40%: high. United Kingdom (GBR) refers to England and Wales only.

Source: OECD (2017a, 2017b) *OECD Environment Statistics* (database).

StatLink http://dx.doi.org/10.1787/888933484688

Figure 8.2. Freshwater abstraction has decoupled from economic growth in many countries

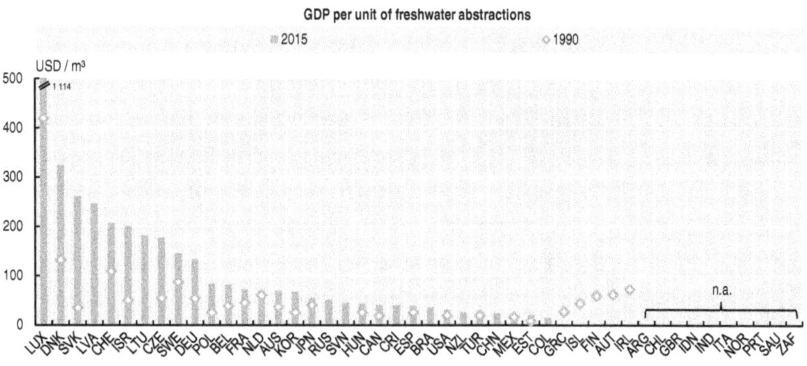

Source: OECD (2017b), "Water: Freshwater abstractions", *OECD Environment Statistics* (database).

StatLink http://dx.doi.org/10.1787/888933484698

on other sources of water (e.g. desalinated sea water). Agriculture in these countries mainly depends on non-renewable groundwater.

Freshwater abstraction is stabilising

Over the 1970s, agricultural and energy sectors in most OECD countries had increased demand for water. Consequently, countries increased water abstraction. In the 1980s, some countries stabilised their abstractions. They adopted more efficient irrigation techniques, reduced water-intensive industries (e.g. mining, steel), increased the use of more efficient technologies and reduced losses in pipe networks.

Since the late 1990s, trends in freshwater abstractions have been generally stable (Figure 8.1b). In some countries this is due to increased use of alternative water sources, including water reuse and desalination.

Abstraction for agricultural uses is decreasing in OECD countries, largely due to improved irrigation

Agricultural water abstraction has decreased in most OECD countries since 2005. This confirms the trend in place since the early 2000s, particularly in countries where agriculture relies largely on irrigation. Some countries achieved major policy reforms in agricultural and water regulations, or introduced energy tariffs for groundwater pumping. Farmers had to adapt both to the new policies and a changing climate. Due to the large weight of agriculture in total water use, reductions in agricultural water abstraction contribute to mitigating water stress in a majority of OECD countries (OECD, 2016).

Freshwater abstraction has decoupled from economic growth in many OECD countries

In all countries for which data are available, national income generated per unit of freshwater abstracted increased in the last two decades (Figure 8.2). The greatest gains occurred in the Slovak Republic, Israel, Poland and the Czech Republic, where productivity levels more than tripled during the period. In Israel, the performance essentially derives from three factors. These include extensive reuse of treated wastewater and pioneering investment in water-efficient technologies (e.g. drip irrigation). And pricing reflects the resource cost, thus shifting towards higher-value water uses. In Central European countries, water productivity gains likely result from improved infrastructure (less leakage) and structural changes in the economy (towards less water-intensive industries).

Robust water allocation can strengthen incentives for innovation in water-intensive activities. Abstraction charges tend to be low in most countries. Therefore, increasing these charges would improve cost recovery. They would also provide a price signal, making low-value and inefficient water uses less attractive. Tradable water permits or abstraction rights exist through either formal or informal water markets. These have been shown to encourage allocating water towards higher-value uses. But safeguards are needed to avoid potentially negative impacts of such trading such as diversion of environmental flows, speculative behaviour from investors who do not reside in the basin, or distributional issues when well-off groups or users "buy and dry" poor ones. Further, transaction costs should be kept as low as possible, whatever the regime in place (OECD, 2015).

Measurability and interpretation

The indicators presented in this chapter give insights into quantitative aspects of water resources. They relate to the following:

- Available **renewable freshwater resource stocks** expressed as the long term annual average availability in cubic metres per capita.
- Total **freshwater abstraction** per capita.

- The **intensity of freshwater resource use** (or water stress), expressed as gross abstraction from groundwater and surface water bodies in percentage of total available renewable freshwater resources (including transboundary inflows) and percentage of internal freshwater resources (precipitation minus evapotranspiration). See also *Glossary*.

These indicators are complemented by the following:

- **Freshwater abstraction in relation to gross domestic product** expressed as gross domestic product per cubic metre of abstracted water, as a proxy for water use productivity.

National-level indicators as shown here may hide significant territorial and seasonal differences. They should be complemented with information at the sub-national (river basin) level. They should also be read in connection with indicators on water quality. Finally, water can affect economic growth through risks of floods and droughts, which are not covered here.

Water resource accounts and water statistics provide information on freshwater resources. These are available for most OECD countries. However, definitions and estimation methods may vary considerably by country and over time. More work is needed to improve the completeness and historical consistency of data on water abstraction and the methods for estimating renewable water resources. Better data on freshwater stored in artificial reservoirs and in underground formations would allow a more complete assessment of water stress. Data on rain water harvesting would be equally useful. As well, more is needed to mobilise data that adequately reflect the spatial distribution of water stress.

Sources

OECD (2017a), "Water: Freshwater resources (long term annual average)", *OECD Environment Statistics* (database), *http://dx.doi.org/10.1787/data-00604-en* (accessed in March 2017).

OECD (2017b), "Water: Freshwater abstractions", *OECD Environment Statistics* (database), *http://dx.doi.org/10.1787/data-00602-en* (accessed in March 2017).

OECD (2017c), "Green growth indicators", *OECD Environment Statistics* (database), *http://dx.doi.org/10.1787/data-00665-en* (accessed in March 2017).

OECD (2016), "Environment Statistics: Water", *OECD Agriculture Statistics* (database), *http:dx.doi.org//10.1787/env-data-en* (accessed in March 2017).

OECD (2015), *Water Resources Allocation: Sharing Risks and Opportunities*, OECD Publishing, Paris, *http://dx.doi.org/10.1787/9789264229631-en*.

Further reading

OECD (2017a), *Groundwater Allocation*, OECD Studies on Water, OECD Publishing, Paris.

OECD (2017b), *Diffuse Pollution in OECD Countries: A Policy Framework for Action*, OECD Studies on Water, OECD Publishing, Paris.

OECD (2016a), *Water, Growth and Finance, Policy Perspectives*, OECD Publishing, Paris, *https://issuu.com/oecd.publishing/docs/water-growth-finance-policy-perspec*.

OECD (2016b), OECD Council Recommendation on Water, *www.oecd.org/environment/resources/Council-Recommendation-on-water.pdf*.

OECD (n.d.), "Green Growth and Water", webpage: *www.oecd.org/greengrowth/greengrowthandwater.htm*.

OECD (n.d.), "Horizontal Water Programme", webpage: *www.oecd.org/water*.

Sadoff, C. et al. (2015), *Securing Water, Sustaining Growth*, report to the OECD-GWP Taskforce on water security and sustainable growth, University of Oxford, UK.

Biodiversity, ecosystems and wildlife resources

Biological resources (terrestrial, aquatic and marine) provide production inputs for many sectors of the economy. They are essential elements of ecosystems and natural capital, and their diversity is key to maintaining life-support systems and quality of life.

Conservation and sustainable use of biodiversity are key concerns nationally and globally. Pressures on biodiversity from human activities take several forms. Pressures can be physical (e.g. habitat alteration and fragmentation through changes in land use and land cover). They can be chemical (e.g. toxic contamination, acidification, oil spills). Or they could be biological (e.g. alteration of population dynamics and species structure through the release of exotic species or commercial use of wildlife resources).

There are also several primary drivers for biodiversity loss. These include land use changes, such as conversion of land from natural or semi-natural state to intensive agriculture and infrastructure. Other drivers are unsustainable use of natural resources, pollution, invasive alien species and climate change.

The main challenge is to ensure an effective conservation and a sustainable use of biological resources. This implies strengthening the degree of protection of habitats and species. Strategies include eliminating illegal exploitation and trade, integrating biodiversity concerns into economic and sectoral policies, and raising public awareness. Strengthening protection also requires removing environmentally harmful subsidies and heightening the role of environmentally related taxes and charges. Finally, it entails payments for ecosystem services, biodiversity offsets and tradable permits (such as transferable quotas for fisheries).

Main trends and recent developments

Many ecosystems have been degraded and wildlife is increasingly threatened

Pressures on biodiversity and threats to global ecosystems and their species are intensifying. In most countries, the number of animal and plant species identified as endangered is increasing. Animal population trends show an overall decline of 58% over 1970-2012, with the greatest losses in freshwater ecosystems (Loh et al., 2008 [Living Planet Index]). Many species are threatened by habitat alteration or loss, including within protected areas. Threat levels are particularly high in countries with high population density and a high concentration of human activities.

The rate of forest habitat loss has slowed in some regions (e.g. the Amazon). However, deforestation in many tropical areas of the world is increasing. Habitats of all types, including grasslands, wetlands and river systems, continue to be fragmented and degraded (CBD, 2014).

Figure 9.1. **Amphibians are under great threat in many countries (2016 or latest available year)**

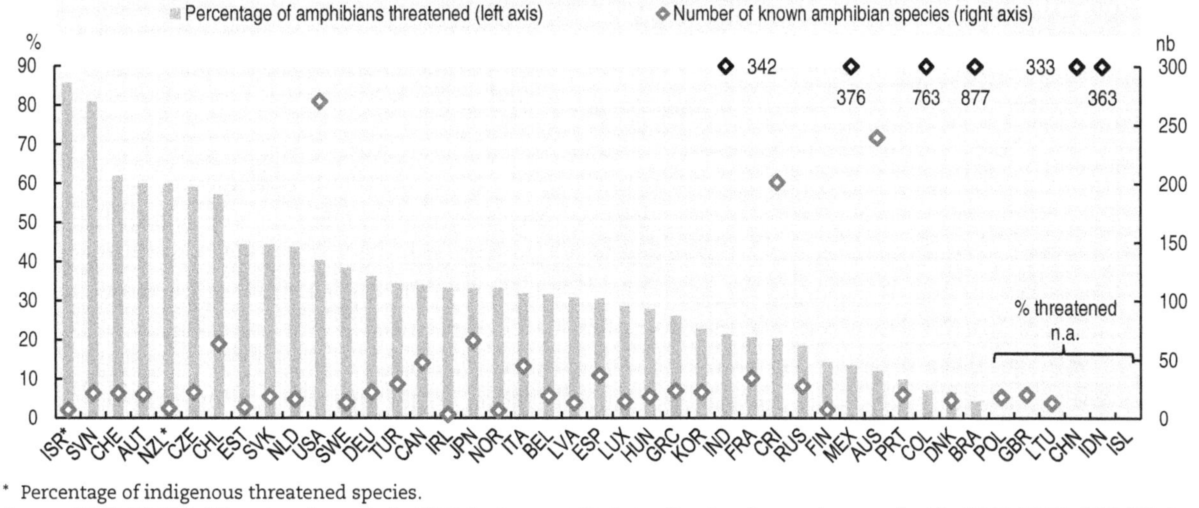

* Percentage of indigenous threatened species.

Source: OECD (2017a), "Threatened species", *OECD Environment Statistics* (database), complemented with: IUCN (2008), "Wildlife in a changing world: An analysis of the 2008 IUCN Red List of Threatened Species"; Brazil Ministry of the Environment (2015), "Fifth national report to the CBD"; Zoological Survey of India (2013), "A Checklist of Amphibians of India with IUCN Red list Status".

StatLink http://dx.doi.org/10.1787/888933484708

Figure 9.2. **Population dynamics of wild birds and wild fish are of concern**

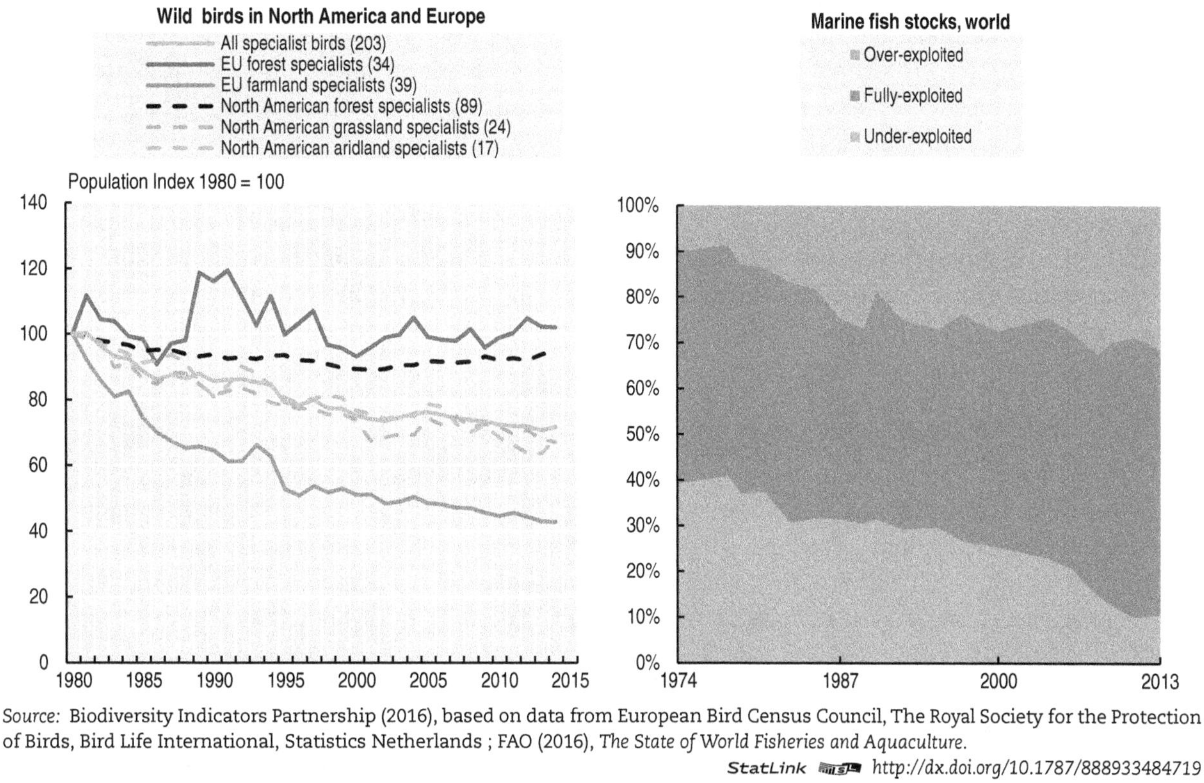

Source: Biodiversity Indicators Partnership (2016), based on data from European Bird Census Council, The Royal Society for the Protection of Birds, Bird Life International, Statistics Netherlands ; FAO (2016), *The State of World Fisheries and Aquaculture.*

StatLink http://dx.doi.org/10.1787/888933484719

Cycads and amphibians are the most threatened species groups

All species groups are moving towards higher risk of extinction, although at varying speed. Cycads, the world's oldest seed plants, and amphibians are, on average, the most threatened groups. But coral species are also increasingly under extinction risk (IUCN Red

List Index). The largest threats to amphibian populations are posed by habitat loss and degradation (due to drainage, loss of wetlands, pollution, etc.), followed by disease and invasive species. Amphibians are sensitive to contaminants (such as pesticides, and industrial and pharmaceutical chemicals) and to variations in climatic conditions. High rates of extinction risk among amphibians signal major deterioration in ecosystem health.

About one-third of the world's amphibian species are known to be threatened or extinct (IUCN, 2016). The threat status is generally higher for indigenous species (e.g. Israel, New Zealand). In seven OECD countries, the majority of amphibian species is threatened. At least 10% of amphibian species are threatened in most other OECD and G20 countries. These include countries with large amphibian populations such as the United States (40%), Indonesia (21%), Mexico (14%) and Australia (12%) (Figure 9.1). Some of the greatest amphibian diversity is located outside the OECD area, in Latin America and the Caribbean and in Asia. Countries such as Brazil, Colombia, Ecuador, Peru, Indonesia and the People's Republic of China (hereafter China) host more than 300 species each.

Wild bird populations declined in Europe and North America

Birds are good indicators of biodiversity for several reasons. They are placed high in the food chain and are they sensitive to land use and climatic changes. Sharp declines in many formerly common and widespread bird species signal broader environmental problems. Data on wild bird populations in Europe and North America show relatively stable trends in widespread forest specialist birds (data for other regions are not available). However, farmland bird populations have declined continuously since the early 1990s in Europe, mostly in farmed lands. There is a similar decline of farmland birds in North America, mostly in grasslands and arid lands. (Figure 9.2a). Overall, specialist birds have declined by 28% since the 1980s and by nearly 41% since the late 1960s.

Agriculture is the major land user in most OECD countries. Agricultural land, if well managed, is a primary habitat for wildlife, particularly for bird and insect species. Agri-environmental programmes can thus be an effective means to revert losses in wild bird populations. Successful approaches include farmland conservation and changes in farm management practices with subsequent reductions in nutrient surpluses and pesticide use (e.g. in the United States).

A third of global fish stocks are overexploited

The proportion of over-exploited stocks increased to 31%, significantly more than in the 1970s. Overexploited stocks yield less than their maximum potential due to excessive fishing in the past. More than half of all stocks (58%) are fully exploited, producing catches at or close to their maximum sustainable limits. Between the 1970s and 2010s, stocks that are not fully exploited, i.e. moderately exploited or under-exploited, declined from 40% to 10% (Figure 9.2b).

Protected areas are increasing, but remain insufficient to meet Aichi targets in 2020

The extent, and management types, of terrestrial and marine protected areas can indicate countries' efforts to safeguard habitats and species as well as landscapes shaped by human-environment interactions that are valued for cultural or other reasons. In many countries, protected areas are increasing, but they are not always representative of national biodiversity or sufficiently connected.

There are large variations among countries in the extent and the management objectives of terrestrial protected areas (Figure 9.3). These can be partly explained by

Figure 9.3. **Extent of protected areas and approaches to their management vary across countries (2017)**

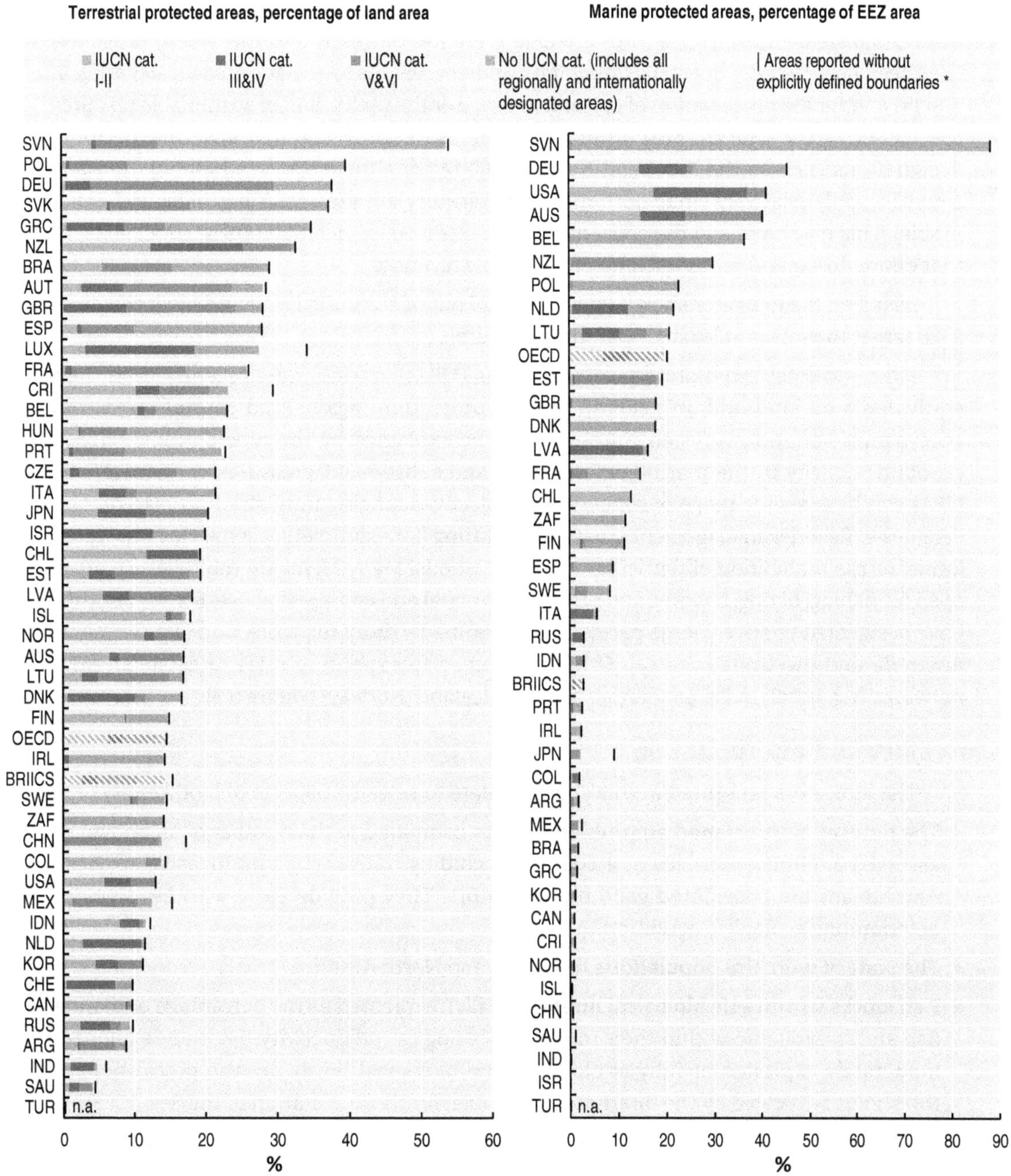

* Shown cumulatively. For some protected areas the data in the WDPA is reported without explicitly defined boundaries. The area they represent cannot be easily accounted for in the graphics presented here, in part because they may overlap other protected areas. The use of explicit geographical boundaries allows a more accurate description of countries' protected areas.

Note: IUCN categories reflect management objectives. Categories I and II refer to strict nature reserves, wilderness areas and national parks. Categories III and IV refer to natural monuments and habitat/species management areas. Categories V and VI refer to protected landscapes/seascapes and areas with sustainable use of natural resources. Other nationally designated areas with no IUCN category are grouped with regionally and internationally designated areas. See *Glossary* for more details on calculation methodology. Data refer to metropolitan or mainland countries, overseas territories are not included. TUR: data not available in the World Database on Protected Areas (WDPA); according to official national sources about 6% of the territory is protected. EEZ = Exclusive economic zone. Landlocked countries are not shown in panel B.

Source: OECD (2017b), OECD calculations using data extracted from the WDPA (January, 2017).

StatLink http://dx.doi.org/10.1787/888933484722

differences in geography, ecology, and the pre-existing patterns of human settlement in the territory. Some countries (e.g. Chile, Costa Rica, Iceland, Colombia) have designated proportionally large areas as strict nature reserves, national parks and wilderness areas (IUCN management categories I-II). Others (e.g. France, Germany and the United Kingdom) use these designations to establish habitats and species management areas (categories III and IV) and for the preservation of cultural heritage or the promotion of sustainable resource use (categories V and VI). Still other countries use mainly regional and international designations such as the European Natura 2000 regional network (e.g. Ireland). In a few countries, only relatively small portions of the territory are protected (e.g. India and Saudi Arabia). This may be due to the concentration of biodiversity-rich habitats in small areas or that efforts to expand protected areas started only recently.

Based on the indicator shown (Figure 9.3), 26 out of 46 countries would meet the Aichi 2020 target to protect at least 17% of their land area.

Efforts to establish marine protected areas (MPAs) started more recently than their equivalents on land and, in general, marine protection lags behind that of terrestrial ecosystems. Variation between countries may be explained by the type and intensity of economic activity in the marine environment and subsequent pressures on biodiversity. MPAs can have a wide range of conservation objectives ranging from strict no-take marine reserves to fisheries management areas incorporating (for example) seasonal closures, catch limits, or the prohibition of particular fishing methods. Many MPAs are multiple-use areas open for fishing, diving, boating, and other recreational and commercial use. Some countries have designated relatively large parts of their marine territory for protection (e.g. Germany, Australia and the United States). Others still need to expand or start to establish MPA networks (e.g. Israel, India, Saudi Arabia, China, Iceland, Norway) (Figure 9.3).

Measurability and interpretation

The indicators presented in this chapter relate to selected aspects of biodiversity:

- The number of **threatened amphibian species** compared to the number of all known or assessed amphibian species in a country (including indigenous and invasive species). Amphibians are considered good bio-indicators. They provide early warning signs of deteriorating ecological conditions.
- The state of **wild bird populations** in Europe and North America.
- **Fish stocks within safe biological limits** (globally), expressed as the percentage of marine fish stocks exploited within their maximum biological productivity (i.e. underexploited, moderately exploited or fully exploited). Safe biological limits are the precautionary thresholds advocated by the International Council for the Exploration of the Sea (ICES).
- The shares of countries' territory (land and inland waters) and exclusive economic zone (EEZ) designated as **protected areas**. Data estimate terrestrial and marine areas dedicated to the protection and maintenance of biological diversity. They also estimate natural and associated cultural resources managed through legal or other effective means.

These indicators provide only a partial picture of the status of biodiversity. They also reflect the level of efforts made to monitor species. For more details see *Glossary*.

Sources

Biodiversity Indicators Partnership (2016), "Global Wild Bird Index", *www.bipindicators.net/WBI* (accessed in February 2017).

Brazil Ministry of the Environment (2015), "Fifth national report to the CBD", *www.cbd.int/doc/world/br/br-nr-05-en.pdf*.

CBD (2014), *Global Biodiversity Outlook 4*, Secretariat of the Convention on Biological Diversity, Montreal.

FAO (2016), *The State of World Fisheries and Aquaculture 2016*, Food and Agriculture Organization of the United Nations, Rome, *www.fao.org/3/a-i5555e.pdf*.

IUCN (2016), "The IUCN Red List of Threatened Species", *www.iucnredlist.org/about* (accessed in January 2017).

IUCN (2008), "Wildlife in a changing world: An analysis of the 2008 IUCN Red List of Threatened Species", *https://portals.iucn.org/library/sites/library/files/documents/RL-2009-001.pdf*.

Loh, J. et al. (2008), "Living Planet Index", in C. Hails (ed.), *Living Planet Report 2008*, WWF International, Gland, Switzerland, *http://assets.panda.org/downloads/living_planet_report_2008.pdf*.

Mackie, A. et al. (2016), "Indicators on Terrestrial and Marine Protected Areas: Methodology and Results for OECD and G20 countries", *OECD Environment Working Papers* (forthcoming).

OECD (2017a), "Threatened species", *OECD Environment Statistics* (database), *http://dx.doi.org/10.1787/data-00605-en* (accessed in February 2017).

OECD (2017b), "Protected areas", *OECD Environment Statistics* (database).

OECD (2017c), "Green growth indicators", *OECD Environment Statistics* (database), *http://dx.doi.org/10.1787/data-00665-en* (accessed in March 2017).

Vié, J.-C., C. Hilton-Taylor and S.N. Stuart (eds.) (2009), *Wildlife in a Changing World – An Analysis of the 2008 IUCN Red List of Threatened Species*, International Union for Conservation of Nature, Gland, Switzerland, *https://portals.iucn.org/library/sites/library/files/documents/RL-2009-001.pdf*.

WDPA (2017), *World Database on Protected Areas* (database), *www.protectedplanet.net* (accessed in January 2017).

WWF (2016), "Living Planet Report 2016: Risk and Resilience in a New Era", WWF International, Gland, Switzerland.

Zoological Survey of India (2013), "A Checklist of Amphibians of India with IUCN Red list Status", *http://indiabiodiversity.org/biodiv/content/documents/document-8e24da1a-e893-4400-9d35-b2f80d1231d5/381.pdf*.

Further reading

CBD (n.d.), Country Profiles, webpage: *www.cbd.int/countries*.

ICES (n.d.), International Council for the Exploration of the Seas, webpage: *www.ices.dk*.

Jansen, J. et al. (2016), European Red List of Habitats, *http://ec.europa.eu/environment/nature/knowledge/redlist_en.htm*.

OECD (2017), "Marine Protected Areas: Economics, Management and Effective Policy Mixes", OECD Publishing, Paris (forthcoming).

OECD (2013), *Scaling-up Finance Mechanisms for Biodiversity*, OECD Publishing, Paris, *http://dx.doi.org/10.1787/9789264193833-en*.

OECD (2012), *OECD Environmental Outlook to 2050: The Consequences of Inaction*, OECD Publishing, Paris, *http://dx.doi.org/10.1787/9789264122246-en*.

Van Winkle C. et al. (2015), "Biodiversity Policy Response Indicators", *OECD Environment Working Papers*, No. 90, OECD Publishing, Paris, *http://dx.doi.org/10.1787/5jrxd8j24fbv-en*.

PART 3

The environmental quality of life

Air pollution, health risks and costs

Access to water supply, sanitation and sewage treatment

Air pollution, health risks and costs

Air pollution is the single greatest environmental health risk worldwide. Reducing risks to human health from degraded air quality, then, is central for improving people's lives and well-being. Fine particulate matter ($PM_{2.5}$), in particular, is the most serious pollutant globally from a human health perspective. Chronic exposure even to moderate levels of $PM_{2.5}$ substantially increases the risk of heart disease and stroke, the leading causes of death in OECD countries. It also increases the risk of respiratory diseases, including lung cancer, chronic obstructive pulmonary disease and respiratory infections (WHO, 2016; Burnett et al., 2014; Brauer et al., 2016). Other pollutants of most concern are small particulates (PM_{10}), ozone (O_3), nitrogen dioxide (NO_2) and sulphur dioxide (SO_2). Emissions from transport, industry, electricity generation, agriculture and domestic (household) sources are the main contributors to outdoor air pollution (EEA, 2016a; Caiazzo et al., 2013).

Air pollution causes millions of avoidable deaths every year. It is therefore urgent to implement policies that reduce emissions of air pollutants and limit the population's exposure to air pollution. Emissions can be reduced by substituting dirty fuels for cleaner ones, focusing development on cleaner industries, reducing consumption of polluting products and adopting cleaner technologies. Behavioural and lifestyle changes are also important. Policies that provide incentives across a broad spectrum of firms and consumers (e.g. emission or energy taxes) tend to be more cost-efficient than those that target a specific product, fuel or technology (e.g. subsidies for electric cars).

Both the sources of air pollution and severity of exposure vary across and within countries. Hence it is important to tailor policies to specific local circumstances. For example, more stringent measures are required in densely populated areas or for emission sources located upwind from urban areas. Such spatially heterogeneous policies help achieve environmental objectives at lower costs than measures that apply uniformly to sources in all locations and to populations at all risk levels. Cost-efficient implementation of air pollution policies deserves attention because it allows a faster transition of countries towards a greener growth model. At the same time, it generates more economic opportunities (jobs, exports, etc.).

Progress can be assessed by measuring the exposure of population to air pollutants, and by assessing the health consequences and their economic costs. The costs of air pollution mainly arise from its detrimental impact on human health. These take the form of shorter life expectancy, increased healthcare costs and reduced labour productivity. Further consequences include reduced agricultural output and damage to ecosystems.

Figure 10.1. **Population exposure to air pollution by $PM_{2.5}$ exceeds guideline in many countries**

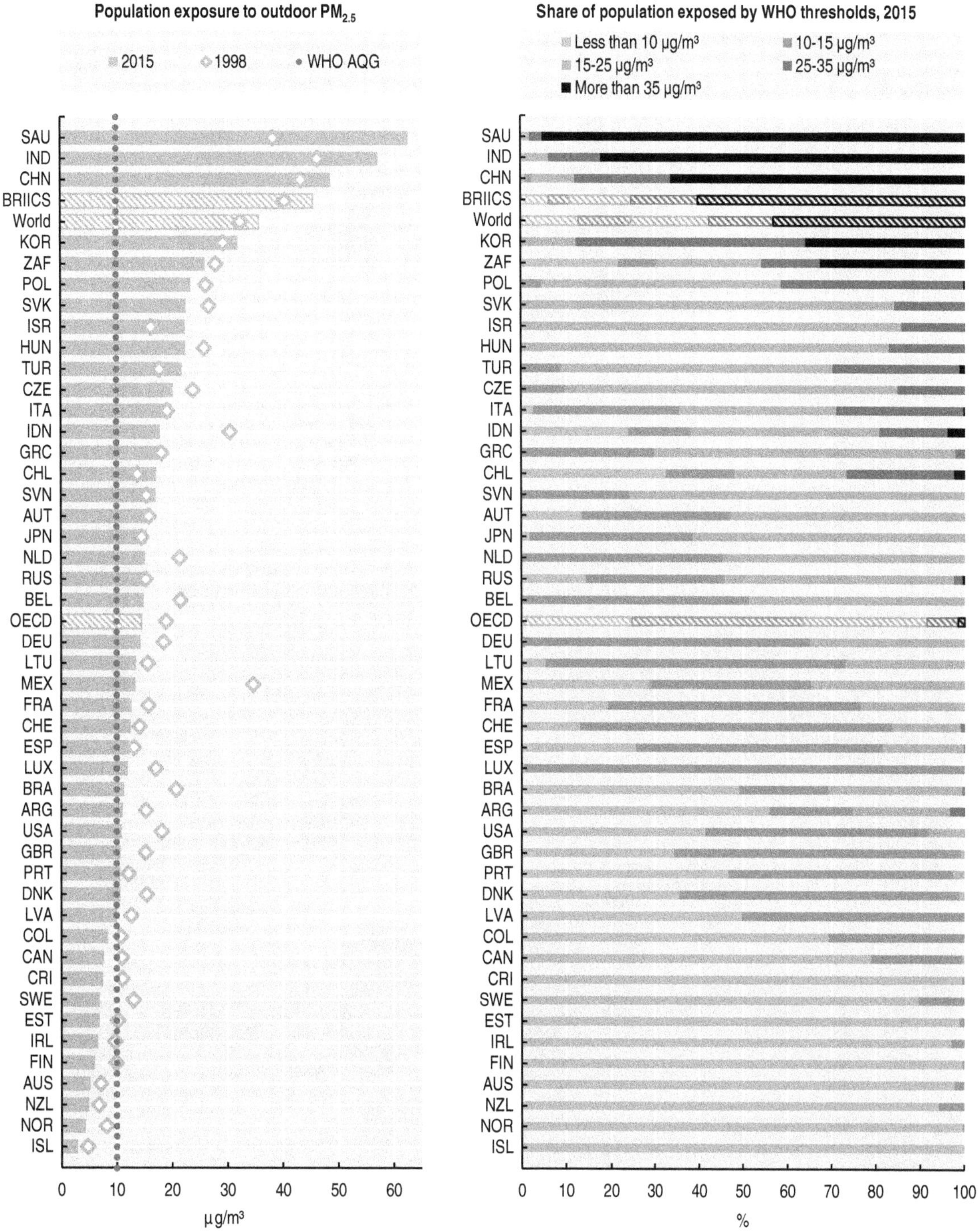

Note: These estimates are for chronic outdoor exposure to $PM_{2.5}$. Internationally comparable measures of average $PM_{2.5}$ concentrations are derived from satellite observations, chemical transport models and ground monitoring stations. Population exposure to air pollution is calculated by weighting concentrations with populations in each cell of the underlying gridded data. These estimates include pollutants from both anthropogenic and natural sources. There is a possibility of over-estimates or under-estimates in certain locations. While satellite observations are less precise than in-situ monitoring, the two data sources are complementary. They allow estimates of concentrations in locations not covered by ground monitoring networks; they also improve the comparability of estimates between different locations.

Source: OECD (2017a), "Exposure to air pollution", *OECD Environment Statistics* (database); OECD calculations based on van Donkelaar et al. (2016) and CIESIN (2016).

StatLink *http://dx.doi.org/10.1787/888933484739*

Figure 10.2. **Population exposure to air pollution by $PM_{2.5}$**

Mean exposure, 2015

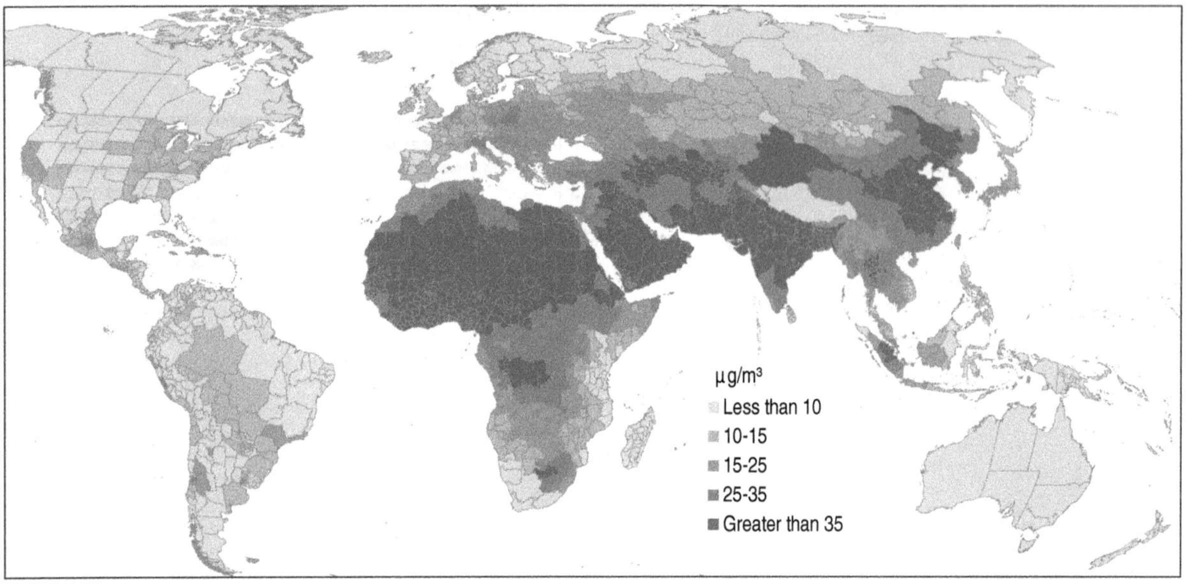

Mean exposure excluding estimated contribution of mineral dust and salt spray, 2015

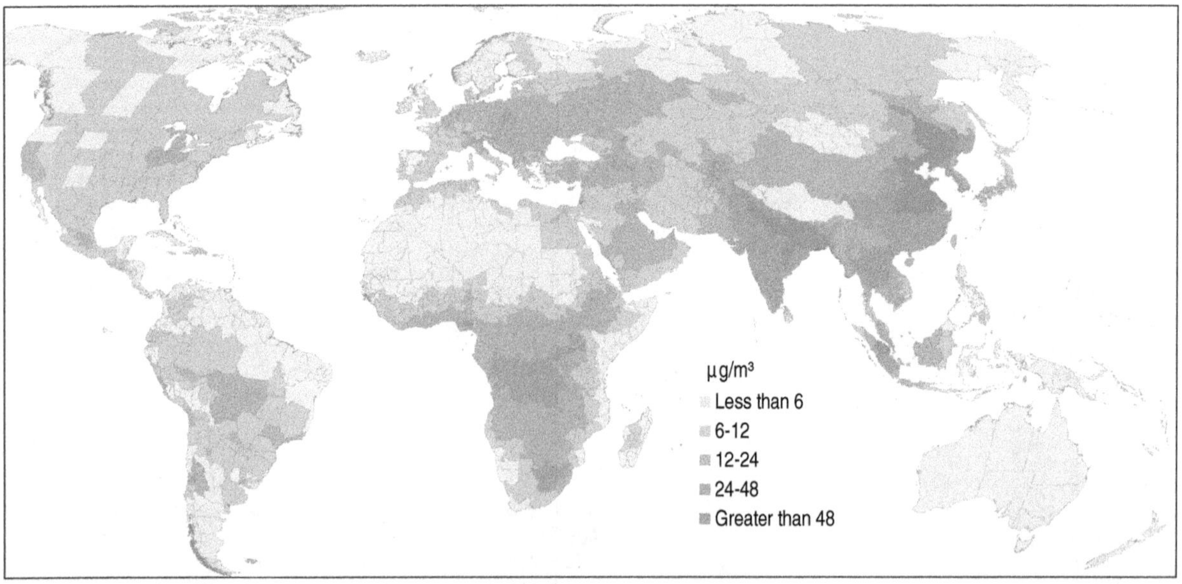

Source: OECD (2017a), "Exposure to air pollution", *OECD Environment Statistics* (database); OECD calculations based on van Donkelaar et al. (2016) and CIESIN (2016). Administrative boundaries: FAO (2015).

StatLink http://dx.doi.org/10.1787/888933484747

Main trends and recent developments

Human exposure to $PM_{2.5}$ remains dangerously high

Despite commendable improvements in reducing exposure, the populations of most OECD countries remain chronically exposed to harmful levels of $PM_{2.5}$ (Figure 10.1). Less than one in three OECD countries meet the WHO Air Quality Guideline for annual average $PM_{2.5}$ exposure of 10 micrograms per cubic metre (µg/m^3). Even this value is not a "safe"

Figure 10.3. **Change in population exposure to air pollution by $PM_{2.5}$ (1998-2015)**

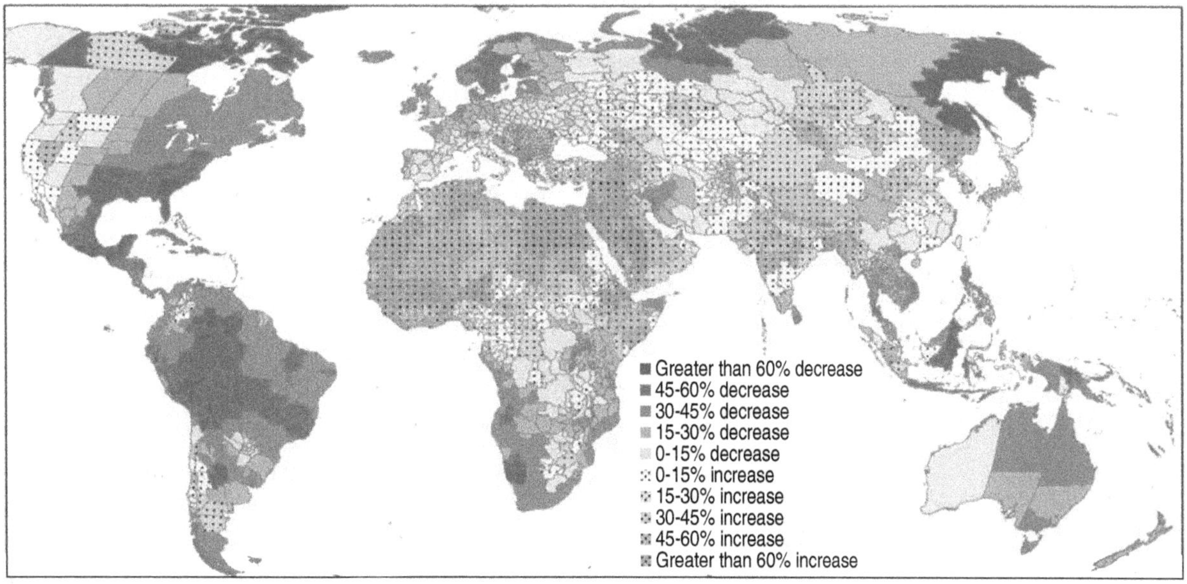

Source: OECD (2017a), "Exposure to air pollution", *OECD Environment Statistics* (database); OECD calculations based on van Donkelaar et al. (2016) and CIESIN (2016). Administrative boundaries: FAO (2015).

StatLink http://dx.doi.org/10.1787/888933484759

level; the 10 µg/m³ guideline is still associated with elevated risk of the diseases listed previously (WHO, 2016). Progress in most OECD countries contrasts with steady increases in $PM_{2.5}$ exposure in the People's Republic of China (hereafter China) and India from already very high, to even more extreme levels.

There has been little improvement in population exposure to air pollution by ozone

Exposure to ground-level ozone (O_3) has serious consequences for human health, contributing to, or triggering, respiratory diseases. These include breathing problems, asthma and reduced lung function (WHO, 2016; Brauer et al., 2016). Ozone exposure is highest in emission-dense countries with warm and sunny summers. In Europe, exceedances of a 70 µg/m³ exposure level in urban areas changed little between 2000-07 and 2008-14. However, some countries with high levels like Italy, Slovenia and Austria appear to be making progress (Figure 10.4). Almost all European countries exceed this O_3 exposure level at some point each year. Determining the causes of O_3 trends is difficult because ozone results from complex interactions between different phenomena. The most important determinants are background atmospheric chemistry, climate, anthropogenic and biogenic emissions of ozone precursors such as volatile organic compounds, and the ratios between different emitted chemicals.

Air pollution is estimated to cause around 0.5 million premature deaths, with a welfare cost equivalent to 3.6% of GDP in the OECD area each year

In OECD countries, exposure to outdoor $PM_{2.5}$ and ozone can be attributed to an estimated 500 000 premature deaths (GBD, 2015). The annual welfare cost associated with these premature deaths can be calculated in terms of what the population would be willing to pay to avoid the fatalities. This amounts to USD 1.7 trillion, equivalent to 3.6% of GDP for the OECD area (Figure 10.5b). Cardiovascular disease from exposure to outdoor particulates

Figure 10.4. **Population exposure to air pollution by O_3 has seen little improvement**

Acute exposure of urban populations to ozone

Cumulative exceedances of daily maximum 8-hour mean exposures above 70 µg/m3 (35 ppb) for all days in a year, based on measurements at ground stations, selected European countries.

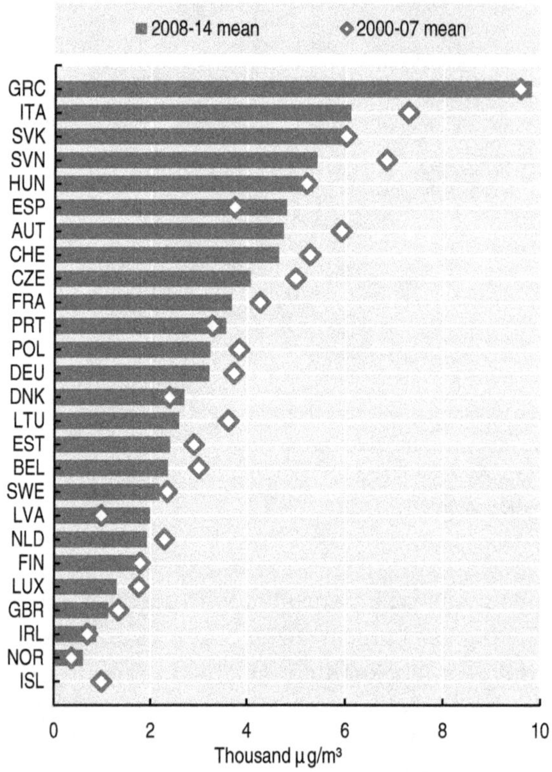

Note: For acute exposure, WHO recommends a maximum daily 8-hour mean exposure limit of 100 µg/m^3 to provide adequate protection of public health. Establishing longer-term health responses to O_3 is complex. There is insufficient evidence to recommend a guideline value for chronic exposure. For some countries the values shown in this figure are not representative of the entire population.

Source: Eurostat (2017), *Urban Population Exposure to Air pollution by Ozone* (database).

StatLink http://dx.doi.org/10.1787/888933484767

causes most of these deaths. Globally, GBD (2015) estimates exceed 4.4 million deaths annually. In some non-OECD economies, such as India, the health risks and welfare costs of exposure to indoor air pollution come close to those of exposure to outdoor air pollution (Figure 10.5d, Figure 10.5e).

The welfare cost from premature deaths is projected to more than double in OECD countries by 2060

According to OECD (2016) annual welfare costs from premature deaths are projected to more than double in OECD countries without more stringent policy action. They are expected to reach USD 3.5 trillion in 2060 (equivalent to 5% of GDP in 2060). In non-OECD economies, costs are projected to increase tenfold. This could reach USD 15-22 trillion in 2060 (equivalent to 7-10% of their GDP in 2060).

Furthermore, the costs to the economy, including through reduced labour productivity, are projected to add an extra USD 3.3 trillion by 2060 (OECD, 2016). Potential benefits of pollution mitigation would thus be very significant.

Figure 10.5. **Air pollution weighs heavily on population's health and welfare**

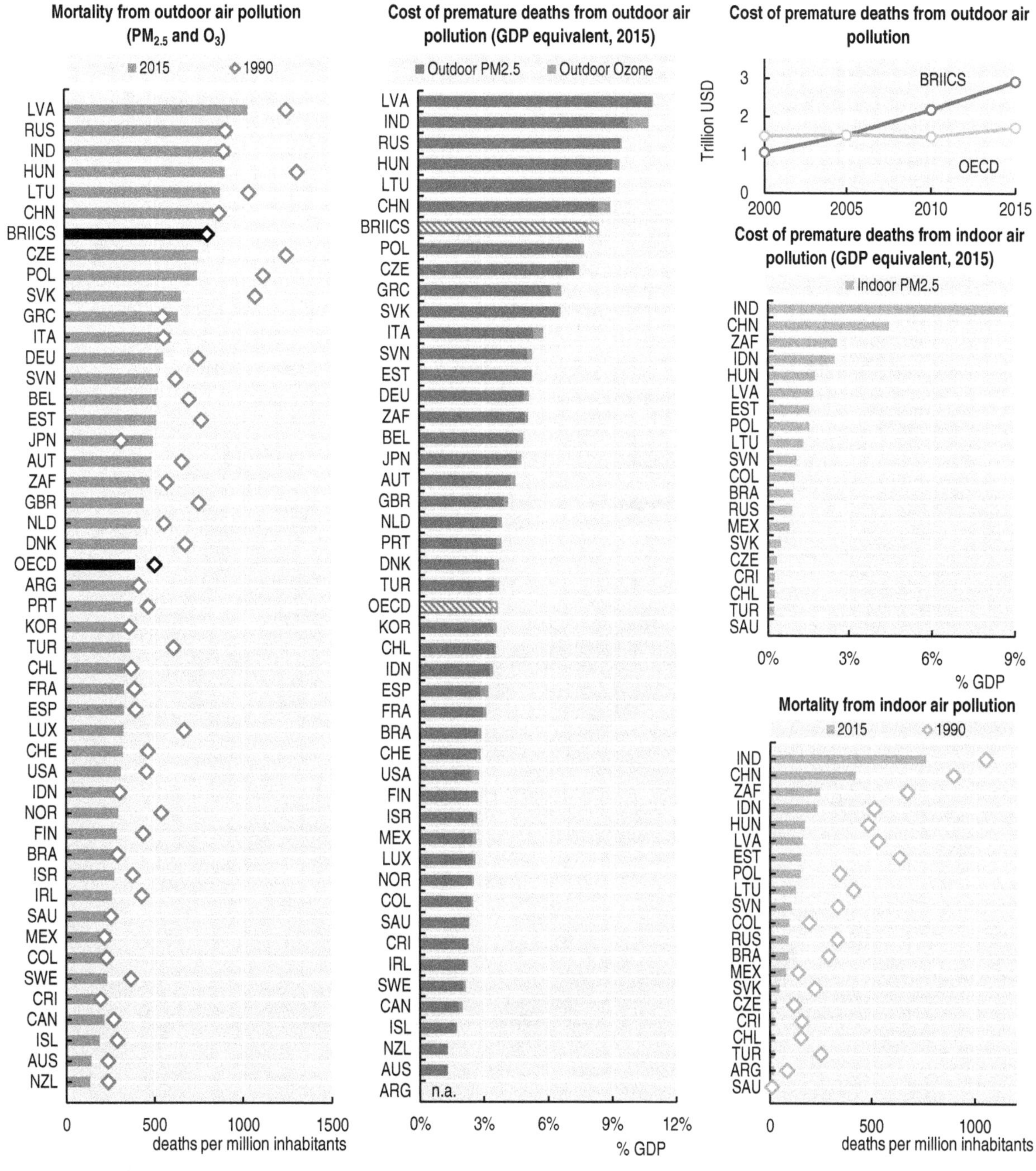

Source (mortality): GBD (2015), *Global Burden of Disease Study 2015 Results*. Mortality data on indoor air pollution from GBD are available for only some countries. They draw on WHO information and national household surveys.

Source (costs): OECD calculations using methodology adapted from OECD (2014). A standard value-of-statistical-life (VSL) estimate is used to calculate the costs of premature mortalities. The country-specific costs presented here account for differences in income levels and income elasticities across countries (elasticity of 0.8 for high-, 0.9 for middle- and 1 for low-income countries). Nevertheless, the underlying VSL estimate might be less reliable when applied to countries with different standards of living or extrapolated over time. VSL also captures non-market values that are unrelated to expenditures and therefore not an integral part of the calculation of GDP. Consequently the cost estimates are compared with GDP only for illustration.

StatLink http://dx.doi.org/10.1787/888933484773

Box 10.1. **Nitrogen dioxide is a persistent problem in cities**

Along with fine particulates and ozone, nitrogen dioxide (NO_2) is the other major constituent of the air pollution mix in OECD countries. Like ozone, NO_2 causes respiratory problems such as bronchitis symptoms in asthmatic children and reduced lung function growth. In 2013, some monitoring stations in Germany, France and the United Kingdom, recorded annual average concentrations over twice the WHO guideline and EU legal limit values. Most European countries have at least one city where the average considerably exceeds limits. NO_2 is predominantly emitted by vehicles. In Paris, for example, road vehicles emit an estimated 62% of NO_2 (Airparif, 2014).

Reducing motor vehicle emissions in densely populated areas could make the greatest impact on NO_2 exposure. Strategies include modal shifts, electrification of vehicle fleets and reduced urban congestion. The public health benefits of more efficient transport are compounded by reductions of other pollutants; in the case of Paris, road traffic generates more than half of particulate emissions.

Figure 10.6. **NO_2 concentrations exceed limits in cities**

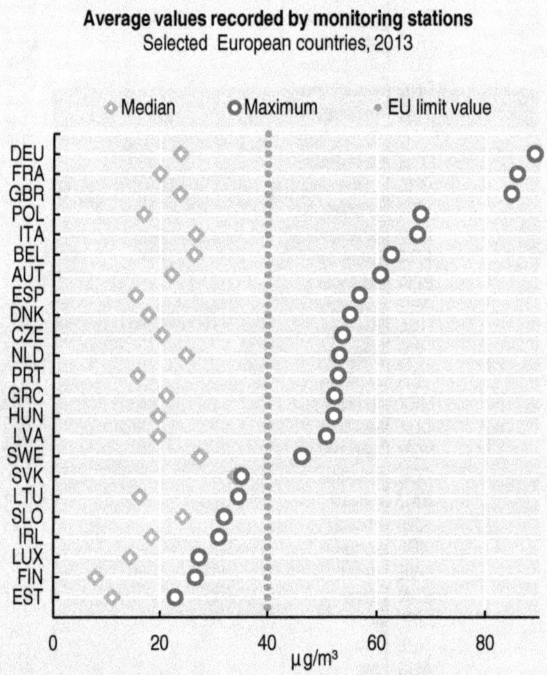

Source: EEA (2016b), *Attainment Situation for* NO_2.

StatLink http://dx.doi.org/10.1787/888933484780

Measurability and interpretation

Exposure to air pollution is assessed against three outdoor air pollutants with the most significant health impacts:

- **Population exposure to outdoor $PM_{2.5}$** is derived using pollutant concentration estimates. These use chemical transport models (which, in turn, rely on several emissions databases), satellite-based measurements of aerosol optical depth and measurements from ground stations. This hybrid approach has the advantage of being available for areas that lack a sufficient density of ground-based air monitoring stations. It is also more comparable between different areas than estimates derived from ground-based measurements stations alone. The estimates include particulates originating from both natural and anthropogenic sources. Population exposure is calculated by weighting concentrations with population in each cell of the resulting gridded concentration data.

- **Population exposure to ground-level ozone** Acute O_3 exposure estimates in urban areas are average ground station measurements weighted by neighbouring population. The indicator refers to the annual sum of daily maximum 8-hour mean concentrations above a threshold (70 µg/m^3 or 35 parts per billion) at urban background stations in agglomerations and calculated for all days in a year. Current WHO air quality guidelines for ozone (O_3) are 8-hour mean concentrations of 100 µg/m^3.
- **Concentrations of NO_2** measured at ground-based monitoring stations.

The health impacts from exposure to air pollution are then evaluated:

- **Cost of outdoor air pollution:** The cost of the health impact of air pollution is evaluated in terms of what the population at large would be "willing to pay" to avoid premature deaths from exposure to outdoor air pollution (the cost estimates take only $PM_{2.5}$ and O_3 into account). These welfare costs are calculated using estimates of the "Value of a Statistical Life". These, in turn, are derived from a meta-analysis of a large number of studies of individual willingness-to-pay to reduce the risk of premature mortality. Cost estimates represent the cost of premature mortalities. They exclude any morbidity impacts (labour productivity losses, treatment costs and willingness to pay to avoid pain and suffering from illness). They also exclude impacts other than those on human health (e.g. on built structures, agricultural productivity, ecosystem health). The social cost of air pollution is thus greater than the cost of mortalities presented in this chapter. Yet the available evidence suggests that mortality costs account for the bulk of the total costs to society. See also *Glossary*.

Exposure indicators provide only a partial view of air pollution severity and consequences aggregated across the entire population. Importantly, there is generally no "safe level" of exposure for many pollutants. Even where guideline or target exposures are met, substantial public health and economic benefits can be realised through further improvements in air quality.

Better estimates are needed for exposure to both outdoor and indoor air pollution. Particular attention should be paid to exposure of sensitive groups and quantitative impact on human health (and associated distributional and equity issues). Although many important gaps remain, available data are improving. This heightened quality is driven by two trends. First, epidemiological evidence of the severity of the impacts of air pollution on human health is increasingly strong. Second, hybrid approaches to measuring pollutant concentration present new opportunities to use different types of data from several different sources. This allows for more robust estimates of pollutant concentrations.

Sources

Airparif (2014), "The State of the Air (Paris)", *www.airparif.asso.fr/etat-air/air-et-climat-quelques-chiffres*.

Brauer, M. et al. (2016), "Ambient air pollution exposure estimation for the global burden of disease 2013", *Environmental Science and Technology*, Vol. 50/1, pp. 79-88.

Burnett, R.T. et al. (2014), "An integrated risk function for estimating the global burden of disease attributable to ambient fine particulate matter exposure", *Environmental Health Perspectives*, 122: 397-403.

Caiazzo, F. et al. (2013), "Air pollution and early deaths in the United States. Part I: Quantifying the impact of major sectors in 2005", *Atmospheric Environment*, 79: 198-208.

CIESIN (2016), Gridded Population of the World, version 4 (GPWv4), Center for International Earth Science Information Network, *http://dx.doi.org/10.7927/H4X63JVC*.

EEA (2016a), Air Quality in Europe – 2016 Report, *www.eea.europa.eu/publications/air-quality-in-europe-2016*.

EEA (2016b), Attainment situation for NO_2, *www.eea.europa.eu/data-and-maps/daviz/attainment-situation-for-annual-limit-1#tab-chart_1*.

Eurostat (2017), *Urban Population Exposure to Air Pollution by Ozone* (database), *http://ec.europa.eu/eurostat/tgm/table.do?tab=table&init=1&plugin=1&language=en&pcode=tsdph380* (accessed in February 2017).

FAO (2015), Global Administrative Unit Layers (GAUL) 2014 version, FAO-GeoNetwork, Food and Agriculture Organization of the United Nations, *www.fao.org/geonetwork/srv/en/metadata.show?id=12691 (accessed in March 2016)*.

GBD (2015), "Global Burden of Disease Study 2015 Results", Institute for Health Metrics and Evaluation, Seattle, United States, *http://ghdx.healthdata.org/gbd-results-tool* (accessed in February 2017).

Mackie, A., I. Haščič and M. Cárdenas Rodríguez (2016), "Population Exposure to Fine Particles: Methodology and Results for OECD and G20 Countries", *OECD Green Growth Papers*, No. 2016/02, OECD Publishing, Paris, *http://dx.doi.org/10.1787/5jlsqs8g1t9r-en*.

OECD (2017a), "Exposure to air pollution, *OECD Environment Statistics* (database), *http://dx.doi.org/10.1787/env-data-en* (accessed in March 2017).

OECD (2017b), "Green growth indicators", *OECD Environment Statistics* (database), *http://dx.doi.org/10.1787/data-00665-en* (accessed in March 2017).

OECD (2016), *The Economic Consequences of Outdoor Air Pollution*, OECD Publishing, Paris, *http://dx.doi.org/10.1787/9789264257474-en*.

OECD (2014), *The Cost of Air Pollution: Health Impacts of Road Transport*, OECD Publishing, Paris, *http://dx.doi.org/10.1787/9789264210448-en*.

van Donkelaar et al. (2016), Global Estimates of Fine Particulate Matter using a Combined Geophysical-Statistical Method with Information from Satellites, Models, and Monitors, *Environmental Science and Technology*, *http://dx.doi.org/10.1021/acs.est.5b05833*.

WHO (2016), Ambient Air Quality and Health (factsheet), World Health Organization, Geneva, *www.who.int/mediacentre/factsheets/fs313/en*.

Further reading

Roy, R. (2016), "The cost of air pollution in Africa", *OECD Development Centre Working Papers*, No. 333, OECD Publishing, Paris, *http://dx.doi.org/10.1787/5jlqzq77x6f8-en*.

US EPA (2011), *The Benefits and Costs of the Clean Air Act from 1990 to 2020*, United States Environmental Protection Agency, Washington, DC, *www.epa.gov/cleanairactbenefits/feb11/summaryreport.pdf*.

Access to water supply, sanitation and sewage treatment

Globally, inadequate access to safe water supply and sanitation acts as a large drag on economic growth and well-being. It affects people's health, increasing mortality and morbidity. It also reduces labour productivity, increases healthcare costs and undermines freshwater ecosystems.

In developing and emerging economies, the main challenge is to extend water supply and sanitation services to rural areas and the poor. In OECD countries, the main challenge is often to renew and upgrade existing (and often ageing) infrastructure. This is particularly vital in light of climate change, which makes water demand and availability more uncertain, and can also increase rainwater run-off in urban environments. Strengthened infrastructure would allow countries to maintain relatively high levels of water supply and sanitation services in the face of population dynamics and climate change. As a related concern, existing wastewater treatment facilities must be better equipped for increasingly stringent environmental and health regulations, as well as for new and emerging contaminants.

In that context, proper financing of water services remains a challenge, including in OECD countries. A first step is to combine revenues from water tariffs, transfers from public budgets and transfers from the international community (i.e. the 3Ts). This should aim to recover the costs of investment, operation and maintenance of water infrastructure as much as possible and where efficient. Well-designed tariffs for water supply and sanitation services should cover the operation, maintenance and renewal costs of infrastructure and a progressive proportion of capital costs, where possible. Targeted social measures, outside the water bill, are best suited to address redistributive consequences and affordability.

Main trends and recent developments

Access to public wastewater treatment has progressed unevenly across countries

Across the OECD area, the share of population whose wastewater is connected to a municipal sewage treatment plant rose from about 60% in the early 1990s to almost 80% today. About 72% benefit from at least secondary treatment. Settlement patterns, economic and environmental conditions, and starting dates vary, however. This means the share of the population connected to waste water treatment plants and the level of treatment also vary significantly across countries. Some countries have reached the economic and technical limits in terms of sewerage connection. They must find other ways of serving small, isolated settlements, including through effective independent on-site treatment systems (Figure 11.1a).

Figure 11.1. **Access to public sewage treatment, improved sanitation and safe drinking water**

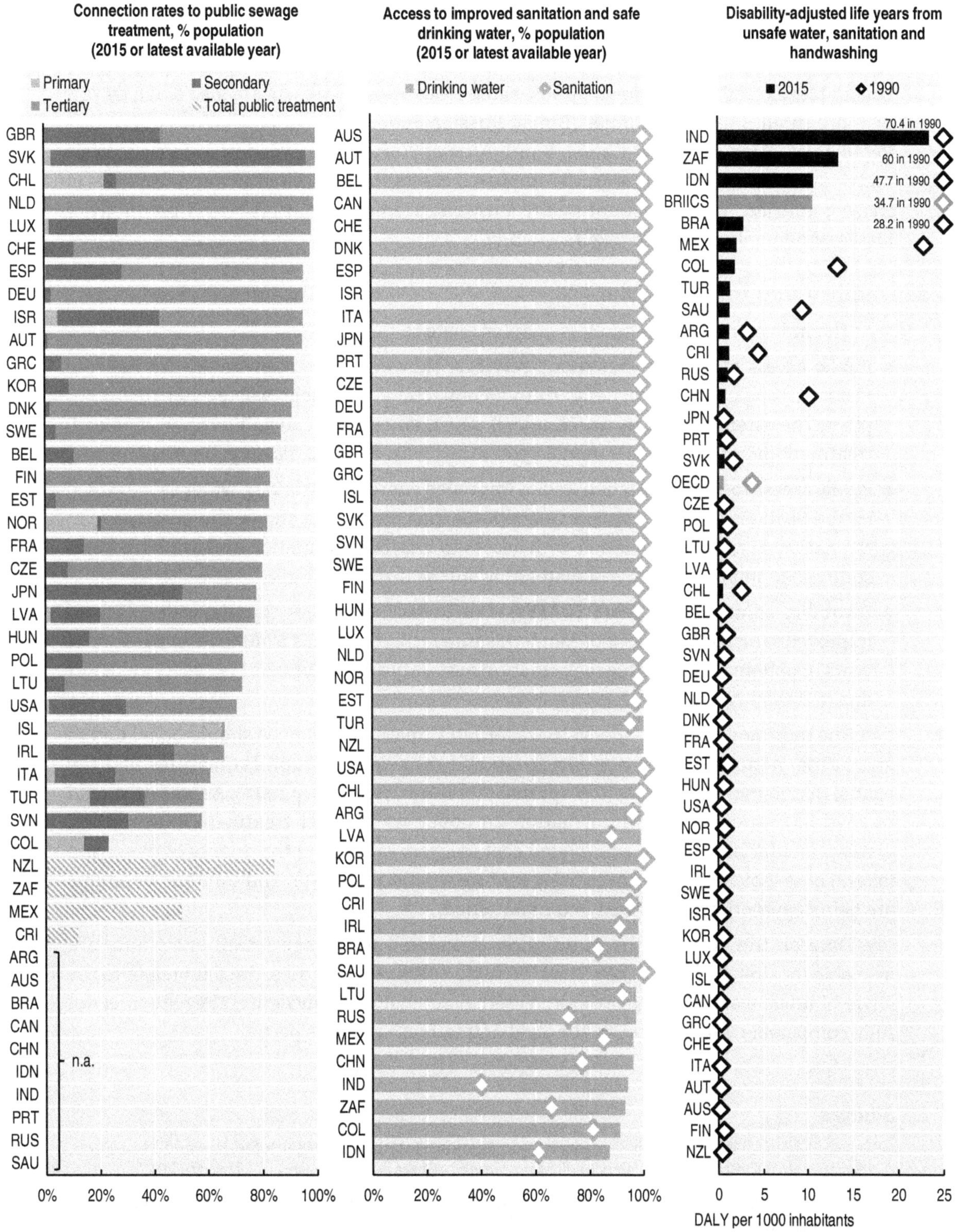

Note: For sewage treatment (panel A) years before 2010 are not considered and United Kingdom (GBR) refers only to England and Wales. Total public treatment shown for countries with no breakdown. Data shown in panel B contain estimates.

Source: OECD (2017a) *OECD Environment Statistics* (database); UN (2017), *Sustainable Development Goals Indicators* (database); GBD (2015), *Global Burden of Disease Study 2015*.

StatLink http://dx.doi.org/10.1787/888933484792

Health impacts from lack of access to improved sanitation and drinking water have been reduced, but remain severe in some countries

Reductions in health impacts, in terms of disability-adjusted life years (DALYs) due to insufficient access to safe water and sanitation, have been important. This is particularly true in Mexico and Turkey (down by 90% since 1990). Health impacts are also down by 70% or more in all BRIICS economies (Brazil, Russian Federation, India, Indonesia, People's Republic of China [hereafter China], South Africa). Progress is needed in Indonesia, India and South Africa to increase access to improved sanitation and drinking water facilities. In these countries, the consequent health impacts, premature mortality and productivity losses remain relatively high (Figure 11.1b-c).

Measurability and interpretation

The indicators presented in this chapter relate to the following:

- **Public access to sewage treatment services**, showing the percentage of the national resident population that benefits from a connection to a public wastewater treatment plant. The extent of primary (mechanical), secondary (biological) and tertiary (chemical) treatment indicates efforts to reduce pollution loads. See also *Glossary*.
- **Public access to basic sanitation and to improved sources of drinking water** as measured by the Sustainable Development Goals (SDG) indicators. This shows the percentage of the national resident population with access to improved sanitation and drinking water sources. An improved source of water may still be unsafe to drink.
- **Disability-adjusted life years (DALYs)** due to lack of access to safe water, lack of improved sanitation and lack of hand-washing facilities. DALYs is defined as the sum of years of potential life lost due to premature mortality and the years of productive life lost due to disability.

The indicator on public access to wastewater treatment services should be related to an optimal national connection rate. It should consider geographical features and the spatial distribution of habitats (the optimal rate is not necessarily 100%). As well, it should be read in connection with information on public wastewater treatment expenditure, water prices for households and related cost recovery ratios, and the quality of rivers and lakes. These indicators may not entirely capture whether the water and sanitation systems are being appropriately operated and maintained.

Data on the share of the population connected to sewage treatment plants are available for almost all OECD countries. In some European countries, the data relate to the share of urban wastewater treated expressed in population equivalents. They are thus not fully comparable. Information on the level of treatment remains partial.

Sources

GBD (2015), "Global Burden of Disease Study 2015 Results", Institute for Health Metrics and Evaluation, Seattle, United States, *http://ghdx.healthdata.org/gbd-results-tool* (accessed in February 2017).

OECD (2017a), "Water: Wastewater treatment", *OECD Environment Statistics* (database), *http://dx.doi.org/10.1787/data-00604-en* (accessed in March 2017).

OECD (2017b), "Green growth indicators", *OECD Environment Statistics* (database), *http://dx.doi.org/10.1787/data-00665-en* (accessed in March 2017).

UN (2017), *Sustainable Development Goals Indicators* (database), *http://unstats.un.org/sdgs/indicators/database* (accessed in March 2017).

Further reading

OECD (2016), *Water, Growth and Finance, Policy Perspectives*, OECD Publishing, Paris, *https://issuu.com/oecd.publishing/docs/water-growth-finance-policy-perspec.*

OECD (2010), *Pricing Water Resources and Water and Sanitation Services*, OECD Publishing, Paris, *http://dx.doi.org/10.1787/9789264083608-en.*

OECD (n.d.), "Green Growth and Water", *www.oecd.org/greengrowth/greengrowthandwater.htm.*

OECD (n.d.), "The Water Challenge: OECD's Response", *www.oecd.org/environment/resources/water.htm.*

WHO/UNICEF (n.d.),"Joint Monitoring Programme for Water Supply and Sanitation", *www.wssinfo.org.*

PART 4

Economic opportunities and policy responses

Technology and innovation

Markets for environmentally related products

International financial flows

Taxes and subsidies

Technology and innovation

Innovation is a key driver of productivity and economic growth. It can help achieve environmental objectives at lower costs, and lead to new business opportunities and markets. It is widely acknowledged that far-reaching innovation will be needed to address climate change and other environmental challenges, and to accelerate the transition to green growth.

The main challenge is to influence the direction of innovation towards more environmentally benign ends. Further, this should be done in a manner that generates the greatest net benefit to society. Policy instruments that encourage innovation include protection of intellectual property, support to basic research and development (R&D), creation of innovation clusters or investment in skilled workforce. These instruments must be complemented with measures that help direct innovation towards more environmentally effective and cost-efficient solutions. One example would be tracing a predictable path for pricing emissions or by tightening emission limits. Another challenge is to mitigate the risk of additional environmental pressures generated by new technology and products. Often the consequences for human and ecosystem health of new materials may not be known.

Public policies may change the opportunity costs of production and consumption. If that happens, they have the potential to induce innovative responses by firms and consumers. Some responses could be to adopt environmentally friendly alternatives, develop new technological solutions or shift towards new management methods. Some policy instruments aim closest to the negative externality (e.g. taxing polluting emissions rather than input use) and provide incentives across a wide spectrum of firms and consumers. These will likely yield innovation at lower cost to society (Johnstone and Haščič, 2013; Haščič and Migotto, 2015).

Additional measures might also be needed. These would help leverage the necessary financing for demonstration projects and market commercialisation. They could also facilitate investment in the supporting infrastructure to speed-up technology diffusion among consumers (e.g. charging stations for e-vehicles). Importantly, outcomes of R&D investment are intrinsically serendipitous. They may take a long time to translate into higher productivity and standards of living (see chapter on *Environmentally adjusted multifactor productivity*).

Main trends and recent developments

R&D budgets are rising, but the share devoted to the environment remains stagnant

Total R&D (public and private) has increased in most OECD countries. This is especially the case in Estonia, where its share on GDP has more than doubled since 2000. Korea and Turkey follow closely (Figure 12.1f). Government budgets for R&D (GBAORD) have also

Figure 12.1. **The environment share of R&D remains stagnant despite a shift towards renewable energy**

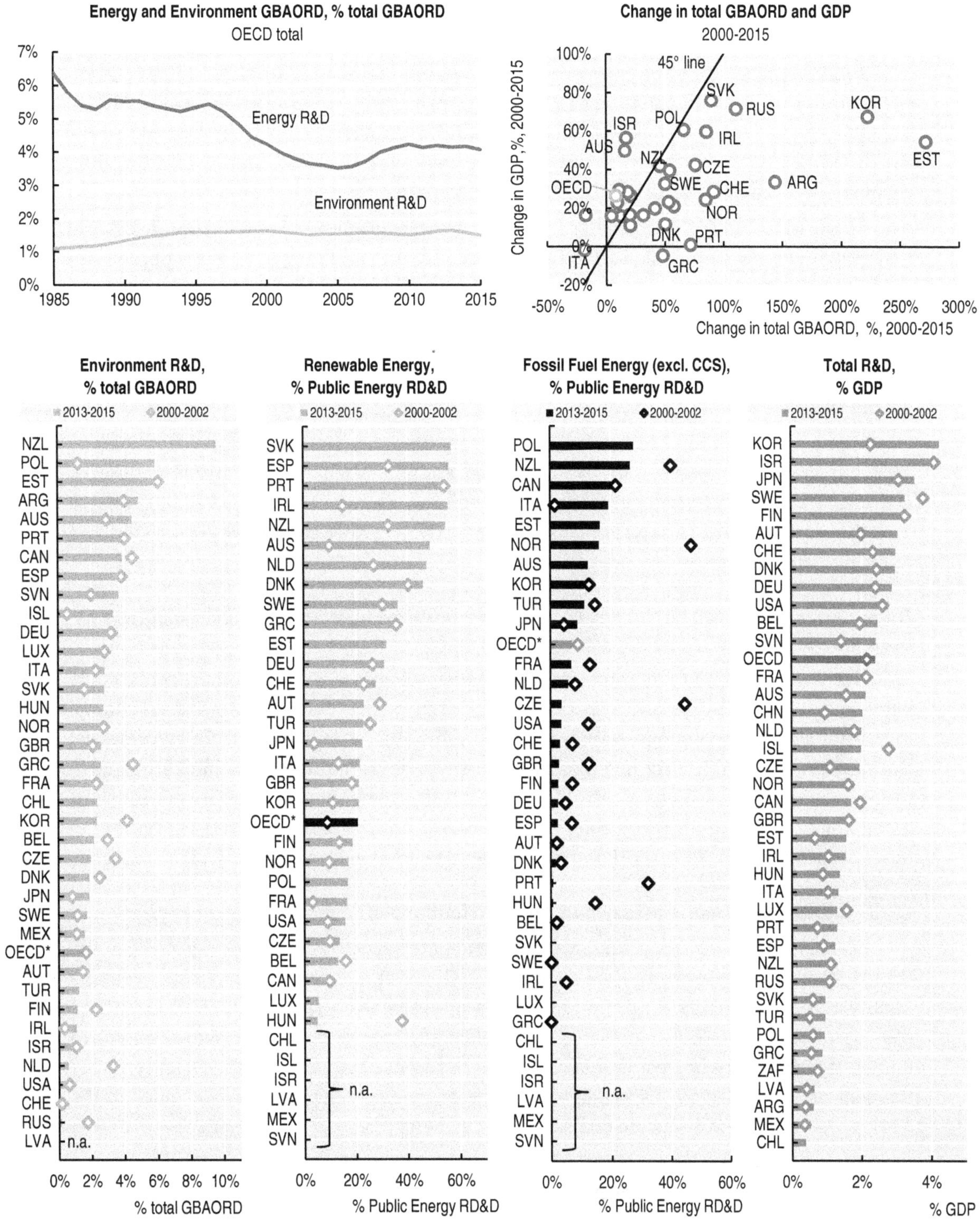

Note: OECD* shows the weighted average across only those OECD countries with available information.

Source: OECD (2016a), "Research and development statistics: government budget appropriations or outlays for R&Ds", *OECD Science, Technology and R&D Statistics* (database); IEA (2016), "RD&D Budget", *IEA Energy Technology RD&D Statistics* (database); OECD (2016b), "Main Science and Technology Indicators", *OECD Science, Technology and R&D Statistics* (database).

StatLink http://dx.doi.org/10.1787/888933484800

increased in many countries since 2000. However, the amount dedicated to environmental and energy objectives has remained stable in the OECD overall (Figures 12.1a-c).

Public expenditure on energy RD&D is shifting towards renewables

Public expenditures on energy-related research, development and demonstration (RD&D) increasingly target renewable energy in most OECD countries. In the Slovak Republic, Spain, Portugal, Ireland and New Zealand, over half of public energy RD&D is now directed towards renewables. In Japan, France and Australia, this share has more than quadrupled since 2000 (Figure 12.1d).

At the same time, there have been sharp cuts in publicly-funded RD&D on fossil fuel energy. Countries such as Ireland, Luxembourg and Greece have now completely phased-out public support for fossil fuel RD&D (excluding carbon capture and storage). In Sweden, the Slovak Republic, Belgium, Hungary and Portugal, it now accounts for less than 1% of public energy RD&D. In contrast, support for fossil fuel RD&D keeps rising in Italy, Japan, Canada and Austria, and it now accounts for over a quarter of publicly-funded energy RD&D in Poland and New Zealand (Figure 12.1e).

Support for greening R&D is often a necessary first step. However, its success must be assessed against outcomes of innovation. Other domains such as chemistry and material sciences influence innovation in green technologies at least as much as research on energy and the environment. Analysis of patenting activity provides one way to assess the (intermediate) outcomes.

Following a rapid growth, inventive activity in environment-related technologies has been slowing down

The development of environment-related technologies (ENV-TECH) grew remarkably between 2000 and 2010. This was particularly apparent with applications to climate change mitigation (CCM) in buildings, transport and energy generation (Figure 12.2a). Worldwide, the number of high-quality inventions in these three domains has trebled since 2000 (doubled for ENV-TECH as a whole). Meanwhile, inventive activity in general (all technologies) has risen by only about 30%. However, inventive activity has been slowing down across all major ENV-TECH domains since 2011, both in levels and as a share on total.

OECD countries still lead the way, but the contributions of China and India are rising fast

A large majority (90%) of green inventions originate in OECD countries, – especially in the United States, Japan, Germany, Korea and France. However, the contributions of the People's Republic of China (hereafter China) and India are increasing rapidly. In some countries development of ENV-TECH represents an increasingly large part of their overall inventive output. It reaches 22% in Denmark, which is almost double the OECD average (Figure 12.2c); this reflects a high degree of specialisation. Denmark thus contributes twice as much to the world stock of ENV-TECH than to technologies in general (RTA = 2.0, Figure 12.2e).

Conversely, countries such as Turkey, Ireland and China contribute much less to the world stock (relative to their overall inventive output). Innovation in several countries, including Portugal and South Africa has slipped compared to the early 2000s (Figure 12.2e, Figure 12.3a). Providing continuous incentives for directing innovation towards environmental objectives remains a challenge. OECD work suggests that stringent, predictable and flexible environmental policies are more likely to provide effective long-term signals to innovators (OECD, 2011).

Figure 12.2. **Following a rapid increase, development of green technologies is slowing down**

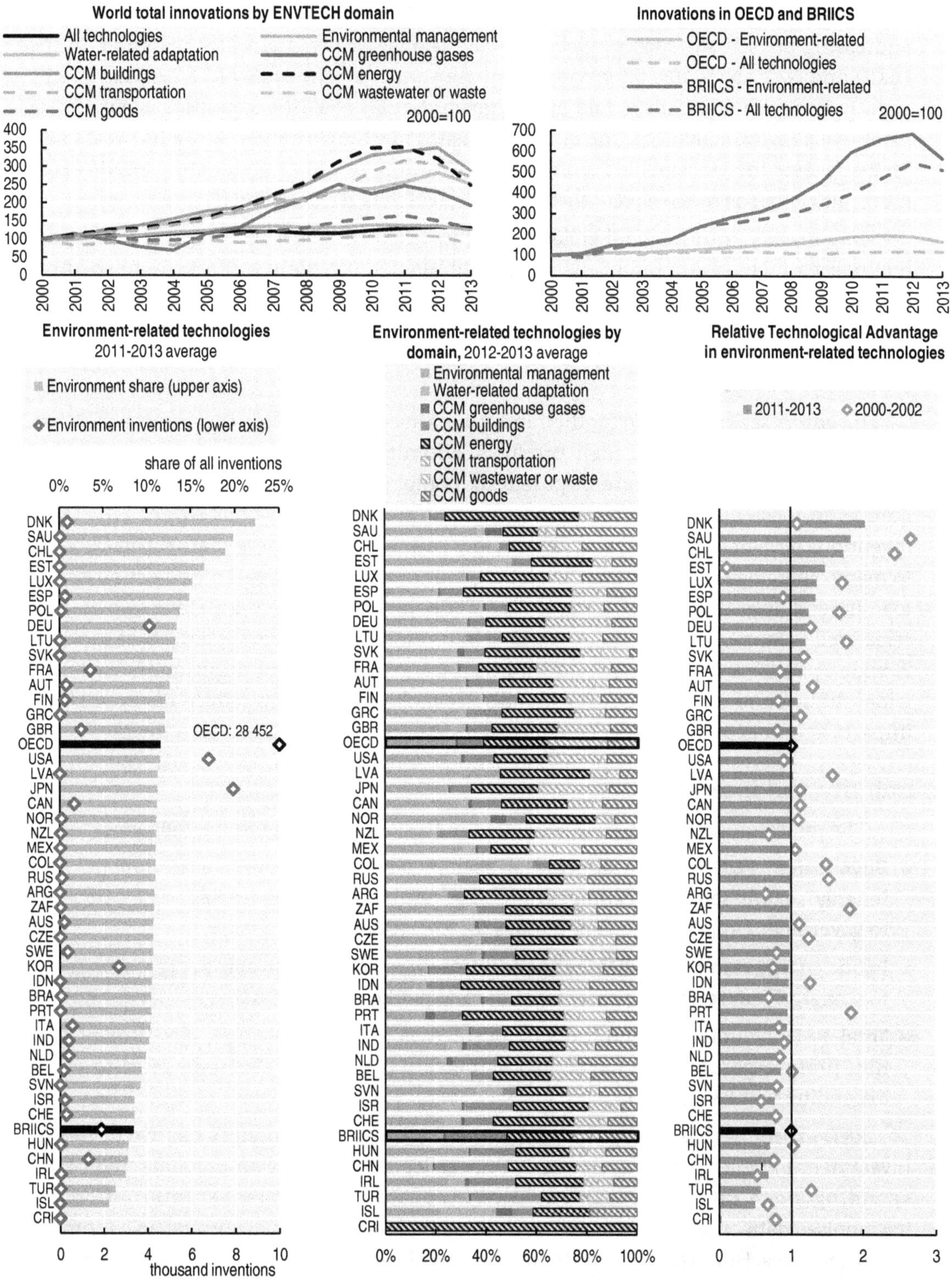

Note: Based on counts of priority patent applications (simple patent families), by inventor's country of residence, with patent family size of two or more (high-value inventions). Data for 2012 and 2013 are provisional. CCM = climate change mitigation.

Source: OECD (2017a, 2017b), "Patents in environment-related technologies", *OECD Environment Statistics* (database); OECD calculations based on EPO (2016).

StatLink http://dx.doi.org/10.1787/888933484818

International collaboration in ENV-TECH is becoming more common, contributing to development of local absorptive capacities

Encouraging collaboration on technology development is particularly pertinent when addressing public bads such as global climate change or regional water pollution. In the OECD and G20, about 10% of cross-border co-inventions concern ENV-TECH. This is only slightly less than what one would expect given that ENV-TECH account for about 11% of inventive activity on average. The difference used to be much greater only a few years ago. This suggests that researchers from different countries now collaborate on ENV-TECH more, and about as much as on other domains, which is encouraging (Figure 12.3b).

Importantly, international collaboration in research and technology can help local businesses take advantage of existing technologies (i.e. help build local absorptive capacity). This, in turn, helps increase the uptake of cleaner technologies globally.

Low patenting activity in many non-OECD economies opens the door to international technology transfer

Inventors seek protection for their inventions in countries where they expect to invest, export or otherwise market their products. Often they do so in multiple jurisdictions (geographic markets). The rate of patenting is highest in the United States, Japan and Europe. In these markets innovators seek patent protection for about 30% of ENV-TECH inventions developed globally, and for as many as 47% in the Chinese market (Figure 12.4). In many emerging economies and developing countries the rate of patent protection is very low. Indeed, less than 1% of world's ENV-TECH inventions have a patent application registered in Brazil, South Africa, Argentina, India or Colombia. This suggests that the door is wide open for a more massive inward technology transfer and diffusion. Achieving a wider diffusion of environmentally friendly technologies can help reduce environmental impacts at lower costs. Further, it can speed up the transition to green growth.

Measurability and interpretation

The indicators of R&D activity presented in this chapter relate to the following:

- **Government R&D budgets** directed at socio-economic objectives "environment" and "energy", expressed as percentages of total government budgets for R&D. The data refer to government appropriations or outlays for R&D (GBAORD).
- **Public energy technology RD&D expenditures** directed at "renewable energy" and "fossil fuel energy", expressed as percentages of total public energy RD&D.
- **Total R&D** including expenditures by businesses, higher education, government and non-profit organisations, expressed as percentage of GDP. The data refer to gross expenditure on R&D (GERD).

R&D expenditure is an input measure that indicates an economy's relative degree of investment in generating knowledge. It thus reflects intent, not an outcome; high R&D spending alone does not mean superior innovation performance. Internationally harmonised data on government R&D following the Frascati Manual are available for most OECD countries. However, at a more detailed level, the coverage of national surveys, as well as sampling and estimation methods, may vary. Significant gaps exist around harmonised data on private-sector R&D expenditure.

The indicators of technological innovation based on patent data presented in this chapter relate to the following:

Figure 12.3. **Bending invention and co-invention towards environment-related technologies**

OECD and G20

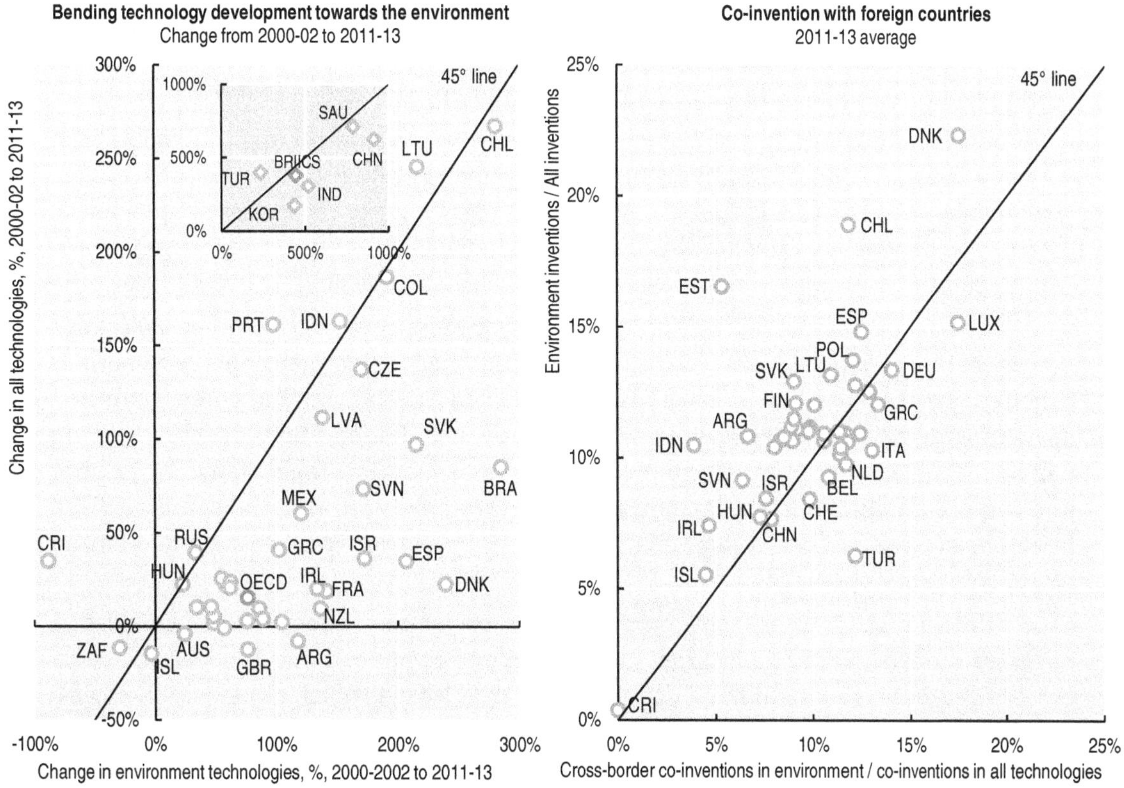

Source: OECD (2017a, 2017c), "Patents in environment-related technologies", *OECD Environment Statistics* (database); OECD calculations based on EPO (2016).

StatLink http://dx.doi.org/10.1787/888933484827

Figure 12.4. **In some large economies only a small share of environment-related technologies are patented**

Share on world stock of patented inventions, 2011-2013 average

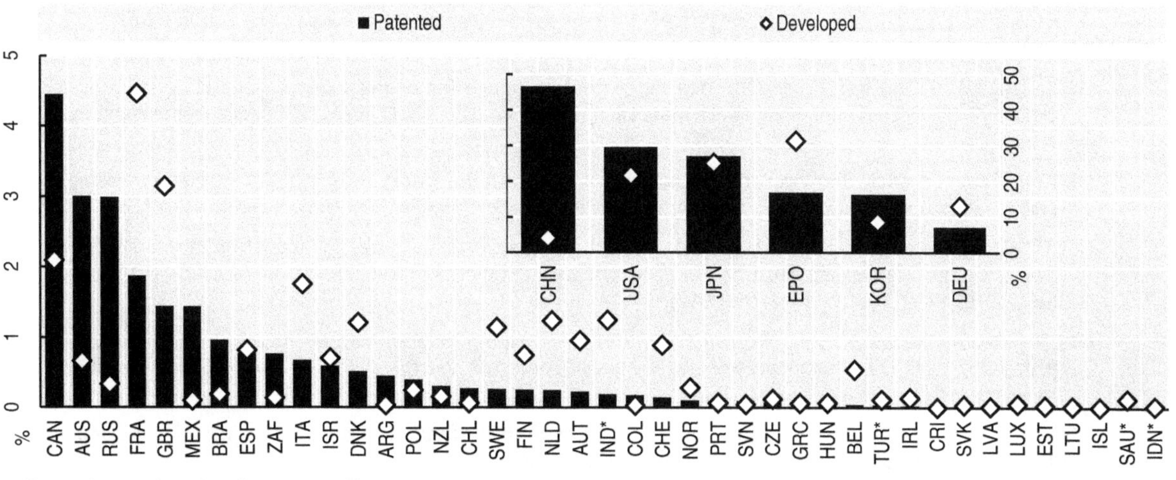

* Indicates incomplete data for patent office.

Note: Patented = % of ENV-TECH patent families protected in a given jurisdiction. Developed = % of ENV-TECH patent families with a country's inventor. EPO = European Patent Office. In Europe innovators can patent via the EPO or national offices.

Sources: OECD (2017b, 2017d) *OECD Environment Statistics* (database); OECD calculations based on EPO (2016).

StatLink http://dx.doi.org/10.1787/888933484839

- **Technology development:** The number of inventions (simple patent families) developed by a country's inventors, independent of the jurisdictions where a patent application has been registered (i.e. all known patent families worldwide are considered).
- **International collaboration in technology development:** the number of co-inventions (simple patent families) developed jointly by inventors from at least two countries.
- **Technology diffusion:** the number of inventions for which a patent application has been registered in a given jurisdiction through national, regional or international routes (equivalents of the priority patent application, pertaining to the same "simple patent family"). It shows the extent to which firms and individuals (domestic or foreign) seek to protect their inventions in the relevant markets. See also *Glossary*.

Patent data present a number of attractive properties compared to other alternative metrics of innovation. They are widely available, quantitative, commensurable and output-oriented. They can also be disaggregated – an important advantage when analysing environment-related technologies. At the same time, not all innovations or inventions are patented. Further, the number of patents by itself does not indicate their relative importance and impact. Analytical techniques have been developed to overcome some of these limitations (e.g. patent family size, relative technological advantage). Yet it is important to carefully interpret these indicators.

Little information is available on non-technological innovation, such as changes in business models, working patterns, managerial and organisational innovations more broadly. Yet these are instrumental for green growth at least as much as new technologies.

Sources

EPO (2016), *Worldwide Patent Statistical Database (PATSTAT)*, Autumn 2016 edition, European Patent Office.

Haščič, I. and M. Migotto (2015), "Measuring environmental innovation using patent data", *OECD Environment Working Papers* No. 89, OECD Publishing, Paris, *http://dx.doi.org/10.1787/5js009kf48xw-en*.

IEA (2016), "RD&D budget", *IEA Energy Technology RD&D Statistics* (database), *http://dx.doi.org/10.1787/data-00488-en*.

Johnstone, N. and I. Haščič (2013), "Policy incentives for energy and environmental technological innovation: Lessons from the empirical evidence", in *Encyclopedia of Energy, Natural Resource and Environmental Economics*, Vol. 1, pp. 98-106, Elsevier, Amsterdam.

OECD (2017a), "Patents in environment-related technologies: Technology development by inventor country", *OECD Environment Statistics* (database), *http://dx.doi.org/10.1787/data-00760-en* (accessed in March 2017).

OECD (2017b), "Patents in environment-related technologies: Summary indicators", *OECD Environment Statistics* (database), *http://stats.oecd.org/Index.aspx?DataSetCode=PAT_IND* (accessed in March 2017).

OECD (2017c), "Patents in environment-related technologies: International collaboration in technology development by inventor country", *OECD Environment Statistics* (database), *http://dx.doi.org/10.1787/data-00762-en* (accessed in March 2017).

OECD (2017d), "Patents in environment-related technologies: Technology diffusion and patent protection", *OECD Environment Statistics* (database), *http://dx.doi.org/10.1787/data-00763-en* (accessed in March 2017).

OECD (2017e), "Green growth indicators", *OECD Environment Statistics* (database), *http://dx.doi.org/10.1787/data-00665-en* (accessed in March 2017).

OECD (2016a), "Research and development statistics: Government budget appropriations or outlays for RD", *OECD Science, Technology and R&D Statistics* (database), *http://dx.doi.org/10.1787/data-00194-en* (accessed in December 2016).

OECD (2016b), "Main Science and Technology Indicators", *OECD Science, Technology and R&D Statistics* (database), *http://dx.doi.org/10.1787/data-00182-en* (accessed in December 2016).

OECD (2011), *Invention and Transfer of Environmental Technologies*, OECD Publishing, Paris, *http://dx.doi.org/10.1787/9789264115620-en*.

Further reading

Andrews, D. and C. Criscuolo (2013), "Knowledge-based capital, innovation and resource allocation: A going for growth report", *OECD Economic Policy Papers*, No. 4, OECD Publishing, Paris, *http://dx.doi.org/10.1787/5k46bh92lr35-en*.

Egli, F., N. Johnstone and C. Menon (2015), "Identifying and inducing breakthrough inventions: An application related to climate change mitigation", *OECD Science, Technology and Industry Working Papers*, No. 2015/04, OECD Publishing, Paris, *http://dx.doi.org/10.1787/5js03zd40n37-en*.

OECD (2015), OECD Science, Technology and Industry Scoreboard 2015: Innovation for growth and society, OECD Publishing, Paris, *http://dx.doi.org/10.1787/sti_scoreboard-2015-en*.

OECD (2015), *The Innovation Imperative: Contributing to Productivity, Growth and Well-Being*, OECD Publishing, Paris, *http://dx.doi.org/10.1787/9789264239814-en*.

Poirier, J. et al. (2015), "The Benefits of International Co-authorship in Scientific Papers: The Case of Wind Energy Technologies", *OECD Environment Working Papers*, No. 81, OECD Publishing, Paris, *http://dx.doi.org/10.1787/5js69ld9w9nv-en*.

Markets for environmentally related products

A well-managed transition to a greener economy is at the heart of the green growth model. It involves a shift to cleaner products and production processes, substitution of dirty inputs for cleaner ones, and a shift to consumption patterns with lower environmental footprints such as the sharing economy. They also comprise increased reuse, repairing and recycling, and overall moderation of consumption – particularly of resource-intensive goods and services.

Achieving this transition cost-efficiently requires considerable strengthening of green taxation and incentivising innovation across the economy. This can be achieved by facilitating market entry and exit, by encouraging an efficient reallocation of labour across sectors and by "greening" of the capital markets. These steps will help direct markets towards greener outcomes in a cost-efficient manner and open-up new opportunities for exports and employment.

Progress towards green growth can be assessed by examining the transformation in economic sectors and shifts from traditional business activities to cleaner alternatives. This chapter discusses markets for environmentally related products. In particular, it examines the opportunities these products can generate across all sectors of the economy (employment, value added and trade). The discussion then turns to a specific subset of these activities – known as the environmental goods and services (EGS) sector. The main purpose of this sector is environmental protection and natural resource management.

Main trends and recent developments

A few industries account for the bulk of pollution, generating little value added and few jobs

The ten most carbon-intensive industries account for 83% of all CO_2 emissions. However, they account for only 28% of employment and 21% of value added, on average, in the EU28 (Figure 13.1). Employment and value added shares of the most polluting industries are generally higher in countries with lower GDP per capita. The concentration of industries is even higher for some of the other pollutants (methane, fine particulates, nitrogen dioxide). Thus, in the absence of optimal policies spanning all sectors of the economy, targeting mitigation efforts on the worst polluters can reduce emissions substantially.

There are signs that international trade might be slowly "greening"

Available data signal a steady increase in the share of environmentally related products in international trade in the OECD area. They also point to a gradual improvement in the trade balance of such products of BRIICS economies (Brazil, Russian Federation, India, Indonesia, People's Republic of China and South Africa) (Figure 13.2).

Figure 13.1. **Several industries account for the bulk of pollution, generating little value added and few jobs**

Cumulative shares of CO_2, CH_4, $PM_{2.5}$, NO_X emissions, employment and value added by industry,
EU28 countries, 2013

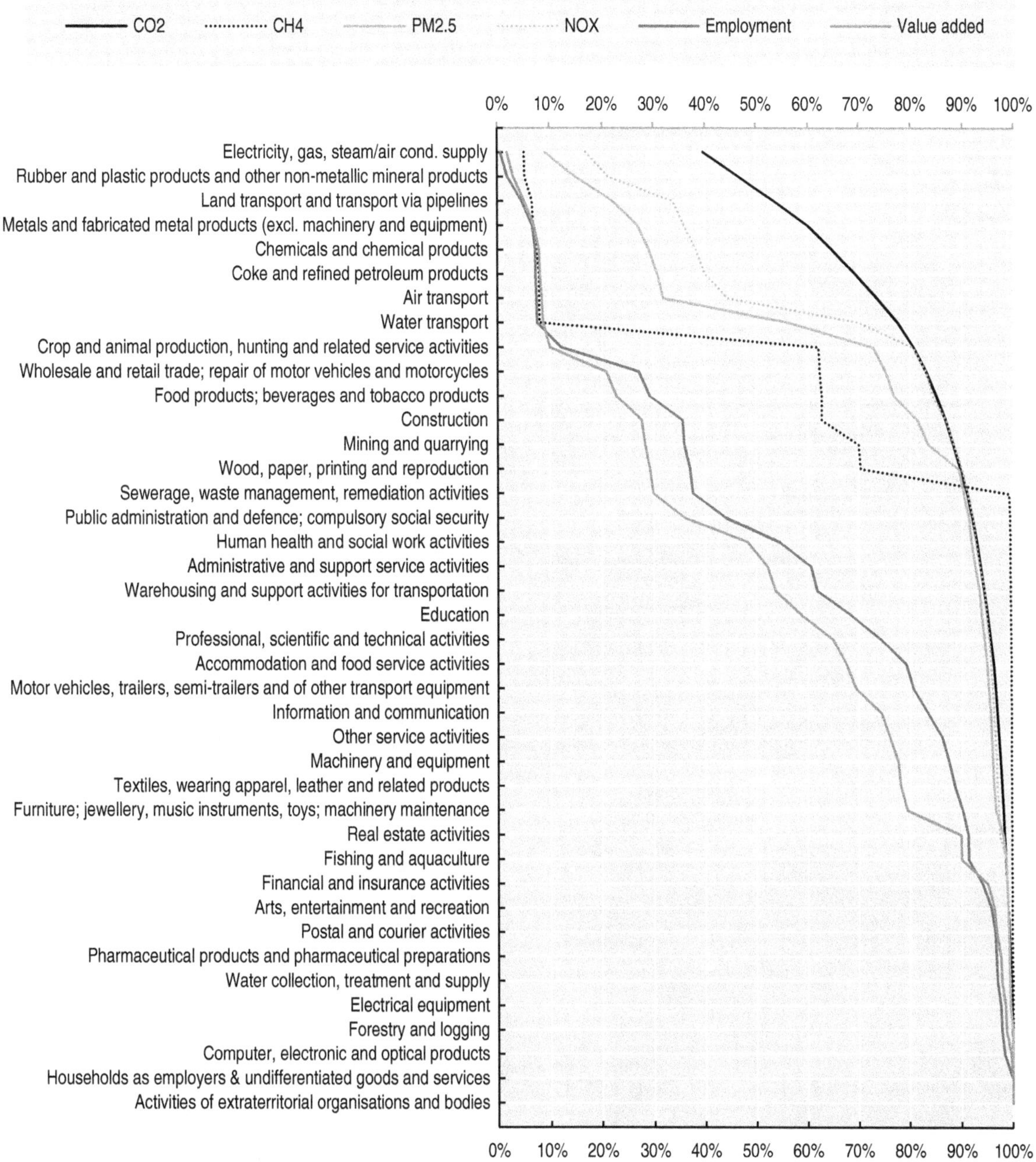

Note: This graph shows the cumulative distribution curves. It depicts the contribution of each sector to total emissions of CO_2, CH_4, $PM_{2.5}$ and NO_X, complemented by sectoral shares of employment and value added. The sectors are sorted in descending order by their share of CO_2 emissions. For example, in 2013 crop and animal production contributed more than 50% of overall methane emissions in the European Union. At the same time, this sector represents only 5% of employment and 2% of value added.

Source: Eurostat (2016a), "Air emissions accounts by NACE Rev. 2 activity"; Eurostat (2016b), "National accounts aggregates by industry (up to NACE A*64)"; Eurostat (2016c), "National accounts employment data by industry (up to NACE A*64)".

StatLink http://dx.doi.org/10.1787/888933484849

Figure 13.2. **Trade in environmentally related products is rising**

OECD and G20

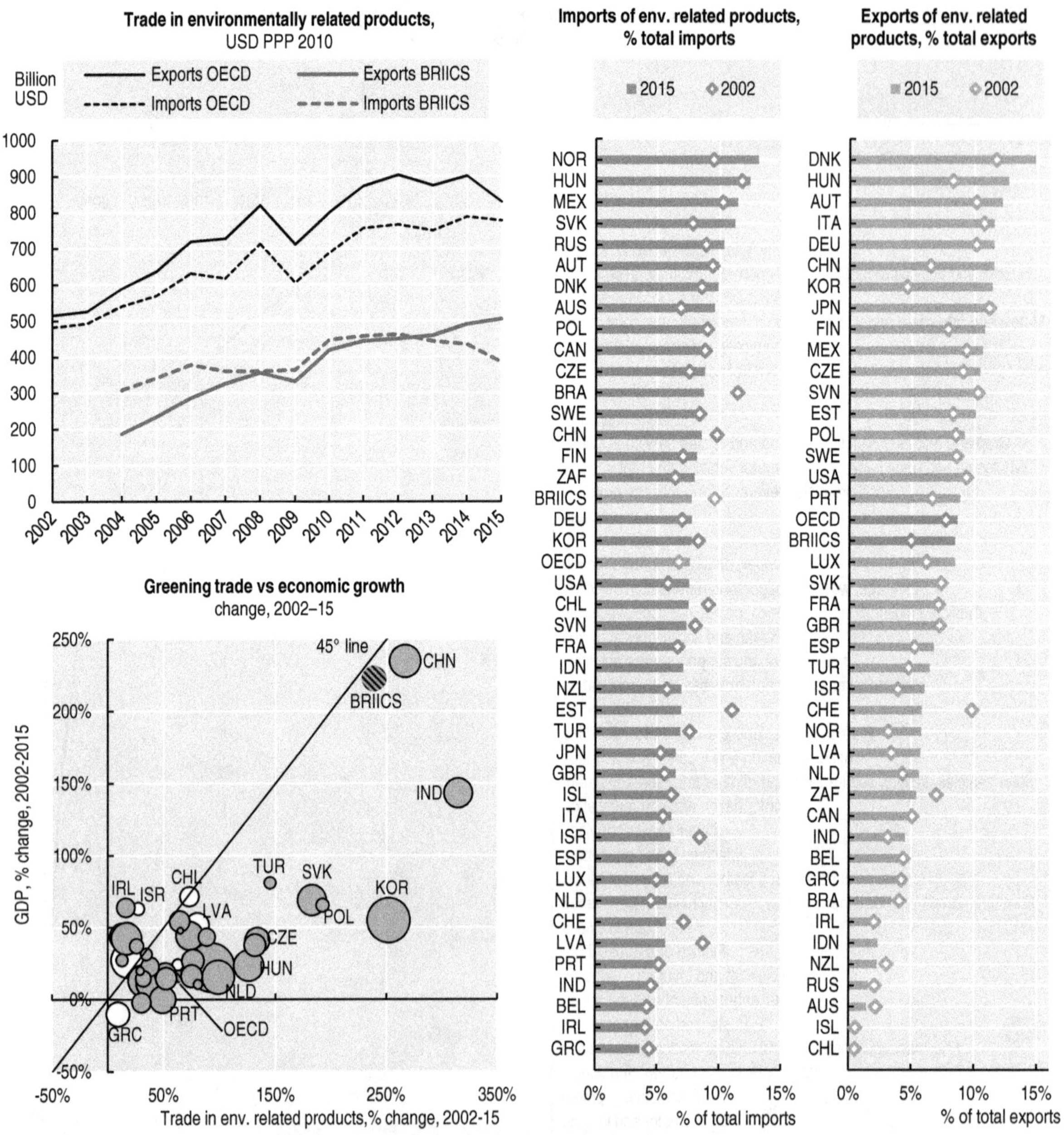

Note: Bubble size shows the change in the share of greener trade. Green (white) bubbles indicate an increase (decrease).

Source: OECD calculations using UN Comtrade (October 2016) and the CLEG list (see Annex 1 in Sauvage, 2014).

StatLink http://dx.doi.org/10.1787/888933484855

Over 2002-15, the importance of environmentally related products in trade increased in more than 20 countries (especially Korea, Norway and Ireland). At the same time, these counties have tightened environmental policies and regulations. This approach has stimulated demand at home and abroad for goods and services in relation to pollution prevention and abatement.

Overall, OECD countries remain net exporters of environmentally related products. Meanwhile, countries have achieved positive economic growth. This suggests that trade in environmentally related products can be accompanied by improvements in economic performance.

Box 13.1. **The labour market effects of climate change policies**

Recent OECD work suggests that ambitious climate change mitigation policies could be good for jobs as well as the environment. Simulation results from the OECD's ENV-Linkages general equilibrium model show that a well-designed emissions trading system could sharply reduce GHG emissions. At the same time, it could allow GDP to keep growing (although at a slightly lower rate). The key is mobility. Workers need to move easily from sectors where employment would drop, notably fossil-fuel industries, to sectors with increasingly more jobs such as renewable energy industries. Countries exporting fossil-based energies would be most affected.

OECD modelling indicates that the impact of GHG mitigation policy on GDP growth is small when the labour market adjusts smoothly to employment opportunities and losses. However, costs rise significantly when workers in declining sectors become unemployable elsewhere due to an incapacity to change and lack of flexibility in labour markets. Environmental policy could be combined with measures to help workers take advantage of new opportunities. One way would be to use revenues from carbon taxes to reduce taxes on labour income. This can generate a "double-dividend" by delivering both lower GHG emissions and higher employment.

Figure 13.3. **Changes in employment implied by ambitious climate change mitigation policies**

% deviation from BAU in 2030

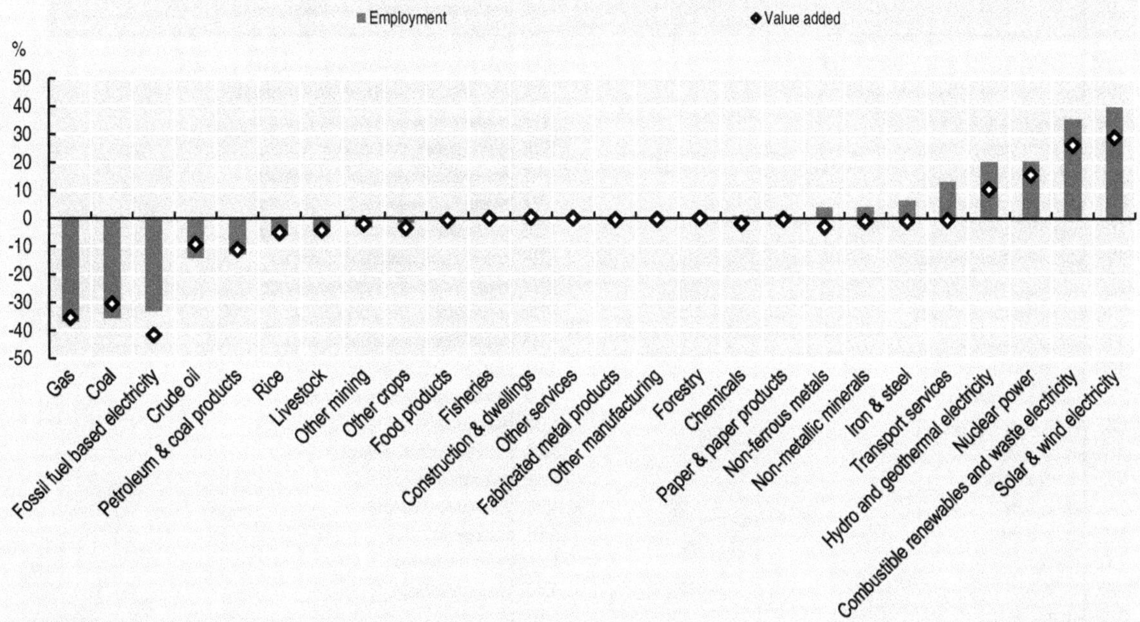

Note: Simulations refer to the OECD area. Simulated impacts in 2030 of GHG mitigation policy are shown as deviations from the business-as-usual (BAU) baseline scenario. They assume no new mitigation policy measures are implemented, and take no account of the impact of resulting environmental damages on economic activity and well-being. Based on the OECD ENV-Linkages model (for more details, see: *www.oecd.org/environment/indicators-modelling-outlooks/modelling.htm*).

Source: OECD (2012), *OECD Employment Outlook 2012.*

StatLink http://dx.doi.org/10.1787/888933484864

The environmental goods and services (EGS) sector

The EGS sector is modest, but is a growing share of the economy

Availability of comparable international data on the EGS sector is limited and allows only for a partial analysis. For instance, sewerage, waste management and remediation activities account for 0.5% of total employment and generate 0.7% of total value added in the European Union. The share is lower in Canada and a few other countries for which data are available (Figure 13.4).

Figure 13.4. **Sewerage, waste management and remediation generate more employment and value added**

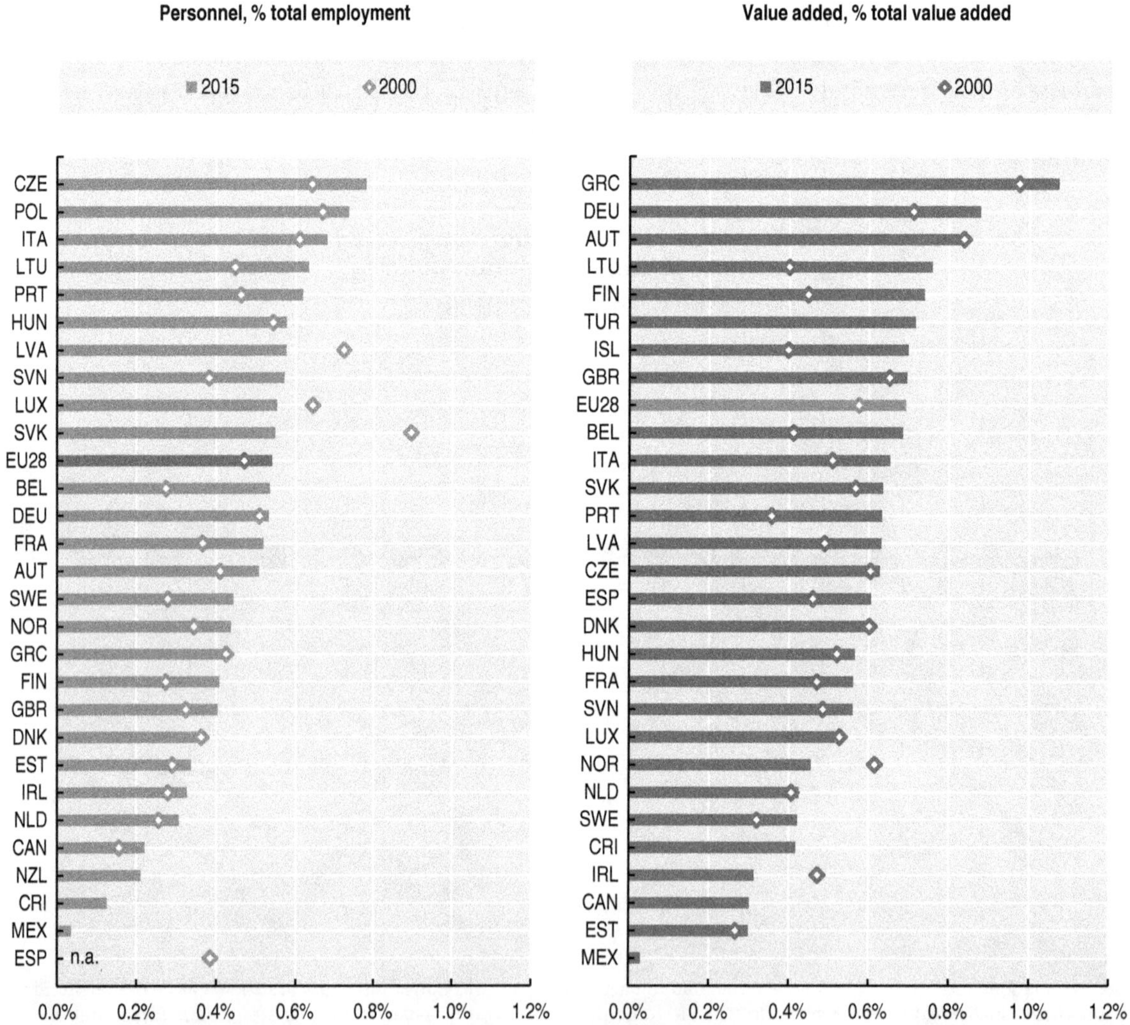

Note: Sewerage, waste management and remediation activities (ISIC Rev. 4, 37-39).

Source: OECD (2016a), "Aggregate national accounts, SNA 2008 (or SNA 1993): population and employment by main activity", *OECD National Accounts Statistics* (database); OECD (2016b), "Aggregate national accounts, SNA 2008 (or SNA 1993): gross domestic product", *OECD National Accounts Statistics* (database).

StatLink http://dx.doi.org/10.1787/888933484870

An estimated 4 million (in full-time equivalent) are employed in environmental protection activities and in water and energy management, an increase of 49% since 2000 (Figure 13.5). The driver for this increase is the growing importance of waste management and energy-related activities (especially renewable energy generation and installations for

Figure 13.5. **Environmental goods and services in Europe (EU28) increased employment and value added**

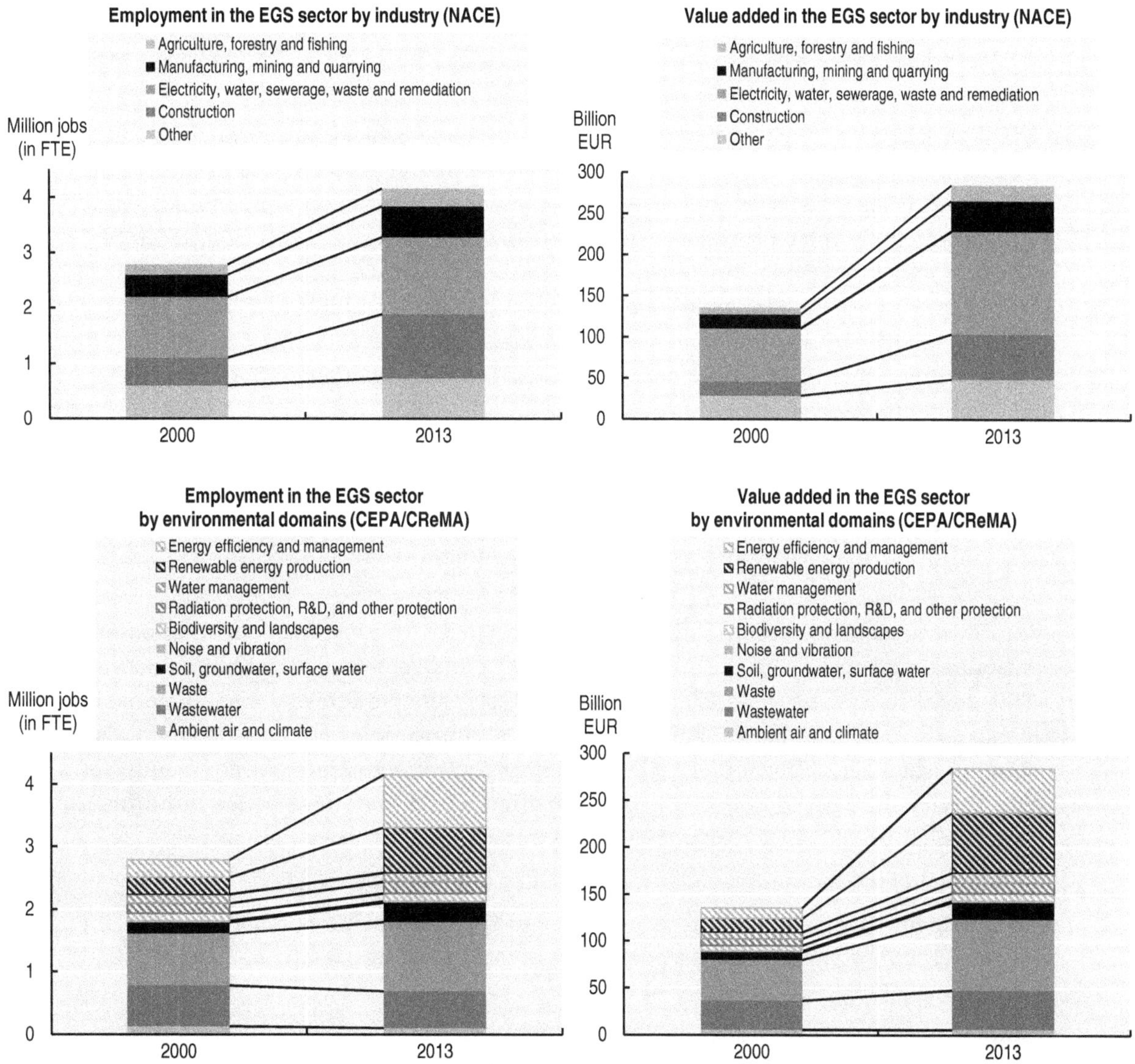

Note: Panels A and B follow the Statistical Classification of Economic Activities in the European Community (NACE) rev.2. Panels C and D follow the Classification of Environmental Protection Activities (CEPA) 2000 and the Classification of Resource Management Activities (CReMA) 2008. Data on value added is expressed in EUR at current prices.

Source: Eurostat (2016d), "Employment in the environmental goods and services sector"; Eurostat (2016e), "Production, value added and exports in the environmental goods and services sector"; Eurostat (2016f), "Production, value added and employment by industry groups in the environmental goods and services sector".

StatLink http://dx.doi.org/10.1787/888933484886

heat and energy savings). Over 2000-13, the contribution of the EGS sector to GDP in terms of gross value added has grown from 1.5% to about 2.2% in the EU. This is a conservative estimate since not all resource management activities are covered.

Measurability and interpretation

OECD economies are transforming. However, it remains challenging to measure the extent and the pace of this change, and the associated economic opportunities, in an internationally harmonised manner.

There are conceptual and statistical difficulties in measuring the "greening" of the economy. These relate to the inherently integrated nature of the phenomenon and lack of sufficiently detailed industry and product classification systems.

The indicators presented in this chapter relate to "greening" of the economy (across all sectors):

- **Trade in environmentally related products**, that is, products that integrate environmental considerations, independently of whether environmental protection is their primary purpose (e.g. energy efficient appliances). The indicator is based on a preliminary list of environmentally related products (the CLEG list, see Sauvage, 2014) that assembles harmonised system (HS) codes drawn from: i) the World Trade Organization (WTO) Friends list; ii) the Asia Pacific Economic Co-operation (APEC) list; and iii) the OECD-PEGS list (a climate-related list designed for the Toronto meeting of the G20). Work is on-going to further refine this CLEG list, in connection with plurilateral negotiations to forge an Environmental Goods Agreement (EGA).
- The most comprehensive assessment can be currently conducted by linking data from **national accounts with the SEEA accounts on air emissions, by industry**. This allows assessing the extent of the transformation of industries (in terms of emission abatement) in relation to their economic outcomes (value added, exports) and the associated employment.
- Ideally, even more detailed breakdown would be needed on the extent of **environmentally sustainable practices** (and the related employment and value added) within industries. This could cover renewable energy generation, sustainable forestry and sustainable fisheries (e.g. with international certification) and organic agriculture. It could also analyse sustainable transport (e.g. electric vehicles), cleaner manufacturing, greening of the service industry (e.g. eco-tourism, certified energy-efficient office buildings). However, internationally comparable data of this type remain extremely scarce.

A subset of the indicators relates specifically to the EGS sector:

- **Employment and value added in selected environmental protection activities** for selected countries, expressed as a percentage of total; sewerage, waste management and remediation (ISIC Rev.4 industries 37-39).
- **Employment and value added in the EGS sector** in the European Union, drawing on Eurostat's definition of EGS, broken down by NACE industries and CEPA/CREMA activities.

These indicators provide only a partial picture of activities relevant for green growth. Not all indicators reflect an internationally agreed classification.

EGS include specific services, connected products and adapted goods, but their definition and measurement scope varies across and within countries. Further efforts are needed to generate internationally comparable data on EGS (turn-over, value added, exports, employment, etc.) in accordance with the recommendations of the Central Framework of the UN System of Environmental Economic Accounting (SEEA). See also *Glossary*.

Sources

Eurostat (2016a), "Air emissions accounts by NACE Rev. 2 activity", *Environment* database, *http://ec.europa.eu/eurostat/data/database* (accessed on 29 November 2016).

Eurostat (2016b), "National accounts aggregates by industry (up to NACE A*64)", *National accounts (ESA2010)* database, *http://ec.europa.eu/eurostat/data/database* (accessed on 29 November 2016).

Eurostat (2016c), "National accounts employment data by industry (up to NACE A*64)", *National accounts (ESA2010)* database, *http://ec.europa.eu/eurostat/data/database* (accessed on 29 November 2016).

Eurostat (2016d), "Employment in the environmental goods and services sector", *Environment* database, *http://ec.europa.eu/eurostat/data/database* (accessed on 23 November 2016).

Eurostat (2016e), "Production, value added and exports in the environmental goods and services sector", *Environment* database, *http://ec.europa.eu/eurostat/data/database* (accessed on 23 November 2016).

Eurostat (2016f), "Production, value added and employment by industry groups in the environmental goods and services sector", *Environment* database, *http://ec.europa.eu/eurostat/data/database* (accessed on 23 November 2016).

OECD (2017), "Green growth indicators", *OECD Environment Statistics* (database), *http://dx.doi.org/10.1787/data-00665-en* (accessed in March 2017).

OECD (2016a), "Aggregate national accounts, SNA 2008 (or SNA 1993): population and employment by main activity", *OECD National Accounts Statistics* (database), *http://dx.doi.org/10.1787/data-00003-en.* (accessed on 31 January 2017)

OECD (2016b), "Aggregate national accounts, SNA 2008 (or SNA 1993): gross domestic product", *OECD National Accounts Statistics* (database), *http://dx.doi.org/10.1787/data-00001-en* (accessed on 31 January 2017).

OECD (2012), OECD Employment Outlook 2012, OECD Publishing, Paris, *http://dx.doi.org/10.1787/empl_outlook-2012-en.*

Sauvage, J. (2014), "The Stringency of Environmental Regulations and Trade in Environmental Goods", *OECD Trade and Environment Working Papers*, No. 2014/03, OECD Publishing, Paris, *http://dx.doi.org/10.1787/5jxrjn7xsnmq-en.*

UN (2016), "United Nations Commodity Trade Statistics Database", *www.comtrade.un.org* (accessed in October 2016).

Further reading

Eurostat (2016), *Environmental Goods and Services Sector Accounts – Handbook*, 2016 edition.

Bruvoll, A. et al. (2012), *Measuring Green Jobs? An evaluation of definitions and statistics for green activities, TemaNord* 2012:534, Nordic Council of Ministers, Copenhagen, *www.norden.org/en/publications/publikationer/2012-534.*

OECD (n.d.), "Greening Jobs and Skills", webpage: *www.oecd.org/employment/greeningjobsandskills.htm.*

United Nations, *System of Environmental-Economic Accounting 2012 – Central Framework, http://unstats.un.org/unsd/envaccounting/seeaRev/SEEA_CF_Final_en.pdf.*

International financial flows

Foreign sources of public and private finance can be useful in countries lacking sufficient access to domestic sources of finance. They can help catalyse investment for environmental projects and technologies, thus fulfilling the twin development-environment objectives. Public and private sources of international finance can also contribute to cross-border exchange of know-how and skills, foster local entrepreneurship and strengthen local absorptive capacity. This, in turn, can facilitate international technology transfer.

There are two main challenges for government. First, to successfully attract foreign sources of finance governments must improve the framework conditions (e.g. rule of law, human capital) and pursue policies that facilitate market entry and exit and do not discriminate among different categories of investors. Second, governments must strengthen the use of public financing to mobilise private finance for projects supporting the transition to greener growth. A particular concern is to minimise the potential for public finance to crowd out private finance (e.g. Cárdenas Rodríguez et al. 2014).

Main trends and recent developments

Official development assistance (ODA) is an important source of government-funded international financial flows. Members of the OECD Development Assistance Committee (OECD-DAC) provide as much as 95% of global development aid. Despite the recent financial crisis, bilateral ODA flows continued to rise to 2015, reaching a total of USD 136 billion. However, the collective efforts of OECD-DAC members fell short of the international ODA target of 0.7% of gross national income (Figure 14.2c).

Environmentally related ODA has increased, from both bilateral and multilateral donors

ODA targeting the biodiversity, climate change and desertification objectives of the Rio conventions has been increasing since the late 1990s. In 2015, DAC members allocated USD 35.5 billion to environmentally related ODA. Most of these funds were for climate change mitigation and adaptation. Much less was directed at biodiversity- and desertification-related ODA. Data on multilateral ODA are more limited, but suggest a similar pattern of rising emphasis on the environment in ODA targeting (Figures 14.1a-b).

ODA targeted at renewables has surpassed ODA for non-renewable energy generation

Since the mid-2000s bilateral donors have strengthened their support for the water and sanitation sector, particularly for environmental protection. ODA targeted at energy generation from renewable sources has increased five-fold since 2000, surpassing ODA for non-renewable energy (Figure 14.1c). Rail transport largely dominates all environmentally related projects supported by ODA in 2015 across all ODA providers.

Figure 14.1. **ODA puts more emphasis on the environment**

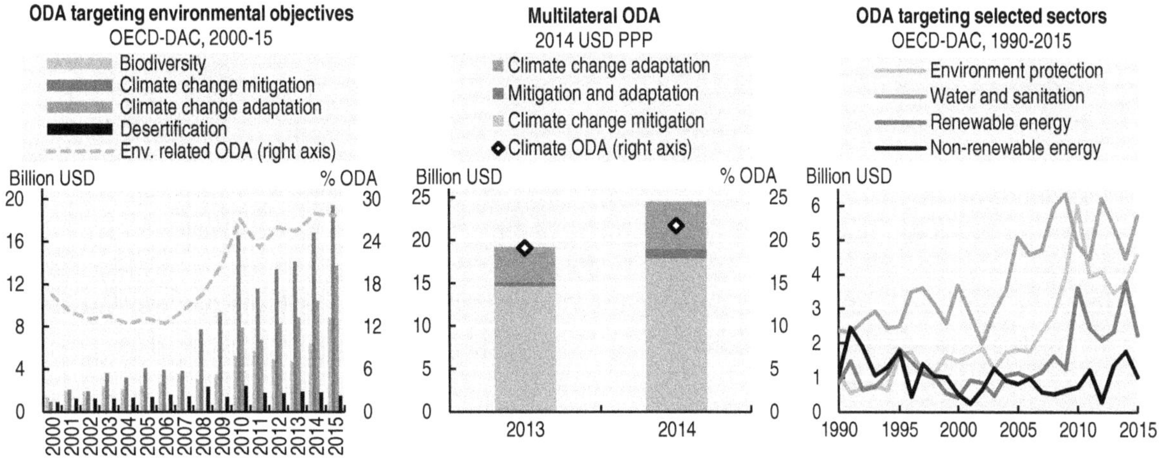

Note: Indicators are constructed from project-level data. Expressed in 2014 USD using PPPs.
Source: Source: OECD (2016a, 2016b) *OECD International Development Statistics* (database).

StatLink http://dx.doi.org/10.1787/888933484892

Figure 14.2. **ODA by donor country**

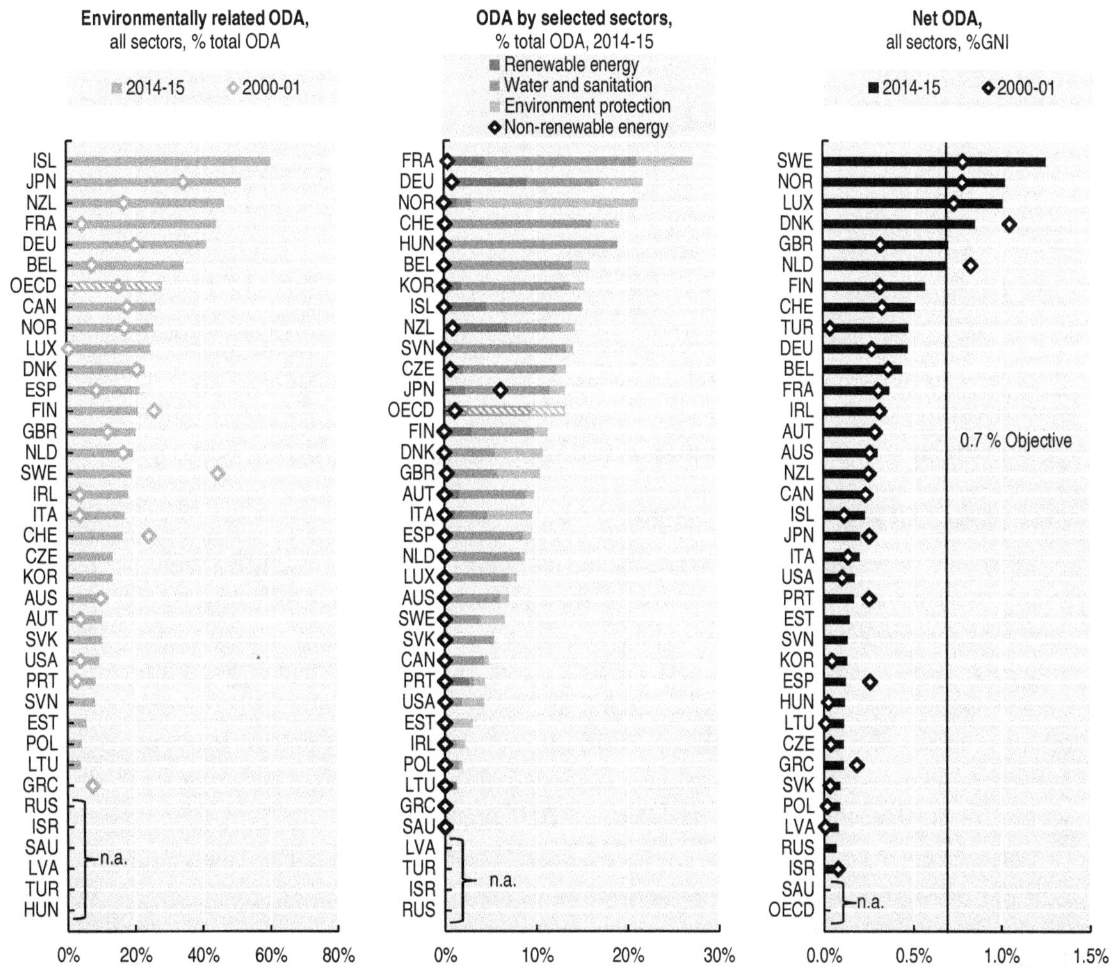

Source: OECD (2016a), *OECD International Development Statistics* (database).

StatLink http://dx.doi.org/10.1787/888933484901

Transactions under the Clean Development Mechanism have declined

Project-based transactions under the Clean Development Mechanism (CDM) declined over 2013-15 to close to nil. This was due to low demand in the European Union emissions trading system and other traditional markets for emission credits from CDM projects. In 2012, the value of new renewable energy projects under the CDM reached a peak of over USD 314 billion. In 2015, however, the transaction value fell below USD 6 billion (Figure 14.3). Throughout the CDM, wind and small hydropower have been the dominant sectors, accounting for 48% and 41% of total investment in renewable energy projects respectively.

Figure 14.3. **Transactions in clean development mechanism projects have declined recently**

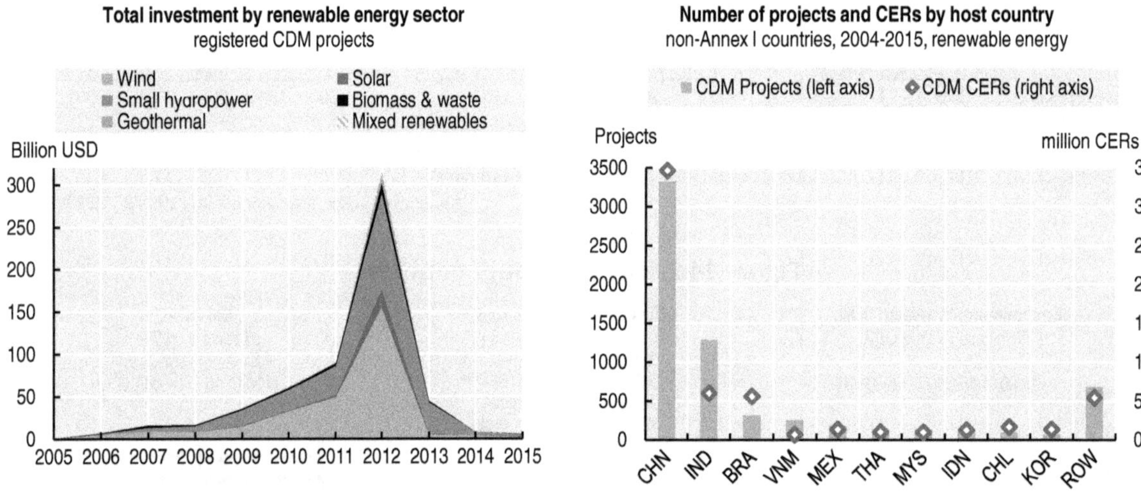

Note: CERs = Certified Emission Reductions.
Source: Source: UNEP-Risoe (2016), data extracted in September 2016.

StatLink http://dx.doi.org/10.1787/888933484911

The People's Republic of China (hereafter China), has been the largest host country for CDM projects (50% of projects and 58% of emission credits issued), followed by India (19.5% and 10.0%) and Brazil (4.8% and 9.3%). The potential of CDM projects to crowd out profitable private investment (additionality) remains a key concern over the CDM mechanism.

Green financial markets are emerging

Sizeable opportunities in international financing have appeared in the field of clean energy. New investment flows, both domestic and international, have more than quadrupled in this field since 2005. In 2015, most funds were invested in projects related to wind (38%) and solar (56%) energy (Figure 14.4). Globally, investment in electricity generation from renewable sources has largely surpassed investment in fossil fuel technology, mainly due to falling cost of wind and solar photovoltaics. Investment in renewables-based capacity is sufficient to cover growth in global electricity demand in 2015, but it is not yet consistent with achieving the objectives of the 2015 Paris Agreement (IEA, 2016).

New opportunities for financing green growth-related projects have also emerged. A number of financial institutions have issued green-labelled bonds, for example. This market is still relatively small compared to global bond markets. However, the issuance of green-labelled bonds amounted to about USD 42 billion in 2015 (Figure 14.5).

Figure 14.4. **Investment in renewable energy increasingly targets non-OECD economies**

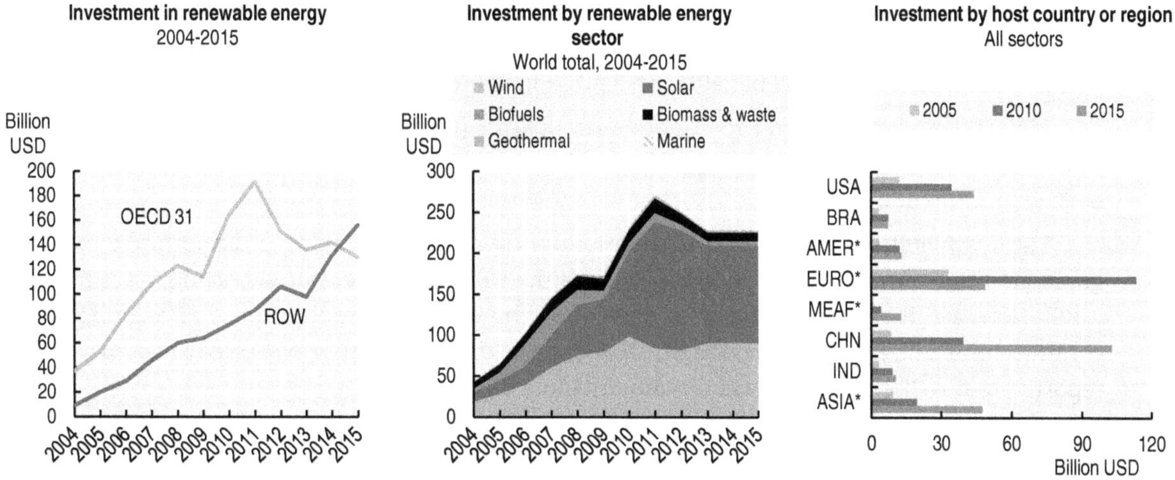

Note: OECD31 = all OECD excl. Mexico, Chile, Turkey and Latvia. ROW = Rest of the World. AMER = America excl. United States and Brazil. EURO = Europe, MEAF = Middle East and Africa, ASIA = Asia excl. China and India. All values are in nominal prices.
Source: Frankfurt School-UNEP Centre/BNEF (2016).

StatLink http://dx.doi.org/10.1787/888933484920

Figure 14.5. **Issuance of green-labelled bonds is growing, particularly in the energy and transport sectors**

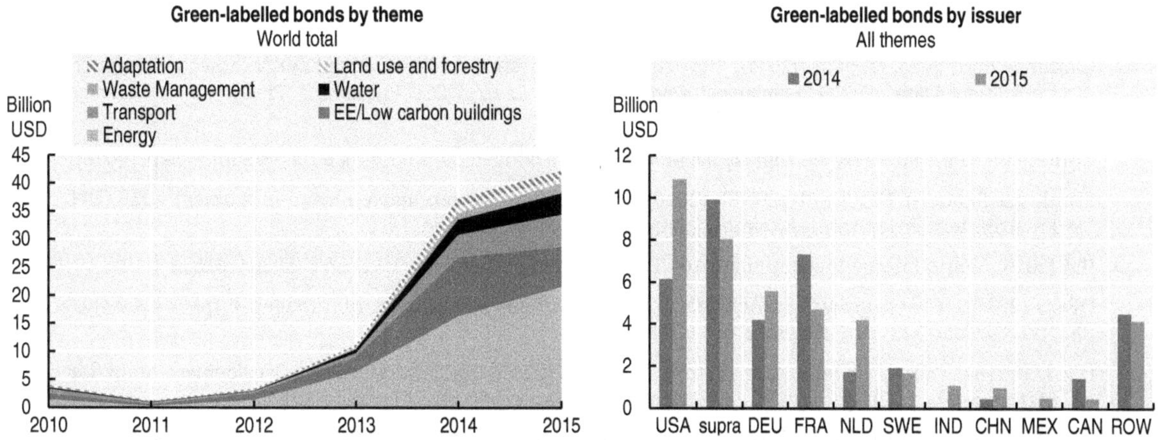

Note: "supra" = supranational (e.g. World Bank, European Investment Bank, etc.). All values are in nominal prices. Country coverage has been improving over time so trends should be interpreted with caution.
Source: Climate Bond Initiative (2016).

StatLink http://dx.doi.org/10.1787/888933484935

Measurability and interpretation

The indicators presented in this chapter relate to the following:

- **Official development assistance**, including ODA directed at selected sectors (environmental protection, renewable energy, water and sanitation), ODA targeting the objectives of the Rio conventions (i.e. related to biodiversity, desertification and climate change mitigation and adaptation) and an additional "environment" marker. Finally, "net ODA" is presented as a share of gross national income. (For further details, see *Glossary*.)
- **CDM:** The structure of Clean Development Mechanism (CDM) projects in the pipeline and the emission credits issued (so-called certified emission reductions or CERs), expressed as a percentage of all projects, by countries and regions.

- **Investment** in renewable energy projects, from both private and public sources, presented in levels of investment by sector and by host country.
- **Green-labelled bonds:** Labelled bonds with proceeds earmarked for projects and assets that deliver environmental benefits, presented in value by theme and by issuer.

Rio markers for ODA refer to donors' *commitments* (i.e. policy objectives). There is no internationally agreed methodology for tracking actual *disbursements* of ODA related to each environmental objective.

The main statistical challenge is the monitoring of financial flows of importance to green growth. Some standards do exist, such as the OECD DAC Creditor Reporting System (CRS). However, it remains difficult to determine the environmental purpose of existing commitments and investment projects. ODA donors are requested to screen each activity reported to the CRS, but data gaps remain for some donors.

There is no internationally agreed methodology for classifying green bonds. The data and definitions from the Climate Bond Initiative are used here only for illustration.

These indicators are limited in that they do not systematically track all the relevant financial flows between countries directly. A "green" FDI-based indicator could help fill this gap. However, the lack of an agreed definition and the patchiness of the data make it impossible to calculate at this stage.

Sources

Cárdenas Rodríguez, M. et al. (2014), "Inducing Private Finance for Renewable Energy Projects: Evidence from Micro-Data", *OECD Environment Working Papers*, No. 67, OECD Publishing, Paris, *http://dx.doi.org/10.1787/5jxvg0k6thr1-en*.

Climate Bond Initiative (2016), *State of the Market* 2016, (Using accompanying data, version 9 Sept. 2016).

Frankfurt School-UNEP Centre/BNEF (2016), *Global Trends in Renewable Energy Investment 2016*, UN Environment Programme-Bloomberg New Energy Finance, Frankfurt.

IEA (2016), World Energy Investment 2016, IEA, Paris, *http://dx.doi.org/10.1787/9789264262836-en*.

OECD (2017), "Green growth indicators", *OECD Environment Statistics* (database), *http://dx.doi.org/10.1787/data-00665-en* (accessed in March 2017).

OECD (2016a), "Creditor reporting system: Aid activities", *OECD International Development Statistics* (database), *http://dx.doi.org/10.1787/data-00061-en* (accessed on 31 January 2017).

OECD (2016b), "Multilateral climate-related development finance", *OECD International Development Statistics* (database), *http://dx.doi.org/10.1787/data-00061-en* (accessed on 31 January 2017).

UNEP-Risoe (2016), *CDM/JI Pipeline Analysis and Database* (database), *www.cdmpipeline.org* (accessed in September 2016).

Further reading

Golub, S.S., C. Kauffmann and P. Yeres (2011), "Defining and Measuring Green FDI: An Exploratory Review of Existing Work and Evidence", *OECD Working Papers on International Investment*, No. 2011/02, OECD Publishing, Paris, *http://dx.doi.org/10.1787/5kg58j1cvcvk-en* (accessed xx Month 2017).

OECD-DAC (n.d.), "Technical Guide to Terms and Data in the Creditor Reporting System", webpage: *www.oecd.org/dac/stats/crsguide*.

UNFCCC (2014), *Clean Development Mechanism: Executive Board Annual Report 2014*, United Nations Framework Convention on Climate Change, *http://unfccc.int/resource/docs/publications/unfccc_cdm-eb_annual_report2014.pdf*.

UNFCCC (n.d.), *CDM Registry*, *http://cdm.unfccc.int/Registry/index.html*.

Taxes and subsidies

Market-based instruments play a key role in facilitating the transition towards green growth. Compared to regulatory instruments, such as emission limits or prescriptive technology standards, environmentally related taxation encourages the lowest-cost abatement across polluters. It also provides incentives for abatement at each unit of pollution. In addition, the revenue raised can be used to support fiscal consolidation or to reduce other taxes (e.g. taxes on labour and capital that distort the labour supply and saving decisions). Shifting the overall tax burden away from labour and capital towards environmentally harmful consumption and production patterns, while maintaining the overall level of redistribution constant, can improve economic efficiency.

Governments levy taxes to raise revenue or to discourage certain behaviour. Historically most environmentally related taxes were introduced primarily to raise revenue. Today, however, they provide important market signals. These aim to influence the behaviour of producers and consumers by shaping the relative prices of substitute goods.

Phasing out government support measures for environmentally harmful products or activities should accompany efforts to green the tax system. Such measures directly undermine efforts to green the tax system by perpetuating wasteful consumption or production patterns. Moreover, they represent an opportunity cost to society: the resources could instead be directed to other more productive uses.

There are two main challenges. First, green tax reform should address environmental externalities across all sources of emissions (or all resource users) in a systematic way. Second, all types of support or preferential tax rates for fossil fuels should be eliminated. This also implies that potentially regressive distributional impacts must be addressed outside of the environmentally related tax through additional targeted measures to protect vulnerable households. In addition, governments should use taxation to provide predictable and transparent market signals to guide long-term investment decisions (e.g. in alternative energy sources). Finally, stronger international coordination can mitigate potential losses in competitiveness of domestic industries. At current carbon prices, limited negative impacts on competitiveness have been found (see *Further reading*).

Main trends and recent developments

The share of environmentally related taxes in total tax revenue and compared to GDP is decreasing

The use of environmentally related taxes is growing but remains limited in many countries. The revenue raised from these taxes represents about 5.2% of all tax revenue, equivalent to 1.6% of GDP in the OECD area. The increase in crude oil prices up until mid-2014 triggered substitution away from motor fuel use. It also made adjustments in nominal

Figure 15.1. **Revenue from environmentally related taxes declined as a share of total tax revenue and compared to GDP**

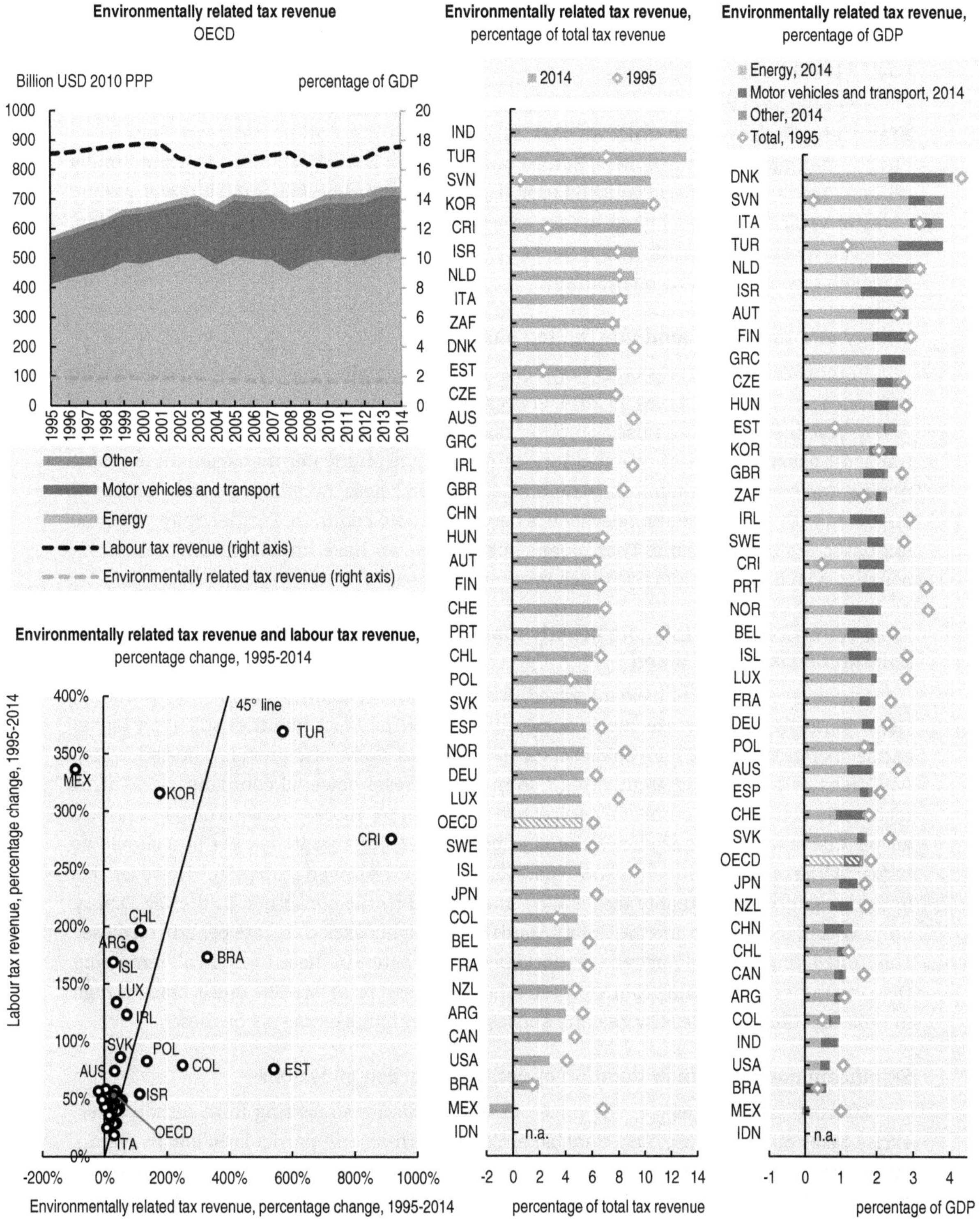

Note: All monetary values are expressed in constant USD using PPPs.

Source: OECD (2016a), "Environmental policy instruments", *OECD Environment Statistics* (database); OECD (2016b), "Revenue statistics", *OECD Tax statistics* (database).

StatLink http://dx.doi.org/10.1787/888933484947

tax rates on motor fuels politically difficult. Yet some countries, such as Slovenia, Costa Rica, Turkey and Estonia strengthened the role of environmentally related taxes and have tripled their share of tax revenue since 1995 (Figure 15.1). During this time period, final consumption of oil products has risen much less than the revenue from environmentally related taxes.

Over the past 15 years, countries such as Israel, Poland, Estonia, Colombia, Costa Rica, Brazil and Turkey have shifted part of their revenue collection from labour to environmentally related activities. Some countries have introduced new environmentally related taxes as part of fiscal consolidation, e.g. taxes on nuclear fuel and air travel, carbon taxes or vehicle tax rates linked to CO_2 emissions and, sometimes, to local air pollution. However, most countries have experienced higher increases in their revenue from labour taxes relative to that of the environment.

Energy and transport dominate the tax base

In most countries, taxes on energy consumption generate most of the revenue among environmentally related taxes. In 2014, energy products, including motor fuels, contributed 70% of revenues. Revenues raised on other tax bases were much lower. Motor vehicles and transport generated 26% of revenue, for example. Waste and water management, forestry, mining and hazardous chemicals generated 4%. Nevertheless, taxation of a wide variety of tax bases with environmental relevance is becoming more common. Further, many of these tax bases are highly elastic. That means such taxes can have important environmental benefits even if they do not raise much revenue.

Most countries tax petrol more heavily than diesel despite the higher carbon and air pollutant emissions of diesel

Excise taxes on diesel have increased in a half of OECD countries while only a third of OECD countries have increased taxes on petrol, in real terms. Most countries still apply higher excise tax rates on petrol than on diesel fuel (Figure 15.2). Some also provide value added tax (VAT) rebates or other preferential tax treatment for diesel-powered company cars. This is regrettable from an environmental perspective. Diesel causes more emissions of CO_2 and local air pollutants than an equivalent volume of petrol, meaning that its tax per litre should be higher. A litre of diesel normally allows more kilometres to be driven than petrol. However, this is a driving-related externality that is fully internalised by the consumer. In the OECD area, only Switzerland, Mexico and the United States have a higher excise tax rate per litre on diesel. The United Kingdom and Australia do not differentiate between these fuels. In all remaining OECD countries the tax rate per litre on petrol is higher than on diesel. The rate is twice as high in Chile and Greece, while New Zealand applies only a minimal excise tax on diesel.

Significant gaps remain in taxation of non-road carbon emissions

Effective carbon rates (i.e. the price of carbon emissions resulting from carbon taxes, excise taxes on energy use, and tradable emission permits) are particularly low in sectors outside road transport. In OECD countries, the average effective rate outside the transport sector is EUR 7.90 per tonne of CO_2. Only 6% of priced emissions are above 30 EUR/t (i.e. a conservative estimate of their cost to society) and 65% of emissions are not priced at all. BRIICS economies (Brazil, Russian Federation, India, Indonesia, People's Republic of China, South Africa), have an average effective rate of 1.30 EUR/t. Only 2% are priced above 30 EUR/t and 81% of emissions are unpriced (see OECD, 2016c) (Figure 15.3).

Figure 15.2. **Motor fuel taxation is increasing in half of OECD countries**

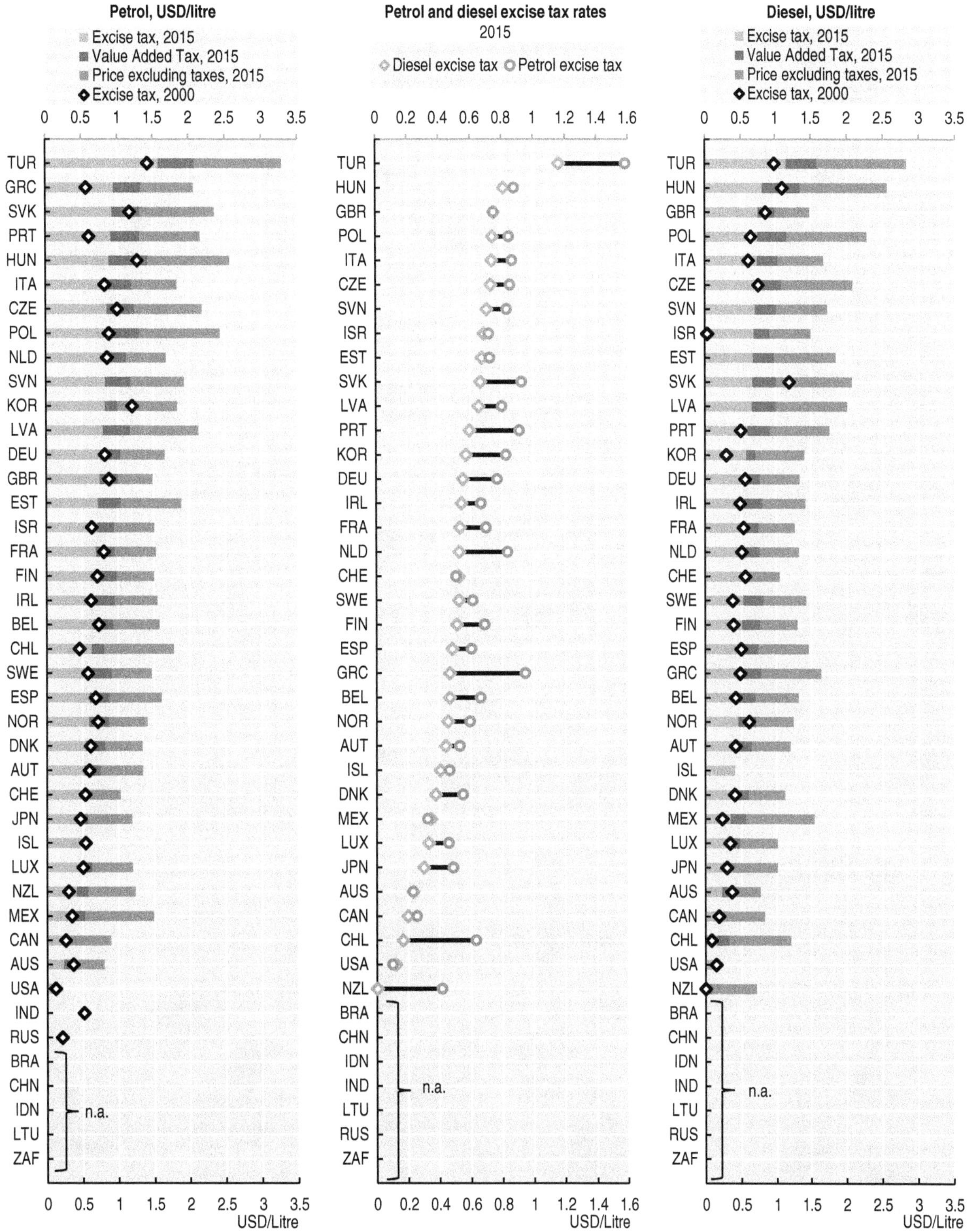

Note: Prices and taxes are expressed in constant 2010 USD using PPPs, deflated using the Consumer Price Index.

Source: IEA (2016a, 2016b), *IEA Energy Prices and Taxes Statistics* (database).

StatLink http://dx.doi.org/10.1787/888933484958

Figure 15.3. **Most carbon emissions are not priced at their climate costs**

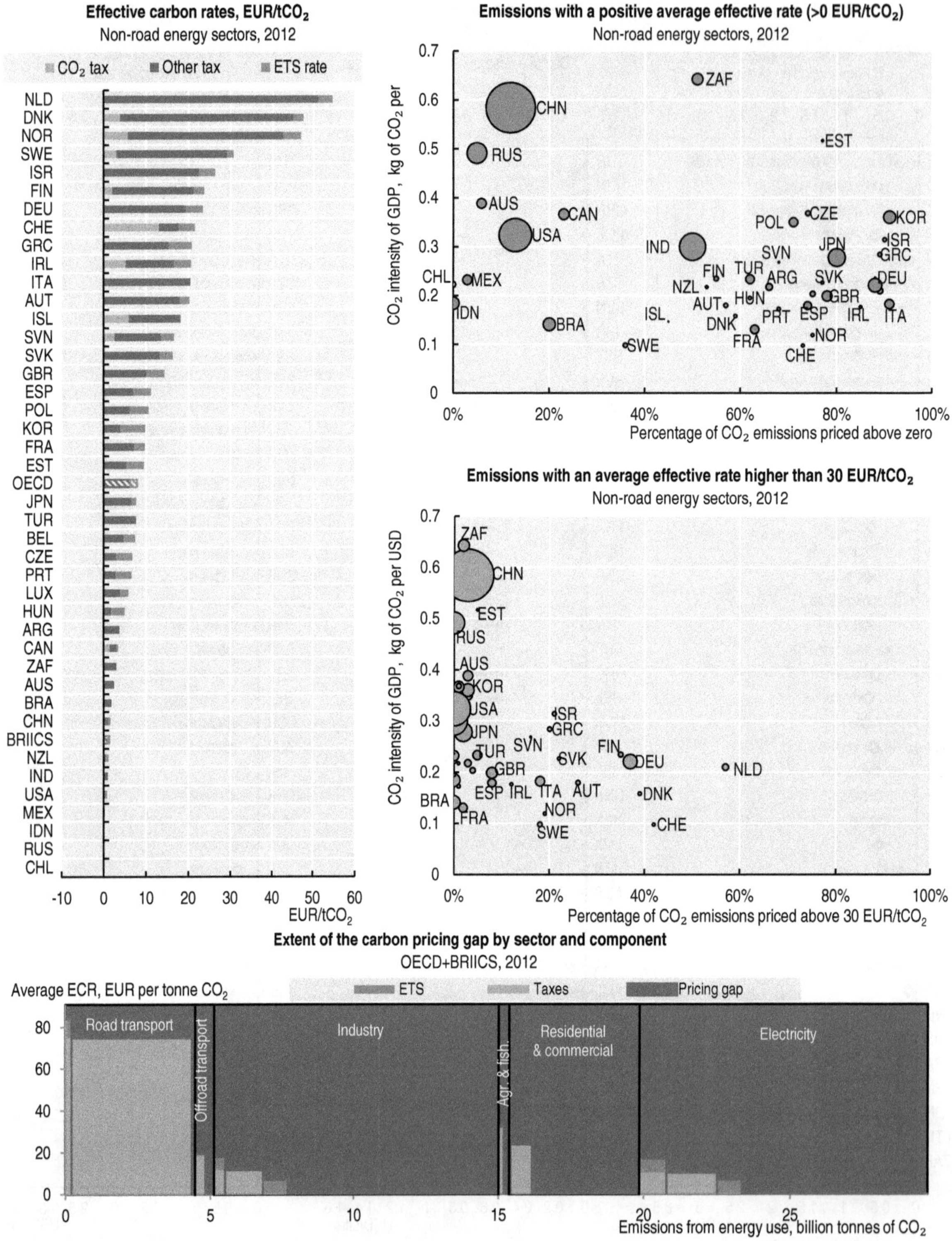

Note: The size of bubbles shows total CO_2 emissions from non-road energy sectors. OECD total represents a weighted average, excluding Latvia (the country became a member of the OECD after the calculations were carried out).

Source: OECD (2016c), *Effective Carbon Rates: Pricing CO_2 through Taxes and Emissions Trading Systems.*

StatLink http://dx.doi.org/10.1787/888933484964

Figure 15.4. **OECD and BRIICS still support fossil fuels**

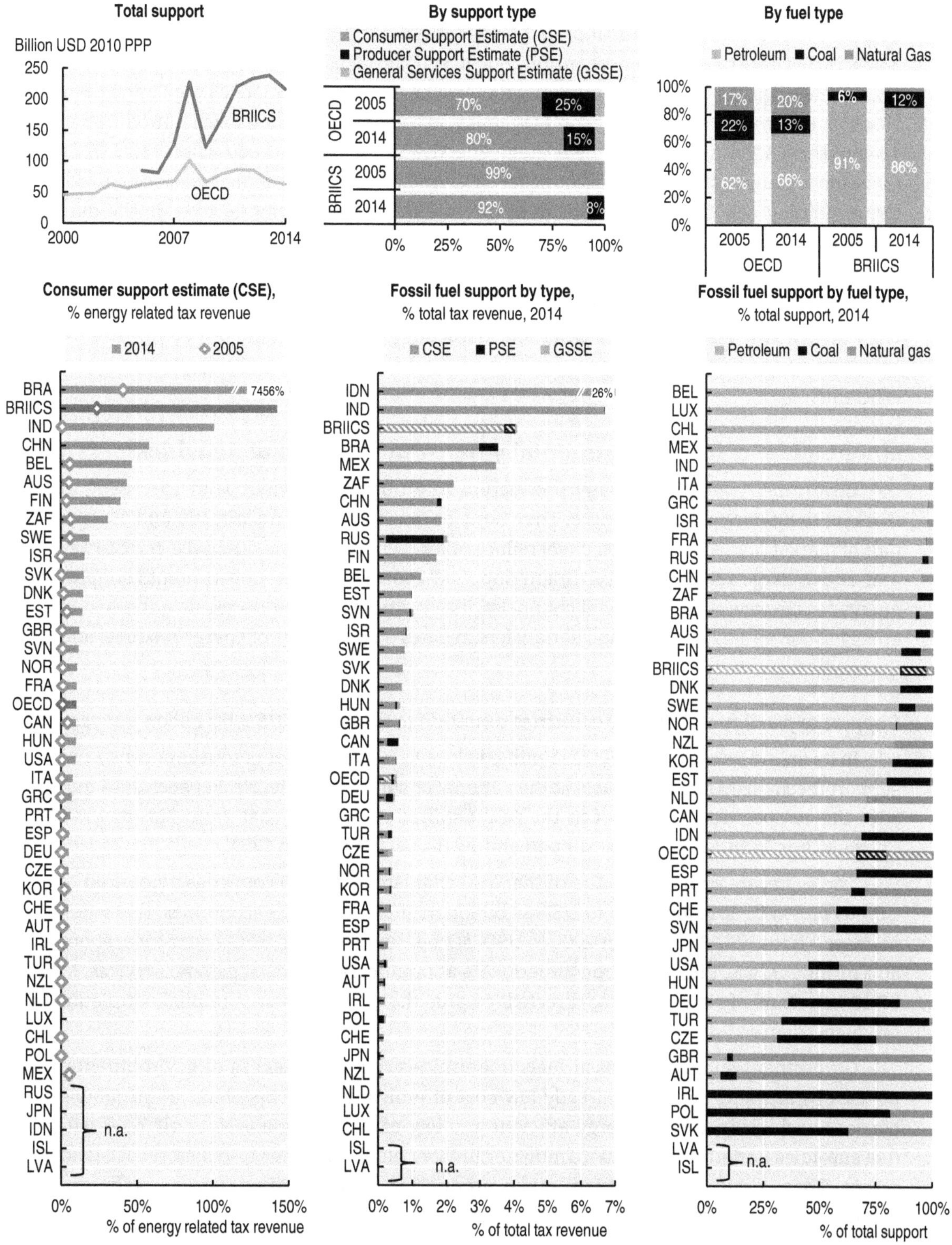

Note: In panel D, the rapid increase for Brazil is due to a fall in energy-related tax revenues (denominator) and an important increase in the CSE (numerator).

Source: OECD (2016d), "Inventory of support measures for fossil fuels".

StatLink http://dx.doi.org/10.1787/888933484976

Road transport has comparatively higher effective carbon rates. For example, OECD countries have an average effective rate of 91 EUR/t. They have 44% of emissions priced above 30 EUR/t and 1% of emissions unpriced (49% and 6% for BRIICS, with an average rate of 30.2 EUR/t). These rates are almost entirely due to specific taxes on road transport fuel. These taxes were originally introduced primarily for reasons other than climate change mitigation. Nevertheless, they have an impact on CO_2 emissions. For example, CO_2 taxes (introduced in 11 countries) account for 2% of the average effective rates for OECD countries. Meanwhile emission trading systems (ETS) account for 21%. And excise and specific taxes account for the remaining 77% of the composition of the rate in non-road sectors. Overall, the data suggest that policies largely fall short of pricing carbon emissions (Figure 15.3d), as well as other negative environmental impacts caused by energy use.

There is wide variation in effective carbon rates and the low levels of taxation of fuels with significant environmental impacts. This suggests important opportunities for countries to reform their energy tax systems and achieve environmental goals more cost-efficiently.

Government support for environmentally harmful products or activities

Governments support energy production in a number of ways. They intervene in markets to influence costs or prices. They transfer funds to recipients directly and assume part of market risk. And they selectively reduce taxes recipients would otherwise have to pay and undercharge for use of government-supplied goods or assets. Governments support energy *consumption* through several channels: price controls intended to regulate the cost of energy to consumers, direct financial transfers, rebates on purchases of energy products and tax relief.

Support to fossil fuels in OECD countries amounts to more than USD 60 billion per year

In its online *Inventory*, the OECD identified close to 800 individual producer or consumer support mechanisms for fossil fuels at the national or sub-national levels. Between 2005 and 2014 the composition of support in the OECD shifted away from coal (from 21% to 13%). Conversely, in BRIICS economies, support shifted *to* coal (from 6% to 12%).

The aggregate estimated value of these mechanisms in OECD countries amounted to USD 63 billion in 2014 (down from USD 84 billion in 2011). In BRIICS economies, this value increased from USD 85 billion in 2005 to USD 217 billion in 2014. In OECD countries, about 80% of support was directed at consumers, 15% at producers and 5% at general services. In BRIICS, the bulk of support is also directed towards the consumption of refined petroleum products (Figure 15.4).

Government support for fossil fuels undermines the effectiveness of environmental policies by bringing down the already low cost of emitting CO_2. This erects a formidable barrier to achieving a more energy-efficient and low-carbon economy. Not only do fossil-fuel subsidies undermine efforts to mitigate climate change, but they also distort costs and prices. These distortions, in turn, make production and use of energy less efficient throughout the economy.

Fossil-fuel subsidies affect allocation of resources across sectors. For example, long-term capital investment can be directed towards those sectors that produce fossil fuels or use them intensively. This can be done at the expense of low-carbon energy and other economic activities more generally.

Policies supporting fossil fuels can impair an economy's long-term productive capacity. Such subsidies can also impose considerable strain on government budgets. Subsidies either increase public expenditure or reduce tax revenue. This is particularly problematic at a time when many countries are taking painful steps to reduce their public debt (OECD, 2015).

The overall level of environmentally harmful support to farmers decreased

In 2015, total annual support to agriculture in the OECD represented about 0.8% of GDP. This encompasses producer, consumer and general services support. In most OECD countries, producer support (PSE) decreased – both, in terms of levels (Figure 15.5a) and compared to GDP (from 1% in 2000 to 0.55% in 2015).

The composition of PSE has changed in two respects that are relevant for the environment. First, since 1990, the potentially most environmentally harmful government support to farmers has declined. On average, in OECD countries, it has dropped from 86% to about 50% of PSE (Figure 15.5b). Countries have made concerted efforts to decouple support from commodity output and prices. However, the potentially least environmentally harmful support accounts for only 7% in the OECD area. Second, support is increasingly tied to environmental conditions (cross compliance). It links the provision (or withdrawal) of support payments to specific farm practices and environmental performance criteria (Figure 15.5c).

Figure 15.5. **The potentially most environmentally harmful government support for agriculture is declining**

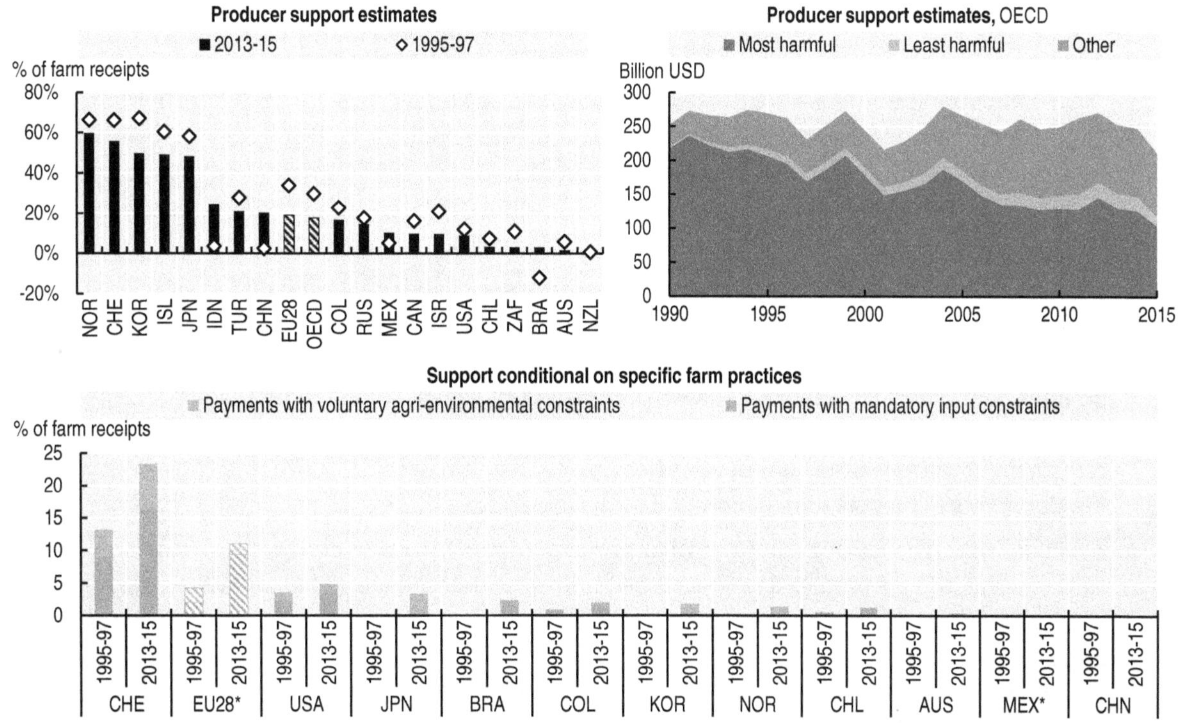

Note: MEX* = 1995-97 is replaced by 1991-93 for Mexico. EU28* = EU15 for 1995-97, EU27 for 2012-13 and EU28 for 2014-15.

Source: OECD calculations based on the classification in OECD (2013) and data extracted from OECD (2016e), "Agricultural support estimates (Edition 2016)", *OECD Agriculture Statistics* (database).

StatLink http://dx.doi.org/10.1787/888933484989

Measurability and interpretation

The indicators presented in this chapter relate to the following:

- **Environmentally related tax revenue**, expressed as a percentage of total tax revenue, and compared to GDP and to labour tax revenue. The structure of the tax base is given as a complement. Labour taxes include taxes on personal income and profits, social security contributions and payroll. See also *Glossary*.
- **Road fuel taxes and prices** expressed in constant 2010 USD using purchasing power parities (PPPs) and deflated using the Consumer Price Index.
- **Effective carbon rates** are expressed in EUR per tonne of CO_2. They are the total price that applies to CO_2 emissions from energy use as a result of CO_2 taxes, specific taxes on energy use and the price of tradable emission permits. The "carbon pricing gap" shows the extent to which effective carbon rates fall short of pricing CO_2 emissions.
- **Support for fossil fuels** is presented by fuel type and by type of support, as defined in the OECD framework for Producer and Consumer Support Estimates. Support estimates are expressed as percentages of total support, compared to total tax revenue and in 2010 USD using PPPs.
- **Support for agriculture** is presented by support type, indicating the potentially environmentally harmful elements of government support to producers. Support considered potentially most environmentally harmful consists of market price support, payments based on commodity output without imposing environmental constraints on farming practices, and payments based on variable input use without imposing environmental constraints on farming practices. For more details, see OECD (2013: pp. 67-68).

The indicators on environmentally related taxes should not be used to assess the "environmental friendliness" of the tax systems. For such analysis, additional information, describing the economic and taxation structure of each country, is required. Moreover, a number of environmentally related taxes can have important environmental impacts, even if they raise little (or no) revenue. In addition, revenue from fees and charges, and from royalties related to resource management, is not included.

The compilation of energy prices is increasingly a challenge. Deregulation of energy markets leads to an important increase in the number of market players. This generates difficulties in collecting price data on an equivalent basis. Cross-country comparisons should be done with care. For instance, using purchasing power parities might exaggerate the differences in fuel prices between countries. Further, consumer price indexes might not reflect the exact evolution of energy prices over time. As a result, this could hide policy developments in fuel taxation in nominal terms (e.g. indexing of excise tax rates in Norway).

The effective carbon rate profiles are amenable for inter-country comparison. Nevertheless, the tax profiles do not account for differentiated value added tax (VAT) rates on energy products within the different countries. Such differentiated rates alter relative prices and should therefore in principle be accounted for. However, the approach focuses on the specific rate to give clear policy recommendations from an environmental pricing point of view. In addition, these rates are expressed irrespective of external costs additional to those of CO_2 emissions. For example, excise taxes can also serve as (imprecise) instruments to internalise congestion, noise and air pollution costs. Ideally, these rates should be compared to the full array of external costs they intend to cover.

Information on fossil-fuel support at national or sub-national levels is available from the *OECD Inventory of Support Measures for Fossil Fuels*. Data on tax expenditures, which represent the majority of the support mechanisms, are not fully comparable across countries. They need to be interpreted with caution, bearing in mind that tax regimes can differ substantially (e.g. depreciation allowances). Fossil-fuel support is often calculated as deviation from the benchmark taxation. However, countries define the benchmark in different ways, making international comparisons difficult. The indicators on government support measures do not provide enough information to judge the environmental impact of specific measures, nor do they indicate which measures should be considered for possible reform or removal. For example, not all support measures for fossil fuel are unambiguously inefficient and some caution is required in interpreting the support amounts.

Agricultural support estimates, available from the *OECD Agriculture Statistics*, are a useful tool for assessing the progress achieved in policy reform. These indicators, however, do not allow measuring the effects on production, consumption, trade and environment. The PSE should not be considered as an indicator of trade distortions. It is an aggregate measure of transfers resulting from a wide variety of policies that support agriculture. These policies may have different effects on quantities produced and consumed, and hence on trade. However, the OECD PSE classification of categories of policy measures has the potential to show the degree of flexibility in production choices that farmers face. This allows better understand how different policies could influence farmers' decisions to produce commodity and non-commodity outputs.

This chapter focuses on market-based policy instruments but regulatory (command-and-control) approaches can also play a role in the transition towards green growth. OECD work on a proxy indicator of Environmental Policy Stringency (EPS) seeks to measure both types of policy responses across 15 environmental domains combined into a composite index over 1990-2015 (see Botta and Koźluk, 2014). Currently, the EPS index covers primarily climate and air pollution policies in energy and transport, but efforts are on-going to integrate also water pollution policies (see *http://oe.cd/eps*).

Sources

IEA (2016a), "End-use prices: Energy prices in national currency per unit", *IEA Energy Prices and Taxes Statistics* (database), *http://dx.doi.org/10.1787/data-00441-en* (accessed in January 2017).

IEA (2016b), "End-use prices: End-use prices: Energy prices for selected non-OECD Countries", *IEA Energy Prices and Taxes Statistics* (database), *http://dx.doi.org/10.1787/data-00683-en* (accessed in January 2017).

OECD (2017), "Green growth indicators", *OECD Environment Statistics* (database), *http://dx.doi.org/10.1787/data-00665-en* (accessed in March 2017).

OECD (2016a), "Environmental policy instruments", *OECD Environment Statistics* (database), *http://dx.doi.org/10.1787/data-00696-en* (accessed in January 2017).

OECD (2016b), "Revenue statistics", *OECD Tax Statistics* (database), *http://dx.doi.org/10.1787/tax-data-en* (accessed in January 2017).

OECD (2016c), *Effective Carbon Rates: Pricing CO_2 through Taxes and Emissions Trading Systems*, OECD Publishing, Paris, *http://dx.doi.org/10.1787/9789264260115-en.*

OECD (2016d), "Inventory of support measures for fossil fuels", *OECD Environment Statistics* (database). *http://www.oecd.org/site/tadffss/* (accessed in September 2016)

OECD (2016e), "Agricultural support estimates (Edition 2016)", *OECD Agriculture Statistics* (database), *http://dx.doi.org/10.1787/83ff9179-en.*

OECD (2016f), *Agricultural Policy Monitoring and Evaluation 2016*, OECD Publishing, Paris. *http://dx.doi.org/10.1787/agr_pol-2016-en*.

OECD (2015), *OECD Companion to the Inventory of Support Measures for Fossil Fuels 2015*, OECD Publishing, Paris, *http://dx.doi.org/10.1787/9789264239616-en*.

OECD (2013), *Policy Instruments to Support Green Growth in Agriculture: A Synthesis of Country Experiences*, OECD Publishing, Paris, *http://dx.doi.org/10.1787/9789264203525-en*.

Further reading

Arlinghaus, J. (2015), "Impacts of Carbon Prices on Indicators of Competitiveness: A Review of Empirical Findings", *OECD Environment Working Papers*, No. 87, OECD Publishing, Paris, *http://dx.doi.org/10.1787/5js37p21grzq-en*.

Botta, E. and T. Koźluk (2014), "Measuring Environmental Policy Stringency in OECD Countries: A Composite Index Approach", *OECD Economics Department Working Papers*, No. 1177, OECD Publishing, Paris, *http://dx.doi.org/10.1787/5jxrjnc45gvg-en*.

Flues, F. and B. Lutz (2015), "Competitiveness Impacts of the German Electricity Tax", *OECD Environment Working Papers*, No. 88, OECD Publishing, Paris, *http://dx.doi.org/10.1787/5js0752mkzmv-en*.

Harding, M. (2014), "The Diesel Differential: Differences in the Tax Treatment of Gasoline and Diesel for Road Use", *OECD Taxation Working Papers*, No. 21, OECD Publishing, Paris, *http://dx.doi.org/10.1787/5jz14cd7hk6b-en*.

Harding, M. (2014), "Personal Tax Treatment of Company Cars and Commuting Expenses: Estimating the Fiscal and Environmental Costs", *OECD Taxation Working Papers*, No. 20, OECD Publishing, Paris, *http://dx.doi.org/10.1787/5jz14cg1s7vl-en*.

OECD (n.d.), *Policy Instruments for the Environment* (database), webpage: *http://oe.cd/pine*.

OECD (n.d.), Environmental taxation, webpage: *http://oe.cd/env-taxes*.

OECD (n.d.), Producer and consumer support estimates, webpage: *www.oecd.org/agriculture/agricultural-policies/producerandconsumersupportestimatesdatabase.htm*.

OECD (n.d.), Environmental Policy Stringency index, webpage: *http://oe.cd/eps*.

Oueslati, W. et al. (2016), "Exploring the relationship between environmentally related taxes and inequality in income sources: An empirical cross-country analysis", *OECD Environment Working Papers*, No. 100, OECD Publishing, Paris, *http://dx.doi.org/10.1787/5jm3mbfzkrzp-en*.

Roy, R. (2014), "Environmental and Related Social Costs of the Tax Treatment of Company Cars and Commuting Expenses", *OECD Environment Working Papers*, No. 70, OECD Publishing, Paris, *http://dx.doi.org/10.1787/5jxwrr5163zp-en*.

Smith, S. and N. Braathen (2015), "Monetary Carbon Values in Policy Appraisal: An Overview of Current Practice and Key Issues", *OECD Environment Working Papers*, No. 92, OECD Publishing, Paris, *http://dx.doi.org/10.1787/5jrs8st3ngvh-en*.

ANNEX

The OECD set of green growth indicators

The list of indicators has been kept flexible so that countries can adapt it to their particular contexts. It also balances the desire to be exhaustive and the need for simplicity. Not all issues of importance to green growth can be measured in quantitative terms. Not all indicators proposed here are equally relevant to all countries.

The set, which has been reviewed by member countries, is neither exhaustive nor final. Indeed, it requires the context of other OECD indicators to acquire its full meaning. In that sense, the indicators specified are a starting point. The list may be modified as the discussion evolves and as new data become available.

The list of indicators includes main and proxy indicators. Each indicator is also accompanied by an evaluation of the measurability of the underlying data:

Type:
- M = **Main indicators** (numbered and in bold), and their components or supplements (numbered)
- P = **Proxy indicators** (bulleted) when the main indicators are not available

Measurability:
- S = **Short term**, basic data currently available for a majority of OECD countries;
- M = **Medium term**, basic data partially available, but calling for further efforts to improve their quality (consistency, comparability, timeliness) and their geographical coverage (number of countries covered);
- L = **Long term**, basic data not available for a majority of OECD countries, calling for a sustained data collection and conceptual efforts.

Group/Theme	Proposed indicators	Type	Measurability	Presented here
The socio-economic context and characteristics of growth				
Economic growth, productivity and competitiveness	**Economic growth and structure**			
	• GDP growth and structure	M	S	☑
	• Net disposable income (or net national income)	M	S/M	
	Productivity and trade			
	• Labour productivity	M	S	
	• Multi-factor productivity	M	M	☑
	• Trade weighted unit labour costs	M	M	
	• Relative importance of trade: (exports + imports)/GDP	M	S	☑ examples
	Inflation and commodity prices			
	• Consumer Price Index	M	S	☑
	• Prices of food; crude oil; minerals, ores and metals	M	S	☑ fuel prices
Labour market, education and income	**Labour markets**			
	• Labour force participation	M	S	
	• Unemployment rate	M	S	
	Socio-demographic patterns			
	• Population growth, structure and density	M	S	☑
	• Life expectancy: years of healthy life at birth	M	S/M	☑ DALYs
	• Income inequality: GINI coefficient	M	S/M	
	• Educational attainment: level of and access to education	M	S	

Group/Theme	Proposed indicators	Type	Measurability	Presented here
The environmental and resource productivity of the economy				
Carbon & energy productivity	**1. CO_2 productivity**			
	1.1. Production-based CO_2 productivity GDP per unit of energy-related CO_2 emitted	M	S	☑
	1.2. Demand-based CO_2 productivity Real income per unit of energy-related CO_2 embodied in final demand	M	S/M	☑
	2. Energy productivity			
	2.1. Energy productivity GDP per unit of TPES	M	S	☑
	2.2. Energy intensity by sector (manufacturing, transport, households, services)	M	S/M	–
	2.3. Share of renewable energy sources in TPES, in electricity production	M	S	☑
Resource productivity	**3. Material productivity (non-energy)**			
	3.1. Demand-based material productivity (comprehensive measure; original units in physical terms) Real income per unit of materials embodied in final demand, materials mix	M	M/L	–
	3.2. Production-based (domestic) material productivity GDP per unit of materials consumed, materials mix • Biotic materials (food, other biomass) • Abiotic materials (metallic minerals, industrial minerals)	P	S/M	☑
	3.3. Waste generation intensity and recovery ratios by sector, per unit of GDP or value added, per capita	M	M/L	☑ municipal waste
	3.4. Nutrient flows and balances (N, P)	M	L	–
	• Nutrient balances in agriculture (N, P) per agricultural land area and change in agricultural output	P	S/M	☑
	4. Water productivity Value added per unit of water consumed, by sector (for agriculture: irrigation water per hectare irrigated)	M	M	–
Multifactor productivity	**5. Environmentally adjusted multifactor productivity** (comprehensive measure; original units in monetary terms)	M	S/M	☑
The natural asset base				
Natural resource stocks	**6. Index of natural resources** Comprehensive measure expressed in monetary terms	M	M	–
Renewable stocks	**7. Freshwater resources** Available renewable natural resources (groundwater, surface water) and related abstraction rates (national, territorial)	M	S/M	☑
	8. Forest resources Area and volume of forests; stock changes over time	M	S/M	☑
	9. Fish resources Proportion of fish stocks within safe biological limits (global)	M	S	☑
Non-renewable stocks	**10. Mineral resources** Available (global) stocks or reserves of selected minerals: metallic minerals, industrial minerals, fossil fuels, critical raw materials; and related extraction rates	M	M	–
Biodiversity and ecosystems	**11. Land resources** Land cover conversions and cover changes from natural state to artificial state	M	M	☑ example
	• Land use: state and changes	P	S	–
	12. Soil resources: Degree of topsoil losses on agricultural land, on other land	M	M	–
	• Agricultural land area affected by water erosion, by class of erosion	P	S/M	–
	13. Wildlife resources (to be further refined)			
	• Trends in farmland or forest bird populations or in breeding bird populations	P	S/M	☑ example
	• Species threat status, in percentage of species assessed or known	P	S	☑
	• Trends in species abundance	P	S/M	☑

Group/Theme	Proposed indicators	Type	Measurability	Presented here
The environmental dimension of quality of life				
Environmental health and risks	**14. Environmentally induced health problems and related costs** (e.g. years of healthy life lost from degraded environmental conditions)	M	L	–
	• Population exposure to air pollution, and the related health risks and costs	P	S/M	☑
	15. Exposure to natural or industrial risks and related economic losses	M	L	–
Environmental services and amenities	**16. Access to sewage treatment and drinking water**	M	S	
	16.1. Population connected to sewage treatment (at least secondary, in relation to optimal connection rate)			☑
	16.2. Population with sustainable access to safe drinking water			☑
Economic opportunities and policy responses				
Technology and innovation	**17. Research and development expenditure of importance to green growth**	M	S/M	☑
	• Renewable energy sources (% of energy-related R&D)		S	
	• Environmental technology (% of total R&D, by type)		S	
	• All-purpose business R&D (% of total R&D)		S	
	18. Patents of importance to green growth (% of a country's patent families worldwide)	M	S	☑
	• Environment-related and total patents		S	
	• Structure of environment-related patents		S	
	19. Environment-related innovation in all sectors	M	M	–
Environmental goods and services	**20. Production of environmental goods and services (EGS)**	P	M	☑ example
	• Gross value added in the EGS sector (% of GDP)			
	• Employment in the EGS sector (% of total employment)			
	• To be complemented with: Environmentally related expenditure (level and structure)	P	M/L	–
International financial flows	**21. International financial flows of importance to green growth** % of total flows and % of GNI	M	L	
	21.1 Official development assistance		S	☑
	21.2 Carbon market financing		S	☑
	21.3 Foreign direct investment		M/L	–
Prices and transfers	**22. Environmentally related taxation and subsidies**	M	S	☑
	• Level of environmentally related tax revenue (% of GDP, % of total tax revenues; in relation to labour-related taxes)			
	• Structure of environmentally related taxes (by type of tax base)		S	☑
	• Level of environmentally related subsidies		S/M	☑
	23. Energy pricing (share of taxes in end-use prices)	M	S	☑
	24. Water pricing and cost recovery (tbd)	M	S/M	–
Regulations and management approaches	25. *Indicators to be developed*	..	..	
Training and skill development	26. *Indicators to be developed*	..	..	

Glossary

This Glossary includes additional information on the main variables and indicators used in this report. An overview by chapter is given below.

Progress towards green growth: an overview

Composition of value added
GDP per capita
Income inequality (Gini coefficient)

Part 1: The resource productivity of the economy

Carbon productivity

Demand-based CO_2 productivity
Production-based CO_2 productivity

Energy productivity

Energy consumption
Energy productivity
Energy supply
Renewable electricity generation
Renewable energy

Materials productivity and waste

Material consumption
Material extraction
Material productivity
Materials or material resources
Municipal waste
Waste composting
Waste recycling

Nutrient flows and balances

Fertiliser consumption
Nutrient balances

Environmentally adjusted multifactor productivity

Environmentally adjusted multifactor productivity (EAMFP)

Part 2: The natural asset base

Land resources

Land cover and land use
Land covered by built-up area

Forest resources

Forest available for wood supply
Forests under certified sustainable management
Growing stock in forest and other wooded land
Intensity of use of forest resources
Trade in forest products (exports)
Value added of forestry

Freshwater resources

Freshwater abstractions
Freshwater resources
Water stress

Biodiversity, ecosystems and wildlife resources

Aichi Targets
Cycads
Exclusive economic zone (EEZ)
Fish stocks within safe biological limits
Global wild bird index
Protected areas
Threatened species

Part 3: The environmental quality of life

Air pollution, health risks and costs

Air pollution by nitrogen dioxide
Air pollution by ozone
Air pollution by particulates

Access to water supply, sanitation and sewage treatment

Public access to sewage treatment services

Part 4: Economic opportunities and policy responses

Technology and innovation

Government R&D budgets
Patent indicators
Public RD&D budgets on energy

Markets for environmentally related products

Environmental goods and services sector (EGSS)

International financial flows

Clean Development Mechanism projects
Environmentally related official development assistance (ODA)
Green bonds
Investment in clean energy

Taxes and subsidies

Budgetary support and tax expenditure for fossil fuel use
Effective carbon rates
Environmentally related taxes
Labour taxes
Producer support in agriculture

Aichi Targets

[Chapter *Biodiversity, ecosystems and wildlife resources*]

In 2010, the Parties to the Convention on Biological Diversity (CBD) adopted a revised and updated Strategic Plan for Biodiversity, including the Aichi Biodiversity Targets, for the 2011-20 period (Nagoya, Aichi Prefecture, Japan). The 20 headline targets are grouped under five strategic goals: i) address the underlying causes of biodiversity loss by mainstreaming biodiversity across government and society; ii) reduce the direct pressures on biodiversity and promote sustainable use; iii) improve the status of biodiversity by safeguarding ecosystems, species and genetic diversity; iv) enhance the benefits to all from biodiversity and ecosystem services; and v) enhance implementation through participatory planning, knowledge management and capacity building. For more information see: *www.cbd.int/sp/targets/*.

Air pollution by nitrogen dioxide

[Chapter *Air pollution, health risks and costs*]

Nitrogen dioxide (NO_2) is one of a group of highly reactive gases known as oxides of nitrogen or nitrogen oxides (NO_x). Other gases belonging to this group are nitric oxide (NO), nitrogen monoxide (or nitrous oxide, N_2O), and nitrogen pentoxide (NO_5). NO_2 is used as the indicator for the larger group of nitrogen oxides. NO_2 is also the main source of nitrate aerosols, which form an important fraction of $PM_{2.5}$ and, in the presence of ultraviolet light, of ozone. NO_2 emissions primarily stem from the burning of fuel (motor vehicles, power plants, heating equipment, etc.). Breathing air with a high concentration of NO_2 can irritate airways in the human respiratory system. Exposures over short periods can aggravate respiratory diseases, particularly asthma, leading to respiratory symptoms (such as coughing, wheezing or difficulty breathing). Longer exposures to high concentrations of NO_2 may contribute to the development of asthma and potentially increase susceptibility to respiratory infections. People with asthma, as well as children and the elderly, are generally at greater risk. For further information see: WHO (2016), Ambient air quality and health factsheet: *www.who.int/mediacentre/factsheets/fs313/en/*; and USEPA (2016), NO_2 Pollution. *www.epa.gov/no2-pollution*.

Air pollution by ozone

[Chapter *Air pollution, health risks and costs*]

Ozone (O_3) at ground level – not to be confused with the ozone layer in the upper atmosphere – is one of the major constituents of photochemical smog. It is a secondary pollutant formed by the reaction with sunlight (photochemical reaction) of pollutants such as nitrogen oxides (NO_x) from motor vehicles, heating and industry, and volatile organic compounds (VOCs) from motor vehicles, solvents and industrial processes. The highest levels of ozone pollution thus occur during periods of sunny weather. Unlike other pollutants, concentrations of O_3 in rural areas tend to be higher than in urban areas. This is due to pollution transport by wind and to ozone degradation by NO_x from vehicle exhausts in urban traffic-heavy areas. Acute exposures (short-term exposure to high concentrations) are most relevant from a health impact perspective. Excessive ozone in the air can have a marked effect on human health. It can cause breathing problems, trigger asthma, reduce lung function and cause lung diseases. For further information see: WHO (2016), Ambient air quality and health factsheet: *www.who.int/mediacentre/factsheets/fs313/en/*.

Air pollution by particulates

[Chapter *Air pollution, health risks and costs*]

The major components of particulate matter (PM) are sulphate, nitrates, ammonia, sodium chloride, black carbon, mineral dust and water. PM consists of a complex mixture of solid and liquid particles of organic and inorganic substances suspended in the air. Small particulates are suspended particulates of less than 10 µm in diameter (PM_{10}) that can penetrate deep into the respiratory tract, causing significant health damage. Chronic exposure to small particulates contributes to the risk of developing cardiovascular and respiratory diseases, as well as lung cancer. Fine particulates, smaller than 2.5 microns in diameter ($PM_{2.5}$), cause even more severe health effects. First, they penetrate deeper into the respiratory tract. Second, they are potentially more toxic as they may include heavy metals and toxic organic substances. There is a close, quantitative relationship between exposure to high concentrations of particulates (PM_{10} and $PM_{2.5}$) and increased mortality or morbidity, both daily and over time.

The data presented in the report are estimates for chronic outdoor exposure to $PM_{2.5}$. Internationally comparable measures of average $PM_{2.5}$ concentrations are derived from satellite observations, chemical transport models and ground monitoring stations. These estimates include pollutants from both anthropogenic and natural sources. Population exposure to air pollution is calculated by weighting concentrations with populations in each cell of the underlying gridded data. Pollution concentrations in densely populated cities will thus carry a bigger weight than pollution in sparsely populated rural areas. This is important to help direct policy action to places where potential health impacts are highest.

There is a possibility of over-estimates or under-estimates in certain locations. While satellite observations are less precise than in-situ monitoring, the two data sources are complementary. They allow estimates of concentrations in locations not covered by ground monitoring networks; they also improve the comparability of estimates between different locations. Concentration estimates derived from satellite observations and modelling may however differ from the concentrations actually measured by national ground monitoring networks.

Budgetary support and tax expenditure for fossil fuel use

[Chapter *Taxes and subsidies*]

Information on fossil-fuel support is available from the OECD *Inventory of Support Measures for Fossil Fuels*. The OECD *Inventory* takes stock of the broad set of measures identified by governments that effectively support fossil-fuel use or production. These terms are defined using the PSE-CSE framework, which has already been used extensively to measure support to other activities, most notably agriculture. The scope of "support" is deliberately broad – broader than some conceptions of "subsidy". It covers a wide range of measures that provide a benefit or preference for a particular activity or product, either in absolute terms or relative to other activities or products. The total support estimate (TSE) includes both direct budgetary transfers and tax expenditures that provide a benefit or preference for fossil fuels relative to other alternatives. It encompasses Producer Support Estimates (PSE), Consumer Support Estimates (CSE), and the General Services Support Estimate (GSSE). Data are also presented by broad fuel category (petroleum, coal and natural gas). Data in the *Inventory* were sourced from official government documents and websites, complemented by information provided directly by government agencies. The charts presented are based on an arithmetic sum of the individual support measures identified for OECD countries, excluding Latvia and Iceland. They include the value of tax relief measured under each jurisdiction's benchmark tax treatment. The estimates do not consider interactions that might occur if multiple measures were to be removed at the same time.

Clean Development Mechanism projects

[Chapter *International financial flows*]

The Clean Development Mechanism (CDM) is one of the Flexible Mechanisms defined in the Kyoto Protocol (IPCC, 2007). It allows a country with an emission-reduction or emission-limitation commitment under the Kyoto Protocol (Annex B Party) to implement an emission-reduction project in developing countries. CDM projects can earn saleable certified emission reduction (CER) credits, which can be counted towards meeting Kyoto targets. The data on CDM projects refer to the total number of CDM-registered projects in the pipeline. Rejected projects are excluded, as are projects where validation has been terminated.

Composition of value added

[Chapter *Progress towards green growth: An overview*]

Value added in agriculture, industry and services are expressed as a percentage of total value added. Agriculture corresponds to ISIC Rev.3 divisions 1-5 and includes forestry, hunting as well as cultivation of crops and livestock production. Value added in industry corresponds to ISIC Rev.3 divisions 10-45 and includes value added in mining, manufacturing, construction, electricity, water, and gas. Value added in services corresponds to ISIC Rev.3 divisions 50-99 and includes value added in wholesale and retail trade (including hotels and restaurants), transport, and government, financial, professional, and personal services such as education, health care, real estate services as well as financial intermediation.

The data on value added come from the Aggregate National Accounts: Gross domestic product dataset of the *OECD National Accounts Statistics Database*, complemented with value added data from the World Bank's *World Development Indicators*.

Cycads

[Chapter *Biodiversity, ecosystems and wildlife resources*]

Cycads are palm-like seed plants of subtropical and tropical regions bearing large male or female cones. They grow very slowly and live very long. Cycads are the most ancient seed plants still living today, with fossils that date to the late Carboniferous period some 300-325 million years ago.

Demand-based CO_2 productivity

[Chapter *Carbon productivity*]

Demand-based CO_2 productivity is defined as the economic value, in terms of GDP (or real national income), generated per unit of CO_2 emitted to satisfy final demand. It is calculated as GDP per unit of demand-based CO_2 emissions (USD/kg). Demand-based emissions reflect the CO_2 from energy use emitted during the various stages of production of goods and services consumed in domestic final demand, irrespective of where the stages of production occurred. Trends in emissions on this basis thus complement the more conventional production-based measures. GDP is expressed at constant 2010 USD using PPPs.

The estimates of CO_2 emissions embodied in final domestic demand are obtained from the OECD dataset on Carbon Dioxide Embodied in International Trade, derived from the *OECD Input-Output Database*. The estimates are calculated for 61 countries (with an input-output table modelled for the "rest of the world") using IEA data on *CO_2 emissions from fuel combustion (2014)* and the *OECD Inter-Country Input-Output (ICIO) system (Edition 2015)*. Using information from both, emission-intensities of production are calculated for each industry in each country. These intensities are then combined with the Leontief inverse of the ICIO system to get emission multipliers for final demand. This can be used to allocate the flows of CO_2 emitted in producing a product; it does not matter how many intermediate processes and countries the product passes through before arriving to its final purchaser. For a more detailed description of the methodology, please consult: *http://oe.cd/io-co2*.

Effective carbon rates

[Chapter *Taxes and subsidies*]

Effective carbon rates are expressed in EUR per tonne of CO_2. They represent the price that applies to CO_2 emissions from energy use as a result of i) CO_2 taxes (i.e. based on the carbon content), ii) specific taxes on energy use (primarily excise taxes), typically set per unit of energy, which can be translated into effective tax rates on the carbon content of each form of energy and iii) the price of tradable emission permits, regardless of the permit allocation method, representing the opportunity cost of emitting an extra unit of CO_2.

The "carbon pricing gap" is presented as a synthetic indicator. It shows the extent to which effective carbon rates fall short of pricing emissions at EUR 30 per tonne of CO_2. Data for OECD and BRIICS are the averages weighted by the level of CO_2 emissions from the respective sector. The OECD total does not include Latvia, as the country became a member of the OECD after the calculations were carried out.

The indicators cover the road sector and non-road energy sectors. The road sector includes only energy used in road transport; non-road energy sectors include: i) Off-road transport (incl. pipelines, rail transport, domestic aviation, and maritime transport); ii) Industry: industrial processes, heating (inside industrial installations) and transformation of energy (incl. fuels used for auto-generation of electricity in industrial installations); iii) Agriculture & fisheries (incl. agriculture, fisheries and forestry); iv) Residential and commercial (incl. energy used for commercial and residential heating (incl. fuels used for auto-generation of electricity); v) Electricity (incl. energy used to generate electricity for domestic use, excluding fuels used in the auto-generation of electricity). For more details see *OECD (2016) Effective carbon rates: Pricing CO_2 through Taxes and Emissions Trading Systems*.

Energy consumption

[Chapter *Energy productivity*]

Energy consumption is expressed in tonnes of oil equivalent. Final consumption reflects for the most part deliveries to consumers. It excludes energy used for transformation processes and for own use of the energy-producing industries. Energy consumption is specified by sectors.

- Consumption in **agriculture** includes deliveries to users classified as agriculture, hunting and forestry by the International Standard Industrial Classification (ISIC).Therefore, it includes energy consumed by such users whether for traction (excluding agricultural highway use), power or heating (agricultural and domestic) [ISIC Rev.4 Divisions 01 and 02].

- Consumption in **services** includes both commercial and public services [ISIC Rev.4 Divisions 33, 36-39, 45-47, 52, 53, 55-56, 58-66, 68-75, 77-82, 84 (excluding Class 8422), 85-88, 90-96 and 99].
- Consumption in **transport** covers all transport activity (in mobile engines) regardless of the economic sector to which it is contributing [ISIC Rev.4 Divisions 49 to 51].
- Consumption in **Industry** includes the following sub-sectors: iron and steel, chemical and petrochemical, non-ferrous metals, non-metallic minerals, transport equipment, machinery, mining and quarrying, food and tobacco, paper, pulp and print, wood and wood products, construction, textile and leather together with any manufacturing industry not included above.
- Consumption in the category **other** includes residential consumption and all fuel use not elsewhere specified.

Energy productivity

[Chapter *Energy productivity*]

Energy productivity is defined as the economic output, in terms of GDP, generated per unit of primary energy used. It is calculated as GDP per unit of Total Primary Energy Supply (TPES) (USD/toe), the inverse of *energy intensity*. This indicator reflects, at least partly, efforts to reduce carbon and other atmospheric emissions as well as structural and climatic factors. GDP is expressed at constant 2010 USD using PPPs.

Energy supply

[Chapter *Energy productivity*]

Total primary energy supply (TPES) is expressed in tonnes of oil equivalent (toe). It comprises indigenous production + imports – exports – international marine bunkers – international aviation bunkers ± stock changes. Primary energy sources include fossil fuels (coal, oil shale, peat and peat products, oil and natural gas), biofuels and waste, nuclear, hydro, geothermal, solar and the heat from heat pumps that is extracted from the ambient environment.

Environmental goods and services sector (EGSS)

[Chapter *Markets for environmentally related products*]

The Environmental goods and services sector is defined as comprising activities to measure, control, restore, prevent, treat, minimise, research and sensitise regarding environmental damage to air, water and soil, resource depletion and problems related to waste, noise, biodiversity and landscapes. The definition includes cleaner and resource-efficient technologies, goods and services, which prevent or minimise pollution, and minimise natural resource use. The scope of the EGS sector is defined according to the classification of environmental protection activities (CEPA) and the classification of resource management activities (CReMA).

The methodological reference is the 2009 Eurostat handbook that has been integrated in the Central Framework of the SEEA, and that builds on earlier work carried out jointly by the OECD and Eurostat (OECD and Eurostat, 1999). The handbook provides guidance to statistical offices in the collection of data on turnover, value added, employment and exports of the EGS sector.

Despite existing definitions and guidelines, setting the boundaries of the EGS sector remains a difficult task, as does its measurement and interpretation. The definition above is essentially a product-based definition. It brings together enterprises producing goods or technologies whose main purpose is environmental. Identifying the main purpose of a technology or product is often difficult so some arbitrariness cannot be avoided. The EGS sector is highly diverse and includes both government and corporate producers. A given production unit may find some of its activities meeting the definition, but not all.

Data on the EGS sector in the European Union result from a data collection by Eurostat and include estimates. They do not cover all resource management activities. For example, the management of forest resources and of wildlife, as well as R&D for resource management are not included. The employment in environmental protection and resource management activities is measured by the full-time equivalent (FTE) jobs engaged in the production of the environmental output. It is defined as total hours worked divided by average annual hours worked in full-time jobs.

Environmentally adjusted multifactor productivity (EAMFP)

[Chapter *Environmentally adjusted multifactor productivity*]

Environmentally adjusted multifactor productivity (EAMFP) is measured using a *growth accounting* framework that includes labour, produced capital and natural capital as factor inputs, and pollution as undesirable by-product. Growth accounting allows decomposing output growth (here GDP growth adjusted for pollution abatement) into the growth contribution of labour, produced capital and natural capital. *EAMFP growth* is then calculated as a residual.

The *growth contributions of inputs* are calculated as the elasticity-weighted growth rates of individual factor inputs. Labour, produced capital and natural capital are all traded in markets. Therefore, under a profit maximisation approach, the elasticities can be calculated from their cost shares in the economy. The *growth contribution of natural capital* is calculated using the cost share of natural capital weighted by the growth rate of natural capital extraction. The cost share of natural capital is calculated using the unit rent (i.e. market price of natural capital minus extractions costs).

The *elasticities of GDP* with respect to pollution are estimated econometrically because pollution does not have an explicit economy-wide price. The *growth adjustment for pollution abatement* is calculated using the estimated elasticities and the growth rate of pollution emissions.

In growth accounting, inputs and outputs are evaluated from the producers' perspective. Thus, this framework makes no account of environmental damages and the social costs of pollution.

In this report, the coverage of environmental services in terms of pollution and natural capital inputs remains partial. It is limited to eight greenhouse gases and air pollutants (CO_2, CH_4, N_2O, NMVOC, SO_x, NO_x, CO, PM_{10}) and 14 types of subsoil assets (hard coal, soft coal, gas, oil, bauxite, copper, gold, iron ore, lead, nickel, phosphate, silver, tin and zinc). Data on produced capital, labour and GDP are taken from the *OECD Productivity Database* complemented with the *Conference Board Total Economy Database*. Data on natural capital are obtained from the *OECD Natural Asset Accounts* and the *World Bank Wealth Accounting and the Valuation of Ecosystem Services (WAVES)* database. Data on air pollutant emisions are taken from the *OECD Air Emission Accounts, OECD Air Emissions by Source, OECD Greenhouse Gas*

Emissions by Source and the *Emissions Database for Global Atmospheric Research (EDGAR)*. Pending better data availability, future work will seek to expand the country coverage and the range of environmental services included. For more details on the underlying methodology, see Cárdenas Rodríguez et al. (2016).

Environmentally related official development assistance (ODA)

[Chapter *International financial flows*]

The OECD Development Assistance Committee (OECD-DAC) has established a comprehensive system for measuring aid targeting the objectives of the Rio conventions, environment and renewable energy. The data on private flows at market terms, such as bank lending and direct investment, are subject to confidentiality restrictions at the level of individual transactions.

Official development assistance (ODA) by sector refers to annual average disbursements as a share of total sector-allocable aid. The *environment protection sector* refers to general environmental protection activities. These comprise environmental policy and administrative management, biosphere protection, biodiversity, site preservation, flood prevention/control, environmental education/training and environmental research. In addition, an activity can target environment as a "principal objective" – if it is an explicit objective of the activity and fundamental in its design. It can target environment as a "significant objective" if it is an important, but secondary objective of the activity. The *water and sanitation sector* refers to water sector policy and administrative management, water resource conservation, water supply and sanitation, basic drinking water supply and basic sanitation, river basin development, waste management/disposal, education and training in water supply and sanitation. *Renewable energy resources* include power generation from renewable sources: hydroelectric power plants, geothermal energy, solar energy, wind power, ocean power and biomass. Non-renewable energy resources include power generation from: coal, oil, natural gas, and non-renewable waste.

Environmentally related ODA refers to annual commitments. It is expressed as a percentage of total ODA. Environmentally related ODA is identified using all relevant markers in the reporting system (i.e. the "Environment" marker and the set of "Rio Markers"). This variable includes only data on bilateral commitments. It is calculated by aggregating up from the level of individual projects in order to avoid double-counting.

- ODA commitments identified using the "***Environment***" marker (activities that target environment as a principal or significant objective) include activities intended to improve the physical and/or biological environment of the recipient country, area or target group concerned. They also include specific action to integrate environmental concerns with a range of development objectives through institution building and/or capacity development. The "Environment" marker was introduced in 1992.
- ***ODA targeting the objectives of the Rio conventions*** is identified using "Rio Markers" (activities that target the Rio objectives as a principal or significant objective). The Rio markers screen for policy objectives of a cross-sectoral nature, including climate change, biodiversity and desertification. Data cover OECD-DAC members and refer to commitments expressed in constant 2010 USD, averaged over two years.
  1. ***Biodiversity-related aid*** is defined as activities that promote conservation of biodiversity, sustainable use of its components, or fair and equitable sharing of the benefits of the use of genetic resources.

2. ***Desertification-related aid*** is defined as activities that tackle desertification or mitigate the effects of drought.
3. ***Climate change mitigation-related aid*** is defined as activities that strengthen the resilience of countries to climate change and that contribute to stabilisation of greenhouse gas (GHG) concentrations by promoting reduction of emissions or enhancement of GHG sequestration.
4. ***Climate change adaptation-related aid*** is identified using a marker, on which reporting started only in 2010. It is defined as aid in support of climate change adaptation, it complements the climate change mitigation marker. It thus allows presentation of a more complete picture of aid in support of developing countries' efforts to address climate change.

Net ODA is expressed as a percentage of gross national income (GNI). Net ODA consists of disbursements of loans made on concessional terms (net of repayments of principal) and grants by official agencies of the members of the DAC, and by non-DAC countries. These loans or grants promote economic development and welfare in countries and territories in the DAC list of ODA recipients. Net ODA includes loans with a grant element of at least 25% (calculated at a rate of discount of 10%). A long-standing ODA target is that developed countries should devote 0.7% of their GNI to ODA.

Environmentally related taxes

[Chapter *Taxes and subsidies*]

Environmentally related taxes include taxes on i) energy products for transport purposes (petrol and diesel) and for stationary purposes (fossil fuels and electricity); ii) motor vehicles and transport (one-off import or sales taxes, recurrent taxes on registration or road use and other transport taxes); iii) other environmentally related taxes, e.g. in relation to waste management (final disposal, packaging and other waste-related product taxes), ozone-depleting substances, measured emissions to air or water, fishing and hunting taxes, and other taxes non-allocated elsewhere. Revenues from auctioning of emission allowances (e.g. from the EU Emissions Trading System) are also part of the "energy tax revenues". Environmentally related tax revenue is expressed as a percentage of total tax revenue, and compared to GDP. The structure of the tax base is given as a complement.

Road fuel taxes and prices are expressed in constant 2010 USD using PPPs and deflated using the Consumer Price Index. Information is available from the *IEA Energy Prices and Taxes Statistics (database)*. Petrol taxes and prices are calculated as the arithmetic average of the unleaded premium 95, unleaded premium 98, and unleaded regular petrol.

Exclusive economic zone (EEZ)

[Chapter *Biodiversity, ecosystems and wildlife resources*]

The perimeters of the exclusive economic zone (EEZ) of a country are defined in the 1982 UN Convention of the Law of the Sea. The EEZ extends 200 nautical miles from the coastline, or to the mid-point between coastlines where the EEZ of different countries would otherwise overlap. There are some exceptions to these rules.

Fertiliser consumption

[Chapter *Nutrient flows and balances*]

Fertilisers are any solid, liquid or gaseous substances containing one or more plant nutrients (such as Nitrogen (N), Phosphorus (P) and Potassium (K), but also Calcium (Ca), Sulphur (S) and Magnesium (Mg)). They comprise inorganic or mineral fertilisers (also called commercial fertilisers, produced by the fertiliser industry) and organic fertilisers such as manure or compost.

Mineral fertilisers, which made their appearance with the industrial revolution, had an important role in sustaining the growing population. Half of the world population is estimated to be fed with crops grown using synthetic fertilisers. Fertilisers can have a negative impact on the environment, leading to eutrophication and pollution of water and soil (e.g. heavy metals, soil acidification and persistent organic pollutants). Also, the production of nitrogenous fertilisers is energy intensive and mineable phosphorus reserves are finite (FAO, 2016).

Fish stocks within safe biological limits

[Chapter *Biodiversity, ecosystems and wildlife resources*]

Fish stocks within safe biological limits represent the proportion of stocks exploited within their level of maximum biological productivity, i.e. stocks that are underexploited, moderately exploited or fully exploited. Safe biological limits are the precautionary thresholds advocated by the International Council for the Exploration of the Sea. The stocks assessed are classified on the basis of various phases of fishery development: underexploited, moderately exploited, fully exploited, overexploited, depleted and recovering. It is still not possible to determine the status of a large number of stocks. More needs to be done to better evaluate the status of fish stocks and to relate it to captures.

Forest available for wood supply

[Chapter *Forest resources*]

This refers to forests where there are no environmental, social or economic restrictions that could have a significant impact on the current or potential supply of wood. These restrictions could be based on legal acts, managerial owners' decisions or other reasons.

Forests under certified sustainable management

[Chapter *Forest resources*]

This refers to forests under independently verified forest management certification. They include forest areas certified under the Forest Stewardship Council (FSC) certification and the Programme for the Endorsement of Forest Certification (PEFC) schemes. They also include forest areas certified under an international forest management certification scheme with published standards and independently verified by a third-party, excluding FSC and PEFC certification.

Freshwater abstractions

[Chapter *Freshwater resources*]

Freshwater abstractions refer to water removed from any freshwater resource, either permanently or temporarily. Mine water and drainage water are included. Water used for hydroelectricity generation is an in-situ use and not included. Water abstractions from precipitation (e.g. rain water collected for use) should be included, but rarely covered in national statistics. For some countries, the data refer to water permits and not to actual abstractions.

Freshwater resources

[Chapter *Freshwater resources*]

Freshwater resources refer to total renewable freshwater resources, i.e. internal flow plus actual external inflow. The internal flow is equal to precipitation less actual evapotranspiration. It represents the total volume of river run-off and groundwater generated, in natural conditions, exclusively by precipitation into a territory. The external inflow is the total volume of the flow of rivers and groundwater coming from neighbouring territories. The data used represent long-term annual averages.

GDP per capita

[Chapter *Progress towards green growth: an overview*]

The Gross Domestic Product per capita (USD/person) is expressed at constant 2010 USD using PPPs. GDP per capita measures a country's economic wealth of the population of a nation. However, as a mean value it does not reflect income distribution. Moreover, it is a "gross" measure of income and no account is taken neither of the depreciation of produced assets nor of the depletion of natural assets. For sources of GDP and population data see the *Reader's Guide*.

Global wild bird index

[Chapter *Biodiversity, ecosystems and wildlife resources*]

Birds are seen as a good indicator of the integrity of ecosystems and biological diversity. Being close to or at the top of the food chain, they reflect changes in ecosystems more rapidly than other species.

The global Wild Bird Index (WBI) is an average trend in a group of species suited to track trends in habitat conditions. A decrease in the WBI means the balance of species' population trends is negative, representing biodiversity loss. If it is constant, there is no overall change. An increase means the balance of species' trends is positive, implying that biodiversity loss has halted. However, an increase may not always indicate an improving environmental situation. In extreme cases, an increase could result from expansion of some species at the cost of others, or reflect habitat degradation. In all cases, detailed analysis must be conducted to interpret the trends accurately. The composite can hide important trends for individual species. Farmland bird population indices are available only for OECD Europe, Canada and the United States. The Biodiversity Indicators Partnership is working to develop the global WBI, building on national data. In general, more accurate and comparable time-series data on wildlife populations still need to be developed.

Government R&D budgets

[Chapter *Technology and innovation*]

The data refer to government budget appropriations or outlays for R&D (GBAORD) that measure the funds that governments allocate to R&D to meet various socio-economic objectives. These are defined on the basis of the primary purpose of the funder. They include control and care for the environment, as well as energy. The selection is based on the socio-economic objectives "energy" and "environment" in the NABS 2007 classification

(Nomenclature for the Analysis and Comparison of Scientific Budgets and Programmes). Additional information on the methodology for internationally harmonised collection and use of R&D statistics can be found in the Frascati Manual.

R&D budgets for control and care for the environment include research on the control of pollution and on developing monitoring facilities to measure, eliminate and prevent pollution. Energy R&D budgets include research on the production, storage, transport, distribution and rational use of all forms of energy. However, they exclude research on prospecting and on vehicle and engine propulsion.

Green bonds

[Chapter *International financial flows*]

Green-labelled bonds are fixed-income financial instruments with proceeds earmarked for projects and assets that deliver environmental benefits. These bonds are labelled as such by the issuer and are therefore easier for investors to identify. Like normal bonds, green-labelled bonds can be issued by governments, multi-national banks or corporations, or supranational entities (i.e. a financing agency backed by multiple governments). The issuing entity guarantees to repay the bond over a certain period of time, plus either a fixed or variable rate of return. It is best practice for bonds to be reviewed or certified by a second or third party. For more information, see *www.climatebonds.net/*.

Growing stock in forest and other wooded land

[Chapter *Forest resources*]

Growing stock is defined as the volume over bark of living trees with more than X cm in diameter breast height (d.b.h. – typically at 130 cm above stump) (or above buttresses if these are higher). Includes stem from ground level or stump height up to a top diameter of Y cm. It may also include branches to a minimum diameter of W cm. The diameters used may vary by country; generally the data refer to d.b.h. of more than 10 cm.

Income inequality (Gini coefficient)

[Chapter *Progress towards green growth: An overview*]

Income inequality among individuals is measured by the Gini coefficient. The Gini coefficient is based on the comparison of cumulative proportions of the population against cumulative proportions of income they receive. It ranges between 0 in the case of perfect equality and 1 in the case of perfect inequality. Income is defined as household disposable income in a particular year. It consists of earnings, self-employment and capital income and public cash transfers; income taxes and social security contributions paid by households are deducted. The income of the household is attributed to each of its members, with an adjustment to reflect differences in needs for households of different sizes.

The source for data on the Gini coefficient is the *Standardized World Income Inequality Database* (SWIID). The SWIID provides comparable Gini indices of net income with the largest geographical and temporal coverage currently available.

Intensity of use of forest resources

[Chapter *Forest resources*]

Intensity of use of forest resources is defined as the ratio of actual fellings to annual productive capacity (i.e. gross increment). Fellings refer to the average annual standing volume of all trees, living or dead, measured over bark to a minimum diameter breast height (d.b.h.) of 0 cm that are felled during the given reference period. This includes the volume of trees or part of trees that are not removed from the forest, other wooded land or other felling site. Gross increment refers to the average annual volume of increment over the reference period of all trees, measured to a minimum d.b.h. of 0 cm.

Investment in clean energy

[Chapter *International financial flows*]

Bloomberg New Energy Finance (*www.bnef.com*) maintains a global database on new financial investment in clean energy, including investors, projects and transactions. These range from R&D funding and venture capital for technology and early-stage companies through to asset finance of utility-scale generation projects.

Investment categories are defined as follows. *Venture capital and private equity* (VC/PE) relates to all money invested by venture capital and private equity funds in the equity of specialist companies developing renewable energy technology. Similar investment in companies setting up generating capacity through special purpose vehicles is counted in the asset financing figure. *Public markets* relate to all money invested in the equity of specialist publicly quoted companies developing renewable energy technology and clean power generation. Investment in companies setting up generating capacity is included in the asset financing figure. *Asset finance* relates to all money invested in renewable energy generation projects (excluding large hydro), whether from internal company balance sheets, from loans, or from equity capital. This excludes refinancing. *Mergers and acquisitions* (M&A) relate to the value of existing equity and debt purchased by new corporate buyers, in companies developing renewable energy technology or operating renewable power and fuel projects.

The types of renewable projects included are all biomass, geothermal and wind generation projects of more than 1MW, all hydropower projects between 0.5 and 50 MW, all solar projects with those less than 1MW estimated separately, all marine (wave and tidal) energy projects and all biofuel projects with an annual capacity of at least 1 million litres.

Labour taxes

[Chapter *Taxes and subsidies*]

Labour tax revenues include total (i.e. supranational + federal/central government + state/regional + local government) revenue from taxes on several categories. First, there are income, profits and capital gains of individuals. Second, there are social security contributions. This would include, for example, taxes on employees, employers, self-employed or non-employed, and other social security contributions that could not be allocated among these fields. Finally, it includes taxes on payroll and workforce.

Land cover and land use

[Chapter Land resources]

"Land cover" refers to the physical surface characteristics of land, such as the type of vegetation or the presence of artificial structures. "Land use" describes the economic and social functions of land to meet demands for food, fibre, shelter, and natural resources. The two concepts are distinct but linked. A land cover like grassland may support many land uses, including livestock production and recreation. Conversely, a single use, e.g. mixed farming, may take in a number of different cover types. These could include grassland, cropped, fallow and artificial land (barns, greenhouses etc.).

Land covered by built-up area

[Chapter *Land resources*]

The term "built-up area" used in this report only refers to the physical *presence of buildings*. It does not include other forms of infrastructure and development such as paved surfaces (roads, parking lots), commercial and industrial sites (ports, landfills) and urban green spaces (parks, gardens). It is therefore not comparable to other definitions of "built-up area" in use.

Material consumption

[Chapter *Materials productivity and waste*]

Domestic material consumption (DMC) measures the amount of materials used in an economy (i.e. the apparent consumption of materials). It is calculated as the domestic extraction used (DEU) minus exports plus imports, and expressed in terms of weight.

Material extraction

[Chapter *Materials productivity and waste*]

Domestic extraction used (DEU) measures the flows of materials that originate from the environment and that physically enter the economic system for further processing or direct consumption (they are "used" by the economy). They are converted into or incorporated in products in one way or another, and are usually of economic value.

Material productivity

Material productivity is defined as the economic output, in terms of GDP, generated per unit of materials used (in terms of DMC). It is calculated as GDP per unit of DMC (USD/kg). In this report material productivity is calculated for non-energy materials only (biomass, metals, non-metallic minerals). GDP is expressed at 2010 prices and PPPs.

Materials or material resources

[Chapter *Materials productivity and waste*]

The term "materials" or "material resources" designates the usable materials or substances (raw materials, energy) produced from natural resources and the products derived therefrom. These usable "materials" include energy carriers (gas, oil, coal), metallic minerals (metal ores and metals), non-metallic minerals (construction minerals, industrial minerals), and biomass (biomass for food and feed, wood). Most indicators presented in this report cover non-energy materials only.

Municipal waste

[Chapter *Materials productivity and waste*]

Municipal waste is waste collected by or on behalf of municipalities. It includes household waste originating from households (i.e. waste generated by the domestic activity of households). It also comprises similar waste from small commercial activities, office buildings and institutions such as schools and government buildings, and small businesses that treat or dispose of waste at the same facilities used for municipally collected waste.

Nutrient balances

[Chapter *Nutrient flows and balances*]

The gross nutrient balances (N and P) are calculated as the difference between the total quantity of nutrient inputs entering an agricultural system (mainly fertilisers, livestock manure), and the quantity of nutrient outputs leaving the system (mainly uptake of nutrients by crops and grassland). Gross nutrient balances are expressed in tonnes of nutrient surplus (when positive) or deficit (when negative). This calculation can be used as a proxy to reveal the status of environmental pressures, such as declining soil fertility in the case of a nutrient deficit, or the risk of polluting soil, water and air in the case of a nutrient surplus.

Main elements in the gross nitrogen balance calculation

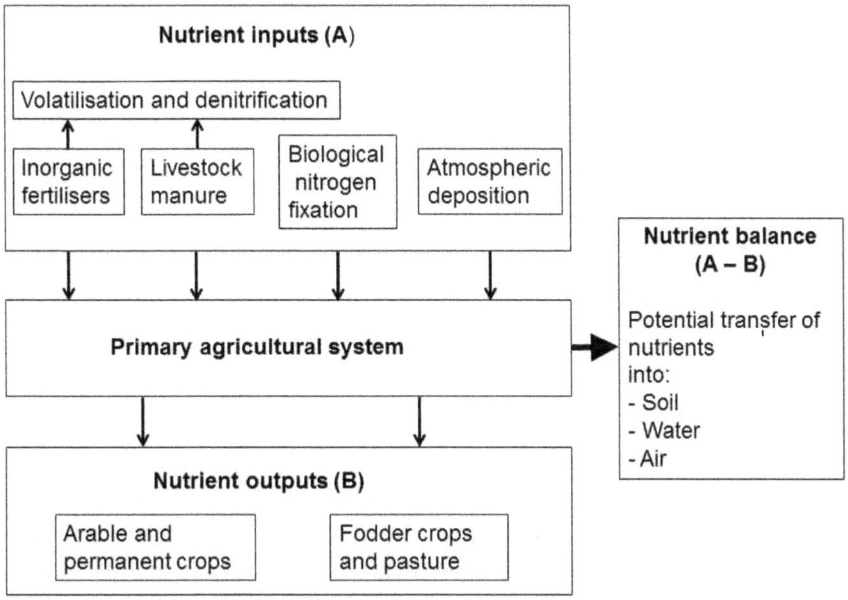

Note: Nutrients surplus to crop/pasture requirements are transported into the environment, potentially polluting soils, water and air. However, a deficit of nutrients in soils can also occur to the detriment of soil fertility and crop productivity.
Source: OECD/Eurostat (2012), *Nitrogen and Phosphorus Balance Handbook*, *www.oecd.org/tad/sustainable-agriculture/agrienvironmentalindicators.htm*

Patent indicators

[Chapter *Technology and innovation*]

The patent indicators presented in this report are based on data extracted from the *Worldwide Patent Statistical Database* (PATSTAT) of the European Patent Office (EPO) using algorithms developed by the OECD (Haščič and Migotto, 2015). Only published applications for "patents of invention" are considered (i.e. they exclude utility models, petty patents, etc.). The relevant patent documents are identified using search strategies for environment-related technologies (ENV-TECH). These strategies developed specifically for this purpose, largely draw upon the expertise of patent examiners at the European Patent Office. The ENV-TECH includes a broad range of technologies relevant to environmental management, water-related adaptation and climate change mitigation.

Patent indicator on technology development

This indicator represents the number of inventions (simple patent families) developed by a country's inventors. It is independent of the jurisdictions where a patent application has been registered (i.e. all known patent families worldwide are considered). The indicator is disaggregated by:

a) *inventor country* – fractional counts by country of residence of the inventor(s);

b) *priority date* – the first filing date worldwide, under the Paris Convention. The priority date is considered to be closest to the actual date of invention;

c) family size – the size of an international patent family (including the first "priority" filing and its equivalents deposited at other patent offices). The family size has been found to be correlated with the value of the invention. Family size "1 and greater" (i.e. all patent priorities) will yield figures based on all available data worldwide, including many low-value inventions; family size "2 and greater" (i.e. "claimed" priorities), used here, will count only the higher-value inventions that have sought patent protection in at least two jurisdictions; etc.;

d) technology domain.

Patent indicator on technology diffusion

This indicator refers to the number of inventions for which a patent application has been registered in a given jurisdiction through national, regional or international routes (equivalents of the priority patent application, pertaining to the same "simple patent family"). It shows the extent to which firms and individuals seek to "protect" their inventions in the relevant markets (including both domestic and foreign inventions). The indicator is disaggregated by:

a) patent office;

b) application date (date of filing);

c) coverage – which allows displaying statistics based on all available data ("full dataset, with no restriction on coverage") or only for offices with data availability above a certain threshold (90%) in a given year ("conservative coverage", used here); is estimated as the proportion of months in a year with the evidence of at least one patent document deposited at the patent office;

d) technology domain.

Producer support in agriculture

[Chapter *Taxes and subsidies*]

Producer support in agricultural is defined as the annual monetary value of gross transfers to agriculture from consumers and taxpayers. These arise from governments' policies that support agriculture, regardless of their objectives and their economic impacts. The Producer Support Estimate (PSE) represents policy transfers to agricultural producers, measured at the farm gate and expressed as a share of gross farm receipts. The Total Support Estimate (TSE) consists of transfers to agricultural producers (measured by the PSE), consumers (measured by the CSE) and support to general services to the agricultural sector (measured by the General Services Support Estimate [GSSE]). Transfers included in the PSE are composed of market price support, budgetary payments and the cost of revenue foregone by the government and other economic agents. Support estimates are expressed as percentages of TSE and as percentage of total tax revenue.

Government support refers to payments made to farmers to manage the supply of agricultural commodities, influence their cost, supplement producers' income and achieve other social and environmental aims. This support to farmers, estimated in terms of the

OECD PSE, can be ranked according to its potential impacts on the environment. The potentially *most* harmful support to farmers comprises: i) market price support, ii) payments based on commodity output, without imposing environmental constraints on farming practices, and iii) payments based on variable input use, without imposing environmental constraints on farming practices.

The potentially *least* harmful support to farmers comprises the payments based on non-commodity criteria and payments for input use linked to constraints on resource use. They are generally beneficial because they are usually designed to help reduce agricultural pressures on the environment. However, neither the total PSE nor its composition in terms of policy categories, indicate the actual impact of policy on production and markets. The actual impacts (*ex post*) will depend on the many factors that determine the aggregate degree of responsiveness of farmers to policy changes – including any constraints on production. For further information, see the OECD *Producer Support Estimates* webpage.

Production-based CO_2 productivity

[Chapter *Carbon productivity*]

Production-based CO_2 productivity is defined as the economic output, in terms of GDP, generated per unit of CO_2 emitted. It is calculated as GDP per unit of production-based CO_2 emissions (USD/kg). Included are CO_2 emissions from combustion of coal, oil, natural gas and other fuels. The estimates of CO_2 emissions are from the International Energy Agency's database of *CO_2 Emissions from Fuel Combustion*. Emissions were calculated using IEA energy databases and the default methods and emission factors given in the *2006 IPCC Guidelines for National Greenhouse Gas Inventories*. GDP is expressed at constant 2010 USD using purchasing power parities (PPPs).

Protected areas

[Chapter *Biodiversity, ecosystems and wildlife resources*]

The protected area indicators presented here are constructed using data extracted from the *World Database on Protected Areas (WDPA)* maintained by the International Union for Conservation of Nature (IUCN) and UN Environment Programme's World Conservation Monitoring Centre (WCMC). A protected area is defined by the IUCN as a clearly defined geographical space, recognised, dedicated and managed, through legal or other effective means, to achieve the long term conservation of nature with associated ecosystem services and cultural values.

IUCN classifications reflect different management objectives. Categories Ia, Ib and II are strict nature reserves, wilderness areas and national parks; categories III and IV include natural monuments and habitat/species management areas; and categories V and VI are predominantly landscape-level designations aimed at preserving traditional human-environment interactions. A number of protected areas have no IUCN categories recorded in the WDPA; these include some nationally designated areas and all regionally and internationally designated areas. Where protected areas overlap, the overlapped area is assigned to the overlapping category that comes first in the following order of precedence: Ia, Ib, II, III, IV, V, VI, no category. Overseas territories are not included. UNESCO Man and Biosphere Reserves are not included, because they may not meet the standard definition of protected areas used by WCMC to calculate protected area coverage. Protected area definitions, although harmonised by the WCMC, may vary among countries. The data do not provide any indication of whether protected areas are effectively managed, ecologically representative, or well-connected and integrated into the wider landscape or seascape.

The WDPA dataset is not necessarily a complete representation of all the conservation areas, which have been designated in a country; the quality of the WDPA depends on the accessibility of accurate, comprehensive, up-to-date conservation areas information from data holders. Mismatches between on the ground conservation areas and conservation areas in the WDPA may be due among others to: new data being quality checked to fit the WDPA standards, data not submitted to the WDPA yet, new conservation area boundaries not being accurately digitised or simply not yet being digitised. Details are described in UNEP-WCMC (2015). World Database on Protected Areas User Manual 1.0, UNEP-WCMC, Cambridge, UK.

Public access to sewage treatment services

[Chapter *Access to water supply, sanitation and sewage treatment*]

Public access to sewage treatment services shows the percentage of the national resident population that is actually connected to a public wastewater treatment plant. It does not take into account independent private treatment facilities (e.g. septic tanks) used where public systems are not economic. Wastewater treatment is the process to render wastewater fit to meet applicable environmental standards or other quality norms for recycling or reuse, or discharge to the environment. Three broad types of treatment are distinguished: primary, secondary and tertiary.

- **Primary** treatment of wastewater by a physical and/or chemical process involving settlement of suspended solids, or other process. The biological oxygen demand (BOD) of the incoming wastewater is reduced by at least 20% before discharge. Total suspended solids of the incoming wastewater are reduced by at least 50%.
- **Secondary** treatment of wastewater by a process generally involving biological treatment with a secondary settlement or other process. It results in a BOD removal of at least 70% and a chemical oxygen demand (COD) removal of at least 75%.
- **Tertiary** treatment (additional to secondary treatment) of nitrogen and/or phosphorous and/or any other pollutant affecting the quality or a specific use of water (microbiological pollution, colour, etc.). The following minimum treatment efficiencies define a tertiary treatment: organic pollution removal of at least 95% for BOD and 85% for COD, and at least one of the following: i) nitrogen removal of at least 70%; ii) phosphorus removal of at least 80%; iii) microbiological removal achieving a faecal coliform density less than 1 000 in 100 ml.

The optimal connection rate is not necessarily 100%. It may vary among countries and depends on geographical features and on the spatial distribution of habitats.

Public RD&D budgets on energy

[Chapter *Technology and innovation*]

The data are obtained from the *IEA Energy Technology RD&D Statistics Database*.

Public RD&D on energy refers to the budgets of public entities (government, public agencies and state-owned enterprises, as defined by the IEA) covering research, development and demonstration (RD&D) programmes that focus on the sourcing, storage, transportation, distribution and rational use of all forms of energy. This covers basic research (oriented towards the development of energy-related technologies), applied research, experimental development and demonstration. Deployment is excluded. Estimates of RD&D are reported from the funder perspective as budget (rather than from the performer perspective as expenditure). As collected by the IEA, RD&D programmes concern energy efficiency, fossil fuels (oil, gas and coal), renewables, nuclear fission and fusion, hydrogen and fuel cells, other power and storage techniques, and other cross-cutting technologies or research.

RD&D budgets for **renewable energy** cover hydro, geothermal, solar (thermal and PV), wind and tide/wave/ocean energy, as well as combustible renewables (solid biomass, liquid biomass, biogas) and other renewable energy technologies (all supporting measuring, monitoring and verifying technologies in renewable energies).

RD&D budgets for **fossil fuel energy** cover oil, gas and coal. They exclude all research, development and demonstration related to CO_2 capture and storage (CCS). They are expressed as a percentage of the total energy RD&D public budget (directed at all forms of energy).

Renewable electricity generation

[Chapter *Energy productivity*]

Renewable electricity is calculated as the output of electricity produced from renewable energy sources divided by total output of electricity, expressed as a ratio. Renewables include hydro, geothermal, solar (thermal and PV), wind and tide/wave/ocean energy, as well as combustible renewables (solid biomass, liquid biomass, biogas) and renewable municipal waste.

Renewable energy

[Chapter *Energy productivity*]

Renewable energy is defined by the International Energy Agency (IEA) as energy that is derived from natural processes that are replenished constantly. The definition includes energy generated from solar (photovoltaic, thermal), wind, geothermal, hydropower (large, medium and small) and ocean resources (tide, wave), biofuels (solid, liquid), biogases, and renewable municipal waste. Under the IEA methodology, industrial waste and non-renewable municipal waste are excluded from the definition of renewable energy sources, as are waste heat, net heat generated by heat pumps, and electricity generated with hydro pumped storage.

Threatened species

[Chapter *Biodiversity, ecosystems and wildlife resources*]

Threatened species refer to critically endangered, endangered and vulnerable species, i.e. those plants and animals in danger of extinction or soon likely to be. See the International Union for Conservation of Nature (IUCN) *Red List Categories and Criteria: Version 3.1 Second Edition* for further information. The indicator presented focuses on amphibians. Other major groups (e.g. mammals, birds, fish, reptiles, invertebrates, vascular plants and fungi) are not covered here. Data on threatened species are available for all OECD countries with varying degrees of completeness. The number of species known or assessed does not always accurately reflect the number of species in existence. Countries apply the IUCN standard definitions with varying degrees of rigour. Historical data are generally not comparable or are not available.

Trade in forest products (exports)

[Chapter *Forest resources*]

Exports of forest products refer to products of domestic origin or manufacture shipped out of the country. The category includes exports from free economic zones and re-exports. It excludes "in-transit" shipments. Values are recorded as free-on-board (i.e. FOB).

Value added of forestry

[Chapter *Forest resources*]

This indicator refers to the value added of forestry and logging (activity 02 in ISIC Rev.4) as a percentage of total value added, measured in USD at 2010 prices and PPPs.

Waste composting

[Chapter *Materials productivity and waste*]

Composting is a biological process that submits biodegradable waste to anaerobic or aerobic decomposition, and that results in a product that is recovered (for example as a fertiliser for plants).

Waste recycling

[Chapter *Materials productivity and waste*]

Recycling is defined as any reprocessing of material in a production process that diverts it from the waste stream, except reuse as fuel. Both reprocessing as the same type of product, and for different purposes are included.

Water stress

[Chapter *Freshwater resources*]

Water stress is defined as the intensity of use of freshwater resources, expressed as gross abstraction in percentage of total available renewable freshwater resources (including inflows from neighbouring countries) or in percentage of internal freshwater resources (i.e. precipitation minus evapotranspiration). Water stress can be categorised as:

- Low (less than 10%) means generally no major stress on the available resources.
- Moderate (10-20%) means water availability is becoming a constraint on development and significant investment is needed to provide adequate supplies.
- Medium-high (20-40%) implies management of both supply and demand, and a need for conflicts among competing uses to be resolved.
- High (more than 40%) indicates serious scarcity and usually shows unsustainable water use, which can become a limiting factor in social and economic development.

National water stress levels may hide important variations at subnational (e.g. river basin) level, particularly in countries with extensive arid and semi-arid regions. The national indicator may conceal unsustainable use in some regions and periods, as well as high dependence on water from other basins.

ORGANISATION FOR ECONOMIC CO-OPERATION AND DEVELOPMENT

The OECD is a unique forum where governments work together to address the economic, social and environmental challenges of globalisation. The OECD is also at the forefront of efforts to understand and to help governments respond to new developments and concerns, such as corporate governance, the information economy and the challenges of an ageing population. The Organisation provides a setting where governments can compare policy experiences, seek answers to common problems, identify good practice and work to co-ordinate domestic and international policies.

The OECD member countries are: Australia, Austria, Belgium, Canada, Chile, the Czech Republic, Denmark, Estonia, Finland, France, Germany, Greece, Hungary, Iceland, Ireland, Israel, Italy, Japan, Korea, Latvia, Luxembourg, Mexico, the Netherlands, New Zealand, Norway, Poland, Portugal, the Slovak Republic, Slovenia, Spain, Sweden, Switzerland, Turkey, the United Kingdom and the United States. The European Union takes part in the work of the OECD.

OECD Publishing disseminates widely the results of the Organisation's statistics gathering and research on economic, social and environmental issues, as well as the conventions, guidelines and standards agreed by its members.

OECD PUBLISHING, 2, rue André-Pascal, 75775 PARIS CEDEX 16
(97 2017 01 1 P) ISBN 978-92-64-26577-6 – 2017

www.ingramcontent.com/pod-product-compliance
Lightning Source LLC
Chambersburg PA
CBHW061216240926
51846CB00006B/1246